MYSTERIES OF THE
CRYSTAL SKULLS
REVEALED

To
Seattle &
I find
my book
here --
The skulls
are an
amazing
journey --
may this
book open
up many
new doors

⚞ Joshua

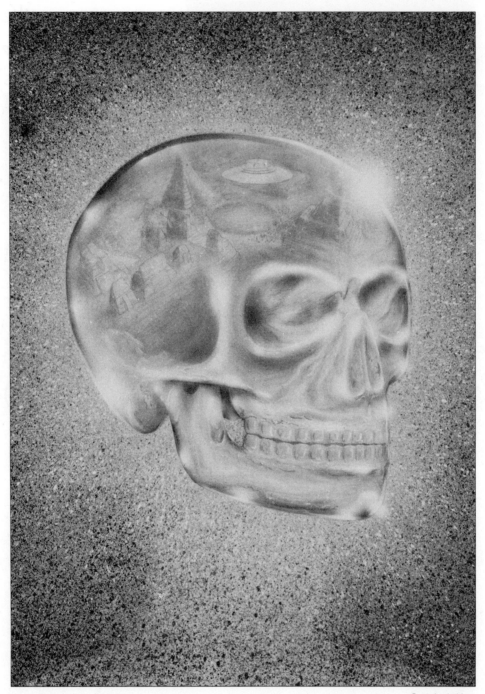

MYSTERIES OF THE CRYSTAL SKULLS REVEALED

Sandra Bowen

F. R. 'Nick' Nocerino

Joshua Shapiro

J & S
Aquarian Networking
Pacifica, California

Mysteries of the Crystal Skulls Revealed

A J & S Aquarian Networking Book (November 1988)
In association with NuSirius Company

J & S Aquarian Networking
Attn: Jeff Cohen & Joshua Shapiro
P.O. Box 1395
Pacifica, CA   94044

Book Design by Li Greiner

Editors -- Jeff Cohen, Barbara Fisher

Cover Painting -- Rodney Birkett

Artists (Illustrations) -- Michael Abbey, Alexandra Kokorich

Crystal Skull Photographs -- Francoise Beaudoin; Sandra Bowen;
Jeff Cohen; Ron Dickinson; J & S Aquarian Networking;
Lois Julian; Steve Mehler; F. R. 'Nick' Nocerino; Joshua Shapiro;
John Shimwell; The Society of Crystal Skulls, Int'l.; R. H. Youngman

Library of Congress
1. Psychical Research - ESP   2. Occult Sciences - Metaphysics
3. Quartz Crystals - Crystal Skulls   I. Title
ISBN: 0-929781-26-0
2nd Edition, First Printing
Printed in the United States

We dedicate this book to the love and support of June Kirkwood, and to the inspiration and guidance of Master LI and many other known and unknown spiritual helpers.

ACKNOWLEDGMENTS

We would like to thank and acknowledge the following people, for without their help this book would not have been possible:

Special recognition is given to Jeff Cohen for his unwavering dedication and assistance to bring this book to completion. He participated in every meeting and phase of the book's development. Jeff accepted every task and completed them expeditiously. We thank him for his competent editing services and for consistently maintaining updated versions of the book on the computer.

We are grateful to Li Greiner for designing our book. His professional publishing advice and guidance was indispensable. Li transformed our preliminary version of this book into a work of art. We appreciate his friendship, encouragement and excellent suggestions on this project, as well as the generous sharing of various resources available to him.

Our heartfelt thanks to Michael Abbey, a visionary artist who brought our book to life through his insight and great talents. Michael's vibrant illustrations were generously provided and they reflect his enthusiasm for this project.

We acknowledge the hard work and efforts of Barbara Fisher, our main editor, who ensured that the material was clear for the reader. We thank her for her support and friendship, as well as joining our group to create a finished product that we are all pleased with.

Many thanks to our good friend, Rodney Birkett, who was able to take our visions and create a wonderful painting for our cover which represents the scope of the book's contents in a single image. And to Alexandra Kokorich, another gifted visionary artist, for supplying additional illustrations to help the reader see some of the many facets contained herein. Also, we thank her for continual support in this project and spiritual guidance.

We thank Larry Byram for his support with the preliminary version of our book. He gave us access to many of the tools necessary to create and print it. We appreciate his help in securing the equipment which made this book possible.

We express our appreciation to Nick's wife, Mrs. F. R. Nocerino, for her valuable suggestions and support in helping to publish this book.

Thanks go to Janine Cohen, who assisted with transcriptions and offered her suggestions for improving this work.

In addition, we wish to express our gratitude to the many contributors to this book: Those who were interviewed, submitted material or allowed us to include their information-- Michael Kant, Jon Klimo, Steve Mehler, and Neville Rowe; and those who supplied photographs-- Francoise Beaudoin, Jeff Cohen, Lois Julien, Steve Mehler, Damien Quinn, John Shimwell and R. H. Youngman. We thank Ruth Fortier, Kathy Grimshaw and Sharon Smith for their encouragement, and Matt Tomas for his assistance in the area of computer graphics. Also, special thanks to Catherine Valentine for recommending an invaluable editor to us.

A special recognition to Anna Mitchell-Hedges, who has shared her Crystal Skull with the world so that people can have a chance to experience it. Also, for allowing the research team the opportunity to work with the Crystal Skull and to share their findings with the public.

Lastly, we greatly appreciate the contributions of time, energy and resources by all the other wonderful people who directly or indirectly supported this book. When we work together, compromise, cooperate and share our collective resources, the projects of Light and Expansion cannot be impeded. We feel blessed to have had this opportunity to work with such dedicated and loving people so that we can share with the world a book about the incredible Crystal Skulls.

Sandra, Nick, Joshua

CONTENTS

APPENDIX

INTRODUCTION

Most contemporary scientists and archaeologists believe that modern civilization and technology represent the most advanced systems our Earth has ever seen. Yet throughout recorded history there have been many baffling discoveries of artifacts, monuments and unusual patterns or designs left by the ancients. We have called some of them Ancient Wonders of the World. But our modern, scientific perspective has not allowed us to completely comprehend the purpose of many of these ancient discoveries.

Think of the pyramids or Stonehenge. Or the unusual discovery of figure drawings etched into the earth and distinguishable only from the air in The Americas (the Nazca Lines) and England (the Cerne Giant). These esoteric remnants of our forebearers challenge the belief in our own unsurpassed advancement. And we believe the Crystal Skulls, the subject of this book, offer an even vaster challenge to any kind of linear theory of progress.

BUT WHAT EXACTLY ARE THE 'CRYSTAL SKULLS'? It is commonly agreed that a Crystal Skull is a human-shaped skull made out of various types of quartz crystal. The Crystal Skulls we will focus on in this book are the ancient ones which are about the size of our own human skull and found among ancient ruins. However, there have been numerous tiny skulls found in the same or similar locations, ranging in size from a large marble to a softball. These smaller skulls do not possess the energy, the power or the air of mystique of the larger ones.

THERE SEEMS TO BE A SPECIFIC REASON WHY QUARTZ CRYSTAL WAS CHOSEN as the material to use for the skulls. Indeed, it is not an easy substance to carve or mold into a shape. If a carver is not careful, an improper cut can shatter the crystal. Quartz was probably chosen in recognition of some of its other powerful physical properties that, in turn, help to catalyze self-awareness.

For those of you unfamiliar with quartz crystal, we have offered a short essay in the Appendix to give a more complete definition. If this is your first introduction to Crystal Skulls or crystals, it might be a good idea to begin your reading there. For now, we will leave you with a few challenging thoughts about the possibilities crystals hold for mankind.

One of the predominant uses of quartz crystals today is in modern electronic devices and machines. In fact, in addition to the computer industry, major advances in the video, film and audio industries utilize the amplification and steady resonant abilities of quartz. Similarly, quartz can work with the human body's system of energy to amplify one's healing abilities or expand psychic awareness. This subtle energy is shown to exist through Kirlian photography, which records the electromagnetic energy emanating from living things. Orientals developed efficient healing systems hundreds of years ago, known as acupuncture and acupressure, in which they charted a system of energy meridian lines that run throughout the body. In addition, there are reports that even some of the so-called primitive tribes in Africa and Australia use crystals today in similar ways for healing and diagnosing illness. Even so, there is still great controversy surrounding the beneficial effects of quartz crystal on the human body, since most scientists and physicians are at odds with holistic, spiritually oriented healers.

Today numerous books are being written about crystals and their ability to be programmed by the human mind. [See Appendix A for a starter list on crystal books.] This programming can include a whole spectrum of affirmations, such as improving life situations, increasing prosperity, clarity of mind, world peace and harmony.

Lastly, quartz crystal has the ability to not only record thoughts and energy, but also visual impressions, as you will see in some of the pictures of the

INTRODUCTION

Crystal Skulls included in this book. The skulls work like a video camera, and through several activation processes they are able to play back these images.

Thus far, of the ancient skulls publicly known, there are three types of quartz which comprise their physical form. First and most common is clear quartz crystal. A few of the Crystal Skulls are made of amethyst (a purple-colored quartz), and one is formed from rose quartz (a pink-colored quartz). To date, all of the Crystal Skulls have been discovered among ancient ruins in Mexico, Central or South America. The symbol of skulls must have made a significant impact upon these cultures because the indigenous peoples continue to carve replicas and miniatures of the ancient skulls in various materials.

As you begin to delve into the material of this book, you will see from our Photogallery how different the contemporary carved crystal skulls are from the ancient ones. Yet this does not even begin to depict the differences which emerge when we turn to the strange and unexplainable phenomena which have occurred around several of the ancient Crystal Skulls.

Many people believe there is only one Crystal Skull, the world-famous Mitchell-Hedges Skull. The media has published photographs of it on numerous occasions. It is the main focus of two previous books which are exclusively devoted to the Crystal Skulls.[1] And it is the skull most widely exhibited throughout the world.

It is the only known Crystal Skull which is not owned by a museum or private collector. The owners (at first, famed explorer, F. A. Mitchell-Hedges, and now subsequently his adopted daughter, Anna) have allowed the skull to be scientifically researched, as well as seen by the public. Individuals have been able to make an appointment with Anna Mitchell-Hedges to see the skull in her home.

The other cause of its fame, we believe, lies in the fact that it is a very skillful replication of a human skull. It even has a detachable jaw. Although there are fine points of discussion about this fact within the growing Crystal Skulls research community, the Mitchell-Hedges Skull is an incredible work of art that no modern carvers have been able to duplicate.[2]

---

[1] Richard Garvin's book, *The Crystal Skull* (published in 1973), and *The Skull Speaks,* by the Anna Mitchell-Hedges Research & Exploration Association (AMHREA, © By Brian Hadley James, published in 1985).

[2] Crystal Skull researcher, Steve Mehler [See Chapter 4], believes the bulges in the temple of the Mitchell-Hedges Skull are very different from the more

THERE ARE SEVERAL OTHER CRYSTAL SKULLS, WHICH WE WILL BRIEFLY MENTION. Much more detailed information is given about each skull in Chapter One. The two other skulls that are available to the public are called Aztec skulls (although archaeologists do not know for sure that the skulls are Aztec creations), and they reside in the British Museum of Man in London, England, and in the Trocadero Museum in Paris, France. They are both clear skulls, but do not have the crystal clarity of the Mitchell-Hedges Skull, nor the compatibility of size and shape with the human skull.

Two other Crystal Skulls which have come to the attention of the authors and contributing writers of this book are the Amethyst Skull and the Mayan Skull (another clear skull). The Mayan Skull was given this name based on F. R. 'Nick' Nocerino's four months of extensive research in 1979/1980. These two skulls were brought to the United States from Mexico. Again, they are not as clear or exact as the Mitchell-Hedges Crystal Skull. The reader will find photographs of most of the skulls in the Photogallery.

A few of the other skulls which will be discussed were encountered by Mr. Nocerino in his extensive travels. During the Second World War, he had a brief opportunity to see another clear skull in France which was in the possession of a secret society. They called the skull, "The Blood of Christ." Also several years after the war, he saw another skull near the Guatemala/Honduras border made out of rose quartz with a movable jaw. It was as perfect as the Mitchell-Hedges Skull (though slightly larger) and well-guarded by the local Mayan natives. Nick will discuss another amethyst skull found near San Jose, Mexico, which is smaller than the previous one mentioned. In addition to these, there are rumors of another three or four Crystal Skulls which are known, but we do not have satisfactory information to report on them at this time.

IT IS OUR GOAL IN THIS BOOK TO MAKE AVAILABLE NEW INFORMATION about the Crystal Skulls. At this time, even though there have been a number of articles in various publications about them [See the Resource Directory in Appendix D], the information given is by no means extensive. We believe this is because our scientists and archaeologists are not sure what to say about them. The origins of the ancient Crystal Skulls and the processes which may have created

---

flattened tendency of modern human skulls. He agrees this could be due to the anatomical changes in humans over time.

INTRODUCTION

them have only been guessed at. Of course there are many theories, many of which we will be sharing in this book, but no one is quite sure which one is correct.

One of the labels that has been showered upon any Crystal Skull, but primarily upon the most well-known one, the Mitchell-Hedges, is "The Skull of Doom." Through our research and findings we do not concur with this notion. We feel that the main problem is due to a misunderstanding of the Crystal Skulls because they do not conform to standard scientific theories.

It so often seems that whatever mankind doesn't understand is regarded as an evil omen or object. If, however, one stays open to psychic possibilities and parapsychological investigation, the result is many more possible answers. We feel that fear of the Crystal Skulls comes from an unwillingness to utilize intuitive measures of investigation. And it is exactly this fear which feeds such notoriety as the "Skulls of Doom." We believe that the Crystal Skulls originally had a beneficial or constructive purpose for the civilizations which created and used them. After hundreds or thousands of years, the true purpose of the skulls was lost and they began to be used for power over the masses.

For the co-authors and contributors of this book, the Crystal Skulls are a sign of life. They are one of the many tangible symbols which demonstrate that the prophecies of a Golden Age are manifesting in our world. As we begin to unravel the secrets and knowledge locked within these vessels of crystal, we feel that once again the true understanding of the Crystal Skulls can be shared. They will be viewed as one of the ancients' most powerful tools which can help us remove the great unrest in our world today.

WHEN WE SPEAK OF USING PSYCHIC TECHNIQUES TO GAIN INSIGHTS into the Crystal Skulls, we must ask the reader's indulgence. As stated earlier, besides being unable to exactly duplicate some of the more finely modeled skulls with even our modern technology, we are also unable to date the skulls because the current form of time-dating using Carbon-14 testing does not work with strictly inorganic material. Thus the only way to estimate the age of the Crystal Skulls, or the possible civilizations which might have created or worked with them, is by using psychometry. This is a process where a psychically sensitized individual "reads" psychic energies or vibrations which are associated with an object. Some of these sensitives would need to physically touch the Crystal Skulls or be in their presence, whereas others feel that they have a mind-link

JOSHUA SHAPIRO

with the skulls. Of course, information gathered in this way is not always able to be traced or empirically verified, but it does introduce new directions and theories to consider.

A good example of being open to a parapsychological approach is discussed in Richard Garvin's book on the Crystal Skulls. Frank Dorland was one of the chief researchers quoted quite extensively in Garvin's book. Mr. Dorland tried every conceivable way to stay away from a psychically oriented study, but there were too many inexplicable phenomena for him to just be scientific in a traditional or conventional way.

IN OCTOBER OF 1970, FRANK DORLAND BROUGHT THE MITCHELL-HEDGES SKULL to Hewlett-Packard in Santa Clara, California, for extensive scientific analysis. Hewlett-Packard has one of the most sophisticated laboratories for crystal research. Again, summarizing the findings given in Garvin's book, their researchers claimed that it would be virtually impossible to duplicate this Crystal Skull. Through their tests, the skull was shown to have an elaborate inner mechanism of prisms and lenses that would refract and reflect light projected upon the Crystal Skull in specific ways. This system of lenses displays a technical competence that has only been achieved recently (please note that this skull was found in 1924, when no computers or lasers existed). After shining polarized light upon the skull while it was bathed in a benzyl alcohol solution, they discovered that whoever carved or made the skull had totally disregarded the natural axis of the crystal itself (the crystal should have shattered).

Another highly puzzling detail was that no matter what temperature the researchers subjected the Mitchell-Hedges Skull to, it always remained seventy degrees Fahrenheit. All of these findings were so astounding that one of the crystalographers at Hewlett-Packard was quoted as saying, "The damn thing simply shouldn't even be."

ANOTHER PHENOMENON CONNECTED WITH THE CRYSTAL SKULLS is their ability to project holographic images within the skull itself. These images can be seen by many with their physical eyes. The process of looking for images in crystal is called scrying. In the many lectures which the co-authors have given about the Crystal Skulls, most participants have reported seeing images in the slides of the skulls that were projected. Again, in Garvin's book, Frank Dorland talked about images he saw (For more information, see Appendix B.) and how the skull would visibly change in color and shape. This again is clearly

INTRODUCTION

exhibited in photographs and slides recorded by the vigorous research done by co-author F. R. 'Nick' Nocerino and his team of assistants, during three weeks of intensive study with the Mitchell-Hedges Skull at Miss Mitchell-Hedges' home in Canada (which included Sandra Bowen), as well as Nick's four months of research with the Mayan Skull.

We have heard accounts of healings received by people who have come to see the Mitchell-Hedges Skull, and they have written to Anna Mitchell-Hedges about their experiences. Another of the contributors to our book, Steve Mehler, had the Amethyst and Mayan Skulls in his home for a few days. He invited many people to visit at that time. Most people who were with the Crystal Skulls reported either some type of healing or an increase in their psychic abilities. As a matter of fact, we have not met anyone who has not experienced some effect when they came into contact with an ancient Crystal Skull.

Our friend and contributor of some of the photos of the British Skull, Lois Julien, told us an interesting story she heard while visiting the British Museum of Man. One of the guards informed her that the cleaning custodians had reported seeing the skull move around in its case all by itself at night, and that they had heard strange sounds coming from the skull as well. So the question arises: What exactly are we dealing with in these Crystal Skulls?

In order to answer this question, we have no choice but to look at the spiritual or psychic aspects of the Crystal Skulls! If the reader wishes to appreciate this book, we must ask for openness to this area of study. We feel it is impossible to even begin to understand what a Crystal Skull is without considering the metaphysical aspects. Today we are finding that science and religion (or spiritual concepts) are beginning to merge together to become one field. Also, all over the world people are awakening or are becoming interested in the spiritual aspect of their being, sensing that it is as real as anything else, even though their spirit may exist in some other dimension which the physical senses do not detect. It has long been prophesied that in the latter part of the Twentieth Century, mankind would have more of an interest in the spiritual or metaphysical.

THUS, YOU WILL FIND IN THIS BOOK not only the personal experiences of several Crystal Skull researchers who have been in the presence of one or more of the ancient skulls, but also information from what are today being called "Channels." You will find a description of channeling, by Jon Klimo in Part III, Introduction to Channeling. Essentially, by channeling we are referring to

JOSHUA SHAPIRO

individuals who are able to act as communicators for various spirit entities to speak through and share their perspectives of reality. Since they exist in spirit, they can (although not always) see many things beyond what we are able to from our perspectives, because on their levels time and space do not exist. In this book, we have included information from trance and conscious channels for extraterrestrials and dolphins, and mind impressions from the Crystal Skulls. We feel it is important to explore all avenues of information, merging them together to give us a better picture of what we are presenting in this book.

As far as channeling goes, it is of course one of the more controversial subjects at the time of the publication of this book. Through the work of actress Shirley MacLaine, her books, seminars, TV mini-series (January, 1987) and media appearances, channeling has been placed into the public eye. It is a source of great hope and great skepticism among the general American population. It all depends on where you are and who you talk to.

From the late 1890's through the early 1980's channeling was called mediumship. The United States has been influenced by many religious movements and individuals who used or were great proponents of trance-like states that yielded valuable information from beyond the world which is plainly visible. The prophetic work of the American, Edgar Cayce, who lived in the early part of this century, has quietly influenced thousands of people. Many Americans have also been interested in the philosophies of the nineteenth century Swedish religious thinker, Swedenborg. So, these ideas and methods of reaching other levels of healing consciousness are not new to Americans, although the name has been updated and the media has chosen to spotlight it as a current fad.

IN NO WAY DO WE FEEL THAT THIS IS A DEFINITIVE BOOK ON THE CRYSTAL SKULLS. The scope of our material is based primarily on spiritual or psychic sources. This information comes either from psychic impressions of those who have been in the presence of a Crystal Skull or from channeled information. We cannot conclusively prove many of the statements made in this book. Also, there is far more scientific and psychic research which needs to be done on the Crystal Skulls whose whereabouts are known, as well as the Crystal Skulls that will emerge into public view in the near future.

But the metaphysical research discussed here does offer some possible avenues for solving the great mysteries of these Crystal Skulls. We do know, and it has been documented by reliable and trustworthy individuals, that the skulls project holographic images, sounds, colors, aromas and change shape.

INTRODUCTION

In addition to our own findings, there are just too many other people reporting similar experiences to us, based on being in the presence of a Crystal Skull (or even working with a photograph), for us to write these phenomena off as hallucinations.

SOME CONTEMPORARY SCIENTISTS ARE UNSURE ABOUT HOW THESE OBJECTS CAME TO BE, and in some cases they deny that the Crystal Skulls exist, or claim that the skulls are frauds. But, there are too many unusual properties which the Crystal Skulls possess, and too many unanswered questions which shouldn't be ignored.

Progress for modern science is too often measured in the physical world. Our entire world culture has become dependent on outward systems interlocking science and technology with transportation, communication and a multitude of questionably useful gadgets. But the systems of ancient cultures may have depended on something quite different. In those times, men and women were closer, more dependent on nature. And it makes sense that their most powerful systems and tools took advantage and explored the inner worlds of nature and the psyche.

SINCE ABOUT 1986, THE INTEREST IN CRYSTAL SKULLS has been growing exponentially. None of the authors has been involved with a subject or a book that has received so much interest from so many people, and which has influenced people enough to volunteer their assistance in every aspect of this book. Whenever we were seeking a particular resource to fill a need in this project, it would miraculously appear within a short time.

We will be writing other books about people's experiences with Crystal Skulls. We feel that these books will not only open many new doors to understanding the mystery of the Crystal Skulls but also may lead us to our origin. We believe that all of us are integrally connected to each other and to the universe, and the Crystal Skulls are one of the keys which will unlock the answers to these long sought-after questions.

We invite you to partake of this work. In this book we have purposely interviewed many different sources to give you various perspectives on the Crystal Skulls. Even as this book goes to press, there is much more we have yet to tell you. So, dear reader, jump in and enjoy!!

Joshua Shapiro
Pinole, CA
November, 1987

JOSHUA SHAPIRO

F. R. 'Nick' Nocerino linking into the energy of the Mayan Crystal Skull during his research.

I was born into a family with a rich background in psychic phenomena and healing which nurtured spiritual/psychic gifts in me. In my early childhood I was exposed to the healing practices and Wicca teachings by very wise, older Italian women in Brooklyn, New York. Wicca is the active remnant of ancient pagan tradition. Two women in particular introduced me to crystals and forecast many events in my life which have come true. At the age of seven, I was given my first "frozen water stones" [rock quartz crystals]. At nine, I began having dreams and mirror visions of Crystal Skulls. These were times of confusion to me because open, voluntary information about the skulls was not easily available. Yet my time spent with these Wiccan teachers reassured me and helped to guide me toward my destiny. Needless to say, I spent a good deal of time with my own thoughts. And I learned one of life's strongest lessons: without desire fueling us, we do not accomplish whatever it is we seek to do.

IT WAS DURING WORLD WAR II THAT I HAD MY FIRST DIRECT CONTACT with three Crystal Skulls, one in England and two in France. It would seem that seeing

3

these would have somehow enticed me to keep records and document my experiences, but at the time, it was more important to survive the war.

When I married in 1947, my life soon took a different course, but I certainly did not end my search to understand what I was trying to accomplish on this earth plane.

TO DATE, I AM THE ONLY PERSON TO HAVE WORKED WITH AND HANDLED nine human-sized ancient Crystal Skulls, along with several hundred smaller ones that are of known ancient origin. A lifetime of extensive travel, study and research has led me on a quest to uncover and tap the knowledge stored within these incredible artifacts. "To see the key, we must see the true lock for it. It is not obvious, for its own protection. Where it was before was a power unto itself and could move through all dimensions." This quote can be attributed to all the Crystal Skulls which I have seen, worked with and researched.

 ## History of the Crystal Skulls

[Editors' notes: (1) The years enclosed in parentheses indicate when Nick was with the Crystal Skulls he is writing about. (2) Some of the dates and places are deliberately left vague at this current printing. This is necessary to protect the well-being of the owners of the skulls.]

FOR NEARLY FORTY YEARS CRYSTAL SKULL INFORMATION WAS KEPT VERY PRIVATE, as was most knowledge concerning crystals and power stones. Fears of condemnation from a culture steeped in Christian values kept many from sharing their knowledge. Of the forty or more Crystal Skull research projects prior to 1980, none were discussed publicly. This knowledge belonged to the individual who owned the skull, the researchers and private students.

It was not until January of 1980 that I did my first public lecture on Crystal Skulls in the vicinity of Mountain View, California. This was followed by a seminar and a crystal conference in February of the same year. Since then I have received constant requests for lectures, articles and television and radio interviews.

TOWARD THE END OF 1982, A FLURRY OF LETTERS AND PHONE CALLS CAME IN from people who had or knew someone who had a Master Skull. I visited most of

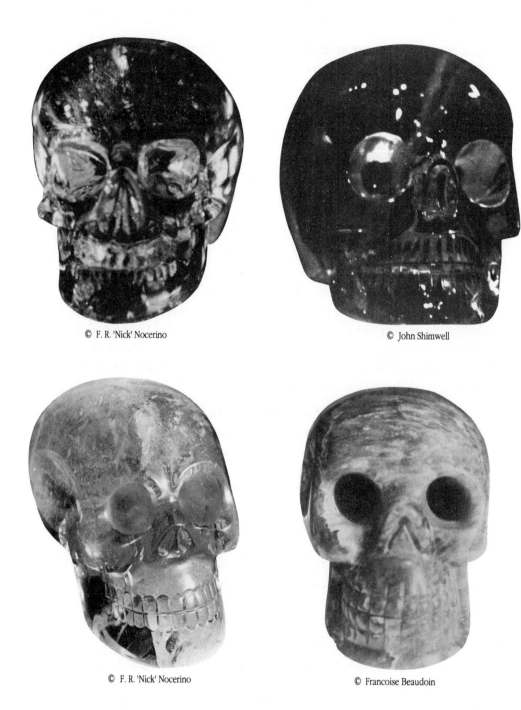

© F. R. 'Nick' Nocerino

© John Shimwell

© F. R. 'Nick' Nocerino

© Francoise Beaudoin

Photographs of four of the ancient Crystal Skulls which are known. Top Left: Mitchell-Hedges Crystal Skull; Top Right: British Crystal Skull; Bottom Left: Mayan Crystal Skull; Bottom Right: Amethyst Crystal Skull.

these people, or got more information, which enabled me to build a reference library on skulls of all sizes and materials.

These alleged Master Skulls rarely turned out to be clear rock quartz crystal, and none have come close to being even half the size of the skulls I had been studying. Of over four hundred skulls I've gone to see or been invited to see, none were the size of a human skull; most were the size of ping-pong balls or smaller, and some were the size of a softball. The skulls have been made of various minerals such as amethyst, emerald, obsidian, rose quartz, ruby, sapphire, topaz, tourmaline, turquoise, rock crystal with tourmaline inclusions, rutilated rock quartz crystal, smoky quartz, rhodochrosite, barite, onyx, malachite, lapis and several other stones which were unknown to me. Some skulls were made of silver, gold, lead, iron, brass, and bronze. I also saw human-sized skulls embedded with stone or seashell chips. And lest it be forgotten, many lead crystal and solid glass skulls.

Despite high hopes, none of these skulls proved, in my estimation, to be skulls from ancient times. Most seem to be of recent origin. Some very definitely could have been made since 1985, such as the skulls coming out of Nepal, Mexico and Brazil. Nearly all the skulls carved in 1986 and 1987 were from carvers in Brazil, Germany and Mexico.

ON ONE OF MY TRIPS TO MEXICO, I WAS ABLE TO SEE about four hundred and fifty skulls made of various stones. All of these were smaller than the size of a tennis ball or a baseball. There was one exception, a dark-green skull about the size of a softball, made of what seemed to be jade. It was taken from a tomb southeast of Mexico City. The owner dated it as being pre-seventeenth century.

Another time when I visited Mexico, I saw two skulls of human size made of amethyst. These were taken from ninth and tenth century tombs in a Central American country. One was the largest amethyst skull I have seen. When doing psychometry on them, time seemed to disappear and the images in my mind depicted scenes that would be thousands of years before Christ or any known civilization. The owner was able to verify my feelings because other artifacts taken out at the time were dated B.C.

IN THE PAST I HAVE OVERSEEN THIRTY-THREE RESEARCH TEAMS in several cities across the United States. The teams generally consist of engineers, doctors, anthropologists and computer scientists. As we worked with Crystal Skulls in research projects, we began to give them names, such as the Mayan Skull

CHAPTER 1

(1979, 1980); the Amethyst Skull *(1982, 1983);* the Master Skull, better known as the Mitchell-Hedges Skull *(1969, 1970, 1985-1988);* the British Skull *(1978, 1981, 1982),* in the British Museum, London, England, better known as the Aztec Skull or the Yucatan Skull; the Paris Skull *(1978, 1981, 1982),* in the Trocadero Museum, Paris, France, also known to the public as the Aztec Skull; the Templar Skull, hidden by a secret organization in France between Carcassonne and the Mediterranean Sea *(1944);* the San Jose Skull from Mexico *(1950);* and to date, the largest skull of all and perhaps the real Master Skull, the clear Rose Quartz Skull with a movable jaw, continually relocating between Guatemala and Honduras *(1949).* Now let's look at each of these skulls. I will give a summary of their physical attributes, a brief history and impressions.

THE **PARIS SKULL** IS A VERY PRIMITIVE CRYSTAL SKULL, perhaps the most primitive of all the ancient skulls. It is a cloudy clear quartz skull, smaller in size than the Mitchell-Hedges. Its mouth and teeth are not well-defined at all. It has a hole that was cut into the top part of the skull which was used to hold a Christian Cross. It is currently in the Trocadero Museum in Paris, France. Its dimensions are 10.95 cm (4- 5/16") high, 14.92 cm (5- 7/8") long, and it weighs 2.48 kg (5 lbs. 8-1/2 oz).

The Paris Skull allegedly was in the Maximilian Collection at one time. [Ferdinand Maximilian Joseph, 1832-1867. Austrian archduke, named emperor of Mexico, 1864.] It was stolen from a tomb, then stolen from the robbers by others, and it was taken from them by a French Officer on duty in Mexico during the French occupation. The French officer is probably the one who gave it to Emperor Maximilian, either by purchase or a gift, and somehow it arrived at the Museum in Paris, France. So little is known about this Crystal Skull since the Museum has no recorded history about it. It is referred to as Aztec. I do not believe it is Aztec or Mayan, but rather from a civilization long before these cultures came into existence.

THE **BRITISH SKULL** IS A CLEAR-CLOUDY CRYSTAL SKULL which appears to be an attempt to imitate the Mitchell-Hedges Skull in shape and size. It is one-piece, and the mouth and teeth are not clearly defined as with the Mitchell-Hedges Skull. It has been theorized that one of the carvers slipped, because the skull has a slight gash. The British Skull presently resides in the Museum of Mankind in London, England.

F. R. 'NICK' NOCERINO

The British Skull is also referred to as Aztec. I disagree, and feel it is much older than the Paris Skull. Not much is known about this skull either; to my knowledge, only one paper has been publicly written about it. It appeared in the July, 1936 issue of MAN, published under the direction of the Royal Anthropological Institute, where it is compared in shape and size to the Mitchell-Hedges Skull. I am not aware of any other records. History is sketchy, but it appears to have been stolen from a tomb and found its way into the hands of a soldier of fortune in Mexico in the late nineteenth century. It was then sold to Tiffany's, a New York jeweler. The Museum of Mankind in London subsequently bought the skull from Tiffany's in 1898 for £120.

THE **MITCHELL-HEDGES SKULL** IS A NEAR-PERFECTLY SHAPED HUMAN-SIZED SKULL. It is comprised of two pieces (the cranium and a detachable jaw) and is made from pure clear quartz crystal, as clear as glass before one begins to work with it. Its dimensions are 13.18 cm (5 -3/16") high, 12.38 cm (4 -7/8") wide, 20 cm (7 - 7/8") long, and it weighs 5.13 kg (11 lbs. 7 oz). Anna Mitchell-Hedges is the owner. She and the Crystal Skull reside in Canada.

The Mitchell-Hedges Skull has its own history. In 1924, on Anna's seventeenth birthday, while she was in British Honduras with her father on an archaeological expedition, she first discovered the Crystal Skull. She noticed something shining, reflecting the sunlight through the rocks of one of the ruins. This location appeared to be a Mayan place of worship, complete with the remnant of an altar. After six weeks of moving stones and debris, they brought out the top part (or cranium) of the Crystal Skull. Three months later in the same location, they found the lower jaw.

When this Crystal Skull was first discovered, the local Mayan natives were so delirious with joy that Anna's father, F. A. Mitchell-Hedges, did not have the heart to keep the skull, so he gave it to them. Later in 1927, as the expedition was concluding, the Mayan High Priest presented the Crystal Skull back to Mr. Mitchell-Hedges as a gift in gratitude for all the clothing, food and medical supplies they had received from him during his expedition. If these events had not occurred, then the Mitchell-Hedges Crystal Skull would have become the property of the museums which were involved.

At this point, it seems that no one in the museums or archaeological fields wants to recognize the Mitchell-Hedges Skull as an ancient artifact. All would like to own it. Little is said about it, and in many cases some have even tried to convince the public that it is glass. I've often wondered why.

CHAPTER 1

THE MITCHELL-HEDGES SKULL IS PERHAPS THE MOST POWERFUL of all the Crystal Skulls
I have seen or worked with. Its pureness and workmanship cannot be
duplicated. We have taken several skulls to crystal laboratories to see if
anyone could duplicate them. The answer was a strong *no*, with comments
that they were fashioned incorrectly in the first place (formed against the axis
of the crystal).

The scrying (where one looks into an object for pictures/images which are
seen by the physical eyes) done with this Crystal Skull provides some very
serious dilemmas for me. It seems to show pictures of several highly civilized
societies, one that lives underwater, a second which lives within the Earth, and
a third one which comes from some place other than our Earth. The world
seems to have changed its geography four times, with mass movements of
people to the East, Southeast and South. What could only be determined to be
North America and South America went through some very traumatic changes.
While ice areas moved into tropical areas, tropical areas moved south and
became ice areas. Each time there was a change, there appeared to be
spaceships (more commonly called UFOs) which removed people. The
spaceships returned at a later date when the land was stable, and people came
out of them. Many people emerged from what appeared to be very large
water areas. Rarely did I see people who went into the Earth come out again.

The real puzzle here is the time periods. Through psychometry I feel that
we are talking about millions of years, but there is no way to be sure.
Furthermore, the Mitchell-Hedges Skull seems to take me to civilizations that
could not exist on our planet. For me, the skull is like a compact computer
with a video monitor and often with accompanying audio sounds.

THE **MAYAN SKULL** IS ANOTHER HUMAN-LOOKING SKULL that is made of clear quartz
crystal which is cloudy. This skull has circular indentations around the ears,
and the back of the head is elongated. Its nose and teeth are not as clearly
defined as with the Mitchell-Hedges Skull and it is one piece. The skull's
dimensions are: 20.48 cm (8 -1/16") long, 12.54 cm (4 -15/16") wide, 10.79 cm
(4 -1/4") high, and it weighs 3.95 kg (8 lbs. 13 oz). The skull is reportedly out
of the United States at this time, but for a few years it had been kept in the
vault of a lawyer in Texas.

The Mayan Skull was allegedly discovered in San Augustine, Acazahuathan,
Departmento De Zacopa, Guatemala in 1912 by Mr. Hector Montano. I
brought the skull to the San Francisco area, on loan from the Mayan priest

who claimed to be its owner. I had contacted this priest in Mexico in August of 1979, prior to his trip to the States, and he had agreed to allow me to research and work with the Mayan Skull if I paid all the expenses! This I agreed to do. I picked up the skull in October of 1979 and had it in my possession for four months.

The Mayan Skull is another one which no one seems to be able to duplicate. In scrying it shows mostly the same things as the Mitchell-Hedges Skull, but only indicates three major geographic changes on Earth. The Mayan Skull also shows some small perversions. Perversion is the term used by Crystal Skull researchers to denote the presence of human sacrifice, mainly for the sake of appeasing gods. In this skull one sees sacrifices and wars which could relate to Earth's history. But then, there are other battles that take place in what seem like the heavens, with spacecraft and people that are certainly alien to the history of Earth as we know it.

THE **AMETHYST SKULL** IS ANOTHER HUMAN-SIZED CRYSTAL SKULL, similar in shape and size to the Mayan Skull. Rather than being a clear quartz skull, this one is a very dark purple amethyst, and is one piece. Also there are holes where the jaw meets the upper face. As with the Mayan Skull, it has circular indentations around the ears, the back of the head is elongated, and the nose and teeth are almost identical in pattern to the Mayan Skull. According to Steve Mehler, its dimensions are about 10-15% smaller than the Mayan Skull and it weighs approximately 3.64 kg (8 lbs.). Currently, this skull is for sale in San Jose, California.

The Mayan priest claimed that the Mayan priesthood had possession of the Amethyst Skull in the Oaxaca area of Mexico. It was brought to the United States around Christmas of 1982, by an agent for the same Mayan priest for a quick sale. I only had one day to work with the skull (in February, 1983), but I found it very interesting. For me this skull seems to have more sounds than images. The audio went through my body and I felt like I was deep underwater.

When the Mayan priest visited my home (after bringing the Amethyst Skull to San Jose, California), he offered to let me work with the skull for $500/week or $50/day for each researcher. Due to a shortage of funds, we were not in a position to make such an arrangement; perhaps at a later date.

THE **TEMPLAR SKULL** IS ANOTHER CLOUDY CLEAR-QUARTZ SKULL. To the best of my knowledge it still might be in the hands of a secret society in France. This society calls the Crystal Skull the "Blood of Christ." When I held this skull, it gave me the sensation of experiencing many wars, possibly in Mesopotamia, Egypt, Palestine and Europe. One interesting aspect of the images I saw within the skull were what seemed like Knights of the Crusades with large red crosses on their armored chests. The best I can recall, it had a great deal of biblical lore and history.

For now I'll say it could be a duplicate of the Mayan Skull in weight and proportion. Nothing has been made public or written about this skull. I have yet to find substantial information other than the fact that I saw and held it. Of course, for me this is history in itself.

THE **SAN JOSE SKULL**[1] IS A ONE-PIECE DEEP PURPLE CLEAR (URAL) AMETHYST SKULL approximately 11 to 12 pounds in weight. It was taken from a ninth or tenth century tomb in Mexico. It was dated as existing prior to the third century, based on other items found with it.

The San Jose Skull projects a great number of images (while scrying or doing psychometry) of what could be battles and rituals of various Indian cultures such as the Toltecs, Mayans, Incas and Aztecs. This skull just has too much perversion; entire scenes were of sacrifices and the vibrations made me feel death. I rarely talk about this one. The so-called Mayan priest that had it, would for a price, remove anyone you wished to have removed! It was his power tool.

THE **ROSE QUARTZ SKULL** IS SOMEWHAT LARGER THAN THE MITCHELL-HEDGES SKULL, but it is just as perfectly shaped. This skull is comprised of two pieces (including a movable jaw) and is made of clear rose quartz crystal. As of July, 1986, it was last seen in Guatemala guarded by the local natives. Like the Mitchell-Hedges Skull, the Rose Quartz Skull seems to be of the purest nature. This skull is reported to be moving between southern Mexico, Guatemala and Honduras.

THERE ARE OTHER SKULLS AND MUCH TO SAY! More detailed material will be published in my forthcoming book about Crystal Skulls and crystals. For now, let me present some conclusions about all the skulls I have seen to date, even those not mentioned:

---

[1] This skull derives its name from San Jose, Mexico, and should not be confused with the Amethyst Skull located in San Jose, California.

F. R. 'NICK' NOCERINO

- ☐ I believe they are intricate computers.

- ☐ They are all made of natural rock-quartz crystal in one form or another.

- ☐ They are all almost duplicates of our human skull in size and shape.

- ☐ They all show UFO activities [See Chapter 2].

- ☐ They all give a very real pictorial relation of a society that may live within the Earth and the oceans.

- ☐ I believe that there are thirteen such ancient rock-quartz Crystal Skulls.

- ☑ All of these skulls come from Central Mexico to south of Central Peru: None have been found anywhere else.

- ☐ All of the skulls, except for the Mitchell-Hedges Skull, were looted from tombs or temples.

- ☐ I believe that if all of the thirteen skulls were put together, we would have a tremendous powerhouse of knowledge to better mankind.

- ☑ All of the skulls can be activated by the use of color and sound codes.

NONE OF THE SKULLS DISCUSSED IN THIS SECTION were made by any known society living in our timespan of recorded history. Where then, did they come from? What is their real purpose? When did they arrive here? Who were they for? Why are they now re-appearing?

Your answers are as good as mine, because I don't know! I believe in my heart and mind that they are appearing now to give the human race a better understanding of itself and from whence it came.

Pinole, California
November, 1987

CHAPTER 1

Interview with F. R. 'Nick' Nocerino

This interview was conducted in Pinole, California in January of 1986, with Sandra Bowen and Joshua Shapiro.

Joshua: Nick, we're eager to talk to you today because you've recently come back from Kitchener, Ontario, Canada, where you researched the Mitchell-Hedges Crystal Skull. We've got a variety of questions to ask, but we'd like to especially focus on the Crystal Skulls' connections to paranormal activities.

Our first question is: what do you believe is the origin of the Mitchell-Hedges Crystal Skull which you researched last November at the home of Anna Mitchell-Hedges?

Nick: Well, I am convinced that the minds which created the Mitchell-Hedges Skull were very powerful. Much more powerful sources created this skull than any of the other skulls I've experienced. I believe that some ancient minds or entities [energies] from this world, or from another world, put this skull together, controlled people and still do control people today.

Sandra: How so?

Nick: When working with the skull the feeling is so strong, on both the mind and body, that you are being probed or observed. At times the skull seems to allow two giant eyes to come through and stare directly at you. Wherever these eyes come from, you can't help but feel they are manipulating your mind.

Joshua: And how do you explain that? I guess I'm trying to get at how the skull was created...

Nick: The skull has been made in such a way that it is beyond our understanding. If I go by what I can see in the skull, I cannot believe it was made by any human beings as we know them; it's almost like somebody mentally formed this skull. It's very possible that it was made elsewhere-- in another dimension or on another planet. However, when all is said and done, there's no way of proving that this skull was made by a far greater intelligence with a greater knowledge than our own.

F. R. 'NICK' NOCERINO

I would say, basically, that whatever culture created the skull is non-existent now, that the creators' energy still exists within the skull and controls it and probably many other skulls as well. There's no doubt that they were able to clear the skull mentally to prepare it for scrying or "reading of images." It takes mental abilities which are less strong to "fog" the skull, and the Mitchell-Hedges Skull requires a "fogging" of energy for images to appear within it.

Joshua: I'd like to clarify that last thought. You've told me a bit about fogging, saying that this particular skull starts out totally clear to the eye. Then, as you continue to focus upon it, energy comes in and the skull changes; it's no longer clear. Is that what you mean by fogging?

Nick: Yes! You see, when you scry there are two things you have to do. You take a piece of crystal and you clear a section. Most crystals are veiled, or cloudy, to start out with. That area will usually cloud more and then eventually clears away. With the Mitchell Hedges Skull, the interesting thing is that it's already clear! It's as clear as glass-- you can look right through it! I know it's very thick, and so forth and so on, but you can look through it! It's just like you're looking through a window. This makes it very difficult to scry because there is no central point to focus on.

Joshua: So, there seems to be two different kinds of fogging, one where the skull starts cleared and the other where the skull is already fogged...

Nick: That's right. A skull can start out fogged due to its absorption of a great deal of unfocussed energy that is just "out there" in the environment. The focussed fogging is what induces the mysterious mechanisms in the skull to produce various unusual phenomena.

Joshua: To say the least!

Nick: But the skull also seems to be able to take energy from the human source or a life source and fog itself up, which then creates the necessary conditions for scrying, so that we can see the pictures which appear within the Crystal Skull. These pictures emerge on several levels with many doorways in each level, and many windows which are very dimensional.

Sandra: Since we've already jumped into the area of paranormal activity, could you tell us a little about the power of crystals?

Nick: The interest and understanding in crystals has really picked up lately... by that I mean the last century. Most people never used crystal balls until the

CHAPTER 1

last two hundred years or so, and more have been used in the last eighty years than ever before.

We use crystals, crystal blocks, crystal balls or various other shapes of crystals because of their ability to integrate mind energies and replay images by changing the crystal so you see these pictures.

It is the polished side of the crystal that is used for your focusing point, because the unpolished sides reflect these focusing points. In other words, they didn't want a clear crystal like people today refer to. They wanted a focusing point to bring in a 'window,' a 'door' or a 'mirror,' and they would focus on that part of the crystal. This focusing point would usually be clouded or veiled, and as it disappeared, the crystal would clear up and then you would see the different pictures and images.

With the Mitchell-Hedges Skull, you see, it starts out clear until you fog it (until you put energy into it), and then you're looking at a pure mirror or window, whatever you want to call it. As you're looking right through it, suddenly the crystal starts getting sutures through it (lines, templates), and pictures/scenes become apparent. Then each one of the sutures begins to produce a different scene, of which none are identical. Overall, there are many picture areas once the fog clears. It gives you a perimeter which you can explore. So now, you're not looking through the skull any longer, rather, you're observing different scenes. But you also see other scenes on top of these scenes. The longer you look at the skull, the more you will see one major scene with other scenes underneath it, or even in it. It doesn't matter whether you're looking at a slide or picture of the Mitchell-Hedges Skull, or whether you're looking at the skull itself-- it becomes dimensional! It actually begins to change!

So it's important that you get into the fogging period. Now, some people's minds go through a 'fogging period' without understanding it. In other words, they never know that there's a fogging taking place (a clouding or veiling if you will; we prefer to call it 'veiling'), and they don't realize that each time (because the phenomenon is so minute in some people's minds) they automatically begin to open up dimensions of the crystal, particularly with the Mitchell-Hedges Skull, and they're looking at seven levels with no trouble. And what the relationships are, or whether they're looking at the past, the present, or the future, I don't know. If these images are of the future, we had better start looking at nature. That's one thing I will say! ...I'm sorry, I didn't mean to get off the subject!

F. R. 'NICK' NOCERINO

© F. R. 'Nick' Nocerino

Mr. Nocerino researching the Mitchell-Hedges Crystal Skull in 1985, at the owner's home in Ontario, Canada.

Joshua: That's Ok! What is the relationship of the Mitchell-Hedges Skull to some of the other skulls you are familiar with?

Nick: I believe that there are twelve other Crystal Skulls besides the Mitchell-Hedges. Some of them were perverted. Now "perverted" is a term we use in connection with the idea that many of these skulls were used in conjunction with human sacrifice rituals. During the [Toltec] period of Mayan history (925 - 1200 A.D.), these sacrifices included bloodletting, shoving the skull into the womb or into the stomach, or taking the heart out and putting the skull in its place, opening the guts [intestines] and spreading them out on a symbolic Tree of Life. Some skulls show sun dehydration sacrifices or people being thrown off temples.

But this particular skull, the Mitchell-Hedges, has not been perverted. I'm positive that this skull was buried for such a long time that it did not go through the primitive period of being perverted. The Crystal Skulls, in general, may be as old as 10,000 to 30,000 years B.C. And I think they were the tools of a much higher civilization than the tombs in which they were found.

I believe those cultures who ended up with the Mitchell-Hedges Skull didn't have the knowledge of the ancients, and their imprints are not that pronounced within the skull. This is a pure, clear artifact. What I would almost call a healing-type skull. There's no doubt that the skull has power (particularly in the right eye) to do damage. It would require a great deal of mind power to use both eyes; a mind power which I am not familiar with today. Therefore, this intuitive feeling again gives me the theory of an ancient civilization, possibly even from some other dimension, creating or depositing the Mitchell-Hedges Skull here on the Earth.

I disagree with Mr. Dorland, that the mouth of the skull was made hundreds or thousands of years later. I think that the skull is a masterpiece in itself and that when you create a masterpiece, you do the entire piece at one time! I do not concur that it was made as one piece and then the jaw was separated. That would allow for too much space in the cutting-- there would be some odd deformity in the mouth, which there is not.

While scrying with the skull, I saw a great deal of sea life, a great number of ocean scenes and I watched lands sink and rise. I got the feeling that no one took a piece of stone (crystal) and physically carved this skull. It's as though it was mentally molded. I know the mind has the potential to do this, but we've lost that capability. I don't know of anyone in this world, in all of the material that I'm reading covering thousands of years (in Archaeology, Anthropology, Sociology, myths, legends, etc.), who could even come close to doing what I think took place with this skull.

So in simple terms, I would say that if the skull *was* made in this world, none of its creators exist now, but that somehow they still have an energy or power over the skull, be it from another dimension or not. Or, if the skull was made in some other world (perhaps on another planet or in another dimension), then it is a doorway for them to look in on us. Now, I know I'm 'out on a limb' when I say this, but that's how I feel.

Sandra: You mention the future and looking at nature... Several books describe an overall plan for the spiritual growth and evolution of the world. For instance, I'm thinking of *The Keys of Enoch,* by J. J. Hurtak (1977). Do you get some sense of that from your study of Crystal Skulls?

Nick: Well, I feel that there's only one simple overall plan for the world which has been distorted by philosophies and theologies. We have one energy source, which today you might learn about in the new book, *Super Force;* if you can understand the mathematical formulas in it! The book states that there is a 'Super Force' and it's capable of utilizing everyone's mind, which therefore is capable of controlling the Elements. The Elements are what destroy this world.

Now, whether these books you mention, which give a plan for the world, are valid or not valid, I don't know. The only plan for this world is to control the Elements (Fire, Earth, Air, Water). And you control the Elements through light, color and sound, the Three Mysteries (Mystery Elements).

People in this world are going crazy, particularly with sound and light. We have all kinds of lasers going around this world right now. We have all kinds of sound, and people going into everything from high-frequency light waves to high-frequency radio waves to God-knows what! And this is not for the betterment of mankind, but the destruction of mankind! Somewhere they're going to reach the vibrations with which light, color and sound balance the Earth. But for now, we need to be concerned with learning how to control these [energies] instead of worrying about a tree or a fish or a snail for the actual preservation of our Earth (because the Earth will constantly evolve and rebuild itself if it has the proper balance of light, color and sound). You see? If it doesn't then you might as well forget about the little fish you're trying to save, or the little tree you're trying to save.

This Universal Force functions very deliberately, very sensibly, and it can react. Now, whether UFOs or other things come from this Universe, I don't know. All I know is that there is something out there that is so gigantic, we can't even imagine it. This Force controls a great deal of what's happening here, and everything moves according to a Universal Plan. There are natural laws that govern this. We don't fly off into space, and nothing is going to fly off into us, until you die. When you die it's the motion that's important. Once the motion stops, you see, then you have problems. As long as the motion takes place, nothing moves out of place. It may tilt a little, but it always gets back to where it belongs. It's very mathematical; it follows a pattern and I wish I knew more about math.

We know, for instance, that every 25,000 or 35,000 years there's a slight magnetic shift in the Earth. This magnetic shift either causes the crust of the Earth to move, or it causes a direct temperature change, and it's almost instantaneous when it happens. Now, this has happened and it's going to happen again. We have now reached a point where we know how to stop meteorites from hitting the Earth. We have a whole plan (most countries have a plan) about how to stop meteorites from hitting our country by exploding them in space. Anybody who follows the science journals knows this. But, I know of nobody who has a plan to figure out what it is that causes the Earth to shift.

CHAPTER 1

One scientific theory involves a 'Death Planet' (or whatever you want to call it), which passes the Earth every so many thousands of years. In its passing it causes the Earth to move in space. The theory is that if we control the Elements, the effects are diminished. It's my belief that when this happens, it can be read in the geological formations of crystals.

Maybe I'm wrong, but there is a planet, which I've known about since I was a kid, that can affect the Earth. Whether this planet can be destroyed, I don't know. All I know is that everything I've read over the last fifty years indicates that the world scientific community has been searching very hard for this planet, and there's been a great deal of money spent to locate it.[2] That's why scientists get very concerned about comets, because when a comet passes, they want to know if it is pulling this planet in. And, if this is so, then it will cause some sort of change in the Earth. See? None of the known effects of comets can really be traced to the comet. When we start tracking the comets, and we try to find out if a particular comet can be attributed to earthquakes or any type of natural disasters, we find out that these things really didn't take place when the comet was around. They took place before or after the comet passed by the Earth, and there stands the problem.

So, these Mystery Elements could destroy us!! And I think that's why we're experiencing UFOs and contact with out-of-our-Universe beings, minds or entities. I don't like to think of them as people like us. I like to think of them as Intelligences that have an understanding far beyond ours, and an understanding of the values of energy-- the Lifeforce. That would be my way of looking at UFOs. And I think the Crystal Skulls are a key, a link to understanding this Lifeforce and the other places and beings where it might exist in the galaxies around us.

Joshua: What are some of the things that crystals tell you about our universe?

Nick: When I gaze into a crystal, I see the galaxy and I see this thing that alters the energy. Also, in crystals I see several universes. And beyond our universe we can count as many as twelve universes where there is a sun which is as big as this entire universe. Its people or planets are pure energy or entities. And in looking at the Mitchell-Hedges Skull, the Mayan Skull, the British Skull, (not so much with the Paris Skull), the other French Skull (the

---

[2]-Robert Jastrow, "Red Giants and White Dwarfs."

F. R. 'NICK' NOCERINO

'Blood of Christ') and various other skulls, I keep seeing this galaxy. I don't know what this means.

Now, I assume that there is a Master Galaxy out there-- a pure Universal Force or Universal Entity. For lack of something better, we might call it 'God,' 'Christ,' 'Buddha,' 'Allah' or anything else you wish to call it.

Then I think to myself, "Is the skull telling me that it came from someplace out there in space?" Hypothetically, I would say yes. "Was it made with pure energy?" Of course, hypothetically, I would say yes. But that doesn't mean that one hundred years from now (or even fifty or ten years from now) someone won't find some way of dating silicon and suddenly make a liar out of me (which doesn't make my theory any less provable or valid). I have to assume that other planets have quartz crystal. I must assume that other places like Earth exist, and if they do, then these extraterrestrials must have a greater intelligence and energy force than we've ever conceived of. There are no norms; there are no variables which can be verified by hard scientific facts.

Sandra: What do you mean by "norms and variables?"

Nick: One could say that the norm is that every 25,000 to 35,000 years something happens. The variable is that there is an unpredictable catastrophe which destroys different parts of the Earth. It creates mountains, leaves lakes, changes oceans, deserts vanish-- all sorts of things happen, and the Crystal Skulls are very precise about that. The only difference is that the Mitchell-Hedges Crystal Skull shows four specific catastrophes, whereas the Mayan Skull showed only three.

Joshua: What do you think that indicates?

Nick: This leads me to believe the Mayan Skull was created thousands of years later than the Mitchell-Hedges Skull, and that the Mayan Skull was eventually found after the last catastrophe by primitive people who, although they might have been advanced in their time period, were not as advanced as the people who made the skull. They therefore perverted it, because the skull to them had a different meaning. Perhaps they believed that all stages and forms of human energy were required to activate the skull's gifts, such as birth, death, anger, happiness, sacrifices, and so forth. This is what I call the 'perversion.' I think we're talking about something that came and went many times, because the Crystal Skull shows many other worlds. I think perhaps

CHAPTER 1

why we see seven levels, and then the many dimensions of those levels, is because it's possible (and again this is only theory) that this skull left and returned seven times in all, to eventually stay where it is. I believe that there are twelve other Crystal Skulls, or twelve other stones (however you want to look at it), whether you want to call them 'skulls' or not.

There is a 'Master Stone'-- I have no doubt. The closest thing to a Master Stone so far seems to be the Mitchell-Hedges Skull; the clearest and purest of the Crystal Skulls. People who want to can take energy from the skull to heal themselves, as some of the letters written to Anna Mitchell-Hedges have indicated (and which also shows that it is not a death skull). Now someone may say that if it heals, it can also kill! That's true, but a healing is also a 'crossing-over' of pain. A healing is a 'crossing-over' of someone who is completely mutilated and in agony, and this gives the person dignity in their crossing. The skull may indeed guarantee death when necessary. Death in itself may be the healing! So we have to understand that 'healing' isn't always to live. To a person riddled with cancer, in complete agony and suffering, a healing may be to cross-over [to an afterlife; to die] with dignity. That's the best way I can explain it.

Sandra: Ok. Now, you've talked about there being these thirteen Crystal Skulls. Where do you think they are? Is the Mitchell-Hedges Skull one of this group of thirteen?

Nick: Yes, I believe there are thirteen 'Power Stones' or skulls or whatever you want to call them. Twelve that may have a certain form or shape (such as a Crystal Skull), and one skull (if they ever find it) which is capable of giving us all the information that is in all the other ancient skulls. And that makes sense to me! The Mitchell-Hedges Skull would definitely be one of these.

I see many pyramids in the skulls. I see Mexican, Chinese, Korean, Nigerian and Egyptian pyramids-- just about every kind of pyramid conceivable. Some of the symbols we see in the skulls have been traced to Korea and Nigeria, but we haven't found any Crystal Skulls in these locations yet. All the skulls that have been found in these locations are human skulls [bone], skulls covered with stone (or something else), or stone skulls that are of minerals other than quartz crystal, such as turquoise, jade, agate and so on.

Sandra: What do you think is the connection between the Skulls and pyramids on this Earth?

F. R. 'NICK' NOCERINO

Nick: Well, I believe that the way humans think about crystals is limited. No one has been able to open a pyramid and find crystals in it anywhere. Yet, in all the pyramids I have visited, I have always scattered crystals inside and outside them. Then I would sit back and watch in hopes of picking up something [psychically] from the crystals. There are probably hundreds of crystals scattered all over the world in different pyramids and someone's going to find it and think that they belong to the pyramid. Now, I know other people before me who have done the same thing. I think there are several people in France and Italy who have scattered crystals in all the pyramids. I have not received any information at this time that one has been found in any of the pyramids.

I believe that there is a Crystal Skull in the pyramids in Peru and British Guiana, and that we'll find another Crystal Skull once we penetrate the Golden City in the Mata Grossa of Brazil. I believe that the cemeteries near the pyramids in Bolivia and Guatemala where hundreds of skulls were found (none larger than a baseball), were training places. You see, we have to understand that pyramids are built upon pyramids, and therefore it's very possible that under the lower pyramids there are more Crystal Skulls.

For instance, many people say there's a Crystal Skull in Egypt. If this is true, then we have to accept the theory that there's a pyramid under the pyramid. Let's say the pyramid is at Giza (where I've spent some time). I always think of pyramids beneath pyramids as reverse pyramids [upside-down]. Now, I've been in the tunnels there during the [Second World] War, and I have the impression that the tunnels all connected somewhere in this world at one time or another. If I can only find the articles in the press from the early '30s that talked about explorers who went into the tunnels and came out in other countries. These were done by the Hearst Press, which claims they never wrote the articles, or that they can't find them. They've only been microfilming copies of their paper for so many years, you know. They claimed they didn't have any old records, but if I could find those, I think it would be a fine connection. Therefore, if there are Crystal Skulls anywhere, it's very possible that the cultures which had them were so ancient, that as other cultures came in, they buried those skulls very deep for safety. Now, eventually, if someone gets down deep enough, they will find all kinds of wonderful artifacts. Someone who just got back from Israel and another person who returned from Egypt were telling me recently that the

CHAPTER 1

archaeologists may have found five cities, one right on top of the other. When I was in Florence [Italy], they had already found three cities. So you know, I think that eventually when we realize that major civilizations always build on top of previous cultures this will uncover many secrets.

Joshua: Do you think Egypt is a good place, besides Central America to look for Crystal Skulls?

Nick: Well, I would say that if I were going to look for a Crystal Skull, I would look in Crete. The fable that was told by one of Plato's students talks about an Atlantean War. He didn't know what they were so he called them 'Atlanteans' (because there's no historical background on anything he was talking about). After the Myceans vanished, due to fighting with the Atlanteans, the Minoans took power. Now if I were an Atlantean in a tribe moving that way (east) through the Aegean and the Mediterranean, I would bring my Power Tools [i.e.- Sacred Objects] with me, which would have included my Crystal Skull. And if that was the greatest civilization of its time, the first thing you'd have to do is conquer them and put yourself in power. So, I would say that somewhere in that area [in the Aegean] there would be a Crystal Skull. Now, if I were to believe what has been written by Le Plongeon[3] or Churchward[4], then from the Gowandaland (or whatever they call it), if the movement of the 'Eri' (or the Earth) went the way of one of the twelve tribes [of Atlantis], I would believe that somewhere (and I would be very positive about this), either in Germany or France, there is a Crystal Skull because I would have brought my Power Tools there with me. These tribes apparently moved and never went back. They were constantly on the move. They moved east and this connected them with everything in the west, therefore, I would expect to find the skull somewhere in the east. I have to be very cautious here because I would think there would be a skull in China and one in India. So, what I'm trying to say is that the Power Tools would have to go with the people who had them.

---

[3]- Augustus Le Plongeon, "Sacred Mysteries Among the Mayas and the Quiches-- Their Relation to the Sacred Mysteries of Egypt." New York.

[4]- Colonel James Churchward, author of Mu series of books, such as *The Lost Continent of Mu, The Children of Mu.*. Churchward was an archaeologist, anthropologist, and an art historian.

F. R. 'NICK' NOCERINO

I don't think the Power Tools all sank underwater when these islands sank (or these continents submerged). I would say that in each continent, outside of the central control place (which I believe was Central America, from about the southern part of the United States down through the center of Brazil) which was the power structure of these twelve tribes, that a skull ended up on each continent. This young lady [Sandra] comes up with these very extensive theories about the skulls. She tells me about all of these skulls that were in Tibet and other places. As I ask this question over and over, I see these seven paths and I think that somewhere there are seven Crystal Skulls dispersed on these continents. Also, I think that the most important thing we're looking for is the Master Stone (assuming that it's not the Mitchell-Hedges Crystal Skull, and it's where I keep going when I astrally project to its location), which lies in Central America.

Now, that's my theory and I can't prove it. I rather like all of Sandra's theories, the 'Crystal Lady' we call her [see Chapter 2]. I think it's possible that there is a Tibetan link to the Crystal Skulls, except that the land-locked position surrounded by the Himalayan Mountain range is a serious factor to consider. Every time I think of the Himalayas (and I've spent time in the Orient in various countries), I see that they are so inaccessible that only until recently were there even roads for vehicles to travel through. And, even now we're not sure they will be able to use radios, because when I was up there radios just never worked. I would definitely consider Crystal Skulls arriving in Tibet from another planet.

It's very possible that from stone tablets found in India and Tibet (of which there are tens of thousands, as described in Churchward's research), we could find a direct link between Tibet and other planets for several reasons. Many of the Juju or Shamans (metaphysicians, witchdoctors or whatever you want to call them) who I talked to, who studied in Tibet or worked in Tibet, told me about caves where there were giants and caves where there were little people [Editors' note: both mummified]. Also, that these caves were deep underground and lit-up by some light that's unknown to mankind today. And whether that's true or not, I don't know. They also told me there are records which no one can read anymore. This is because the keepers who were living in these caves (monks who were stationed in these caves and did nothing but work with the records) used to be constantly replenished by descendants. Now because the Chinese control the country, these monks will not be

CHAPTER 1

replaced for two hundred years. The Tibetans have always been accurate about how long they will be conquered and when they will be freed. So, let's assume it's going to be two hundred years. How do we get into these records? Where are they? The Chinese are certainly looking for them.

Other questions I have are, why will they not allow anybody into the Shensi Pyramids (China)? Why were the Shensi Pyramids protected by the ancient people? Why were foreigners kept out of the area? Why are they closed now and no one is allowed into this area? Are we supposed to assume that suddenly it has become a military area? Or are we to assume that there's something there which we don't know about? Now, if there is a Crystal Skull anywhere in the China area, I would expect to find it somewhere deep within the Shensi Pyramids. That would be my best way of explaining where the other Crystal Skulls might be, or where they might not be.

I have always felt this, particularly when I was flying CBI, the China-Burma-India route in the 40's. We saw gigantic pyramids and they seemed to appear and disappear (maybe we were off-course and then we didn't fly back over them). The government of China has continually denied that the pyramids existed. The U.S. Government has a satellite which passes over this part of China and took pictures which prove that the Shensi Pyramids are there. So, what the heck is the big mystery? Why has this mystery been going on and why are people who used to go into the area (particularly the foreigners) now leaving the area? What's in there? Are we going to find out if it's a simple archaeological dig problem, or are we going to find out what's really true (if we can actually get into it)? If we wait for the Chinese it may be five hundred years before they start digging there. Is a secret there, a secret that Man needs? The Chinese Government knows about it and is looking for that secret. I would say so but I don't know for sure! Yes, I believe there are other skulls and I believe that's where some skulls might be.

Also I think that this newly discovered cave in Belize (formerly British Honduras) will be a very big answer to where some of the other skulls are-- if somebody knows how to cut their way through the jungle again to find it. I feel that the archaeologists and anthropologists who are doing this type of work today don't take it seriously anymore. They work for two or three months and then leave. They would have to work five or ten years just to get into these places, and they're not! They're making quick trips out from schools or something of this order, because nobody wants to 'put up' the money or

F. R. 'NICK' NOCERINO

During his research with the Mitchell-Hedges Skull, Mr. Nocerino used a special technique for listening to the Crystal Skull. In this photograph, Nick is aligning himself with the skull by touching the part of his head where the brain processes sound.

whatever it takes to keep a team out there for several years (they don't make fortunes on these things, the governments do). It's very possible that the Mexican Government has a skull that they've never told anyone about. Instead of all this secrecy, if they were able to find all of these little skulls, why did they make a move to claim that all of them were theirs? I mean, there are so many unanswered questions!

Joshua: What makes the Crystal Skulls different from other skulls or other pieces of crystal, for that matter?

Nick: A Crystal Skull (a rock-quartz Crystal Skull) has a method of establishing rapport with the human mind, with a lifeforce, and immediately extending that energy. This can be measured and it doesn't only extend the energy out like most of the other [non-quartz] skulls do. It extends an entire wall of energy. How high this wall of energy goes, I don't know. I've never been able to climb up on a ladder high enough to measure this, but it certainly goes well

CHAPTER 1

above my head with my arm extended. You know, we were able to test some skulls like that, and it was damn near a mile! That was the one we had for four months, the Mayan Skull. With the Mitchell-Hedges Crystal Skull I felt that had I been two blocks away from it, the wall of energy would have kept going because my aurameter was bent over and would not straighten out. So you know, the force gets stronger and stronger as the human mind works with it.

With the normal stones and small skulls the energy is very different. I don't accept those skulls as ancient programmed Crystal Skulls because I think those are simply perverted imitations. In examining them (which I've done a lot of over the years), I found that the energies are not there like with the ancient Crystal Skulls.

Sandra: Nick, one of my connections with you is in the area of UFOs and the Crystal Skulls. What is your personal or intuitive feeling about this? I know you've worked with people who have had UFO experiences.

Nick: Yes, thousands of them! But you're the first UFO contactee who has ever received information from extraterrestrials that the Crystal Skulls and UFOs are linked, you're the very first.

Sandra: I am?

Nick: Yes, no one that we ever talked with before has received such information from extraterrestrials. Most people who came to me had a UFO experience, but you were the first to connect these two topics, Crystal Skulls and UFOs.

Sandra: I know, but with all the networking of people that he's [Joshua] done...

Nick: It doesn't matter who comes up with them. You've told me more about them than Joshua has. The people I've talked to about UFOs, whether in Europe or in Africa, whether here or somewhere else, looked at them as another intelligence (a concept which few people want to accept). UFOs are simple phenomena they saw and it doesn't matter what other people tell them, that they're nuts or what have you. They had a living experience and that's it. It's true for them. I've seen and photographed UFOs, I have movies of them, I've been on national radio and television with movies and pictures of UFOs. I've had UFO research teams out in the field, forty at a time. And so I had no problem accepting UFOs. But, never have I received information about a

Crystal Skull from a UFO channel or contactee or anything like that. Until you mentioned it.

Sandra: Do you feel that your own source of inner information comes from tapping into your seven other bodies-- your memory banks, your past lives-- or do you actually feel that there are some Space Beings or Higher Consciousnesses who work with you?

Nick: Let me explain it this way. I can be sitting and reading a book, eating a sandwich, or talking with you, when suddenly I see a scenario about a Crystal Skull. It says to me, "There's a skull in the area." And this often happens to me. It doesn't matter whether it's an ancient skull or not; there's always been a Crystal Skull which shows up, and I have always been contacted about it. Now, even when other people have had dreams (and Sandra and my son have had many dreams about Crystal Skulls), they tell me, "Well you're going to see a Crystal Skull and you're going to be contacted about one in six weeks." I usually don't say anything to them because I've already received this information in a vision. One might say I've already been contacted by what I call my skull informant. I have to get as much valid information as I can on something like this, to see where it fits. It doesn't matter whether I've seen the skull already, or if my son or someone else has, and they say, "There's a skull in the area-- it's on the move." It may not be *where* they said it was going to be, it may not be *what* they said it was going to be, but a Crystal Skull always shows up. You see? So there is some validity there to what they are relating to me. But whether they pick it up clairvoyantly or from reading my mind (however they receive it), I don't know. The fact is that it's happening.

You see, right now I have some people who are going to be transmitting to me hundreds of pictures, photos and slides of other skulls. I'm going to have to pay for them, and I will if they do what I've asked them to do. I always prefer to touch the skulls myself in doing the research, but I can obtain good results from pictures. In two cases I can't really get to touch and be with those skulls, but with the other two, I don't know. That has to be worked out. No matter how many skulls I have seen, whether twelve or thirteen, I have to honestly say that wherever there are skulls there seems to be UFO activity. That's number one. Number two, wherever there's UFO activity there's great telekinetic or psychokinetic activity. The skull functions entirely through telekinetic and psychokinetic protection (or however you want to look at this).

CHAPTER 1

There's no doubt that the skull causes me to question people differently, particularly in the last two or three years.

Now, the other thing is that most UFO contactees are very emphatic about their experience. They prefer not to discuss it too openly. People who discuss UFO experiences (particularly to me in the last three years) and mention something about Crystal Skulls, usually mention it because I asked them. I've only done this since I've talked to Sandra, because she had made that a point. So when I ask, "Do you get any information on Crystal Skulls?," they usually answer, "No, but as long as you asked the question..." Then they will go on to say something about there being some Crystal Skulls which are coming out into the open pretty soon. But, the skulls *aren't* coming out into the open. The people who are getting or finding them are keeping them undercover and hidden. You see, that's the big problem! And if things work out, within at least the next year or two at the most, I hope to be connected to three or four other skulls, or spend some time with them. So I don't know whether it's going to take that long, but this will very definitely happen.

Sandra: What kind of information about these Crystal Skulls have you received inwardly or from people you've worked with who have had UFO experiences?

Nick: I never had to be convinced that the skulls and UFOs have some connection, if not a complete connection. Of all the people involved in UFOs, about 2%, maybe 3% actually had physical contact, but the majority of them had what we would call "other-body contacts" (astral projection, astral bodies, mind bodies or the spiritual bodies made contact). That makes the information just as valid, because when it's put down and passes through the bodies into the waking consciousness, it feels and seems very real. Sometimes it has to be brought out [through hypnosis] because it gets into the unconscious and lies between the subconscious and conscious. When I bring it into their consciousness, it becomes very valid.

In putting clients into regression, I have found this is true. Also, I've talked to people in many parts of the world. Whether I'm talking to someone in Paris, or someone in Southern France, or I'm talking to someone in Florence, Italy, they are all telling me the same story, but they don't know each other. Then I come home and I talk to someone in New York, North Carolina, Dallas or the San Francisco Bay area and they're telling me the same story.

F. R. 'NICK' NOCERINO

Therefore, I begin to wonder why it's so difficult to accept the fact that people can actually separate from their bodies and have UFO experiences? Why does it always have to be a physical contact?

I'm finding that a great deal of the information is very valid. That is, if the person understands what is happening and can interpret it correctly. I always have to look at their interpretation, rather than how I would interpret it.

I have been lucky in that I've had physical sightings of UFOs and even taken photos and movies of them. Yet all my contacts with so-called extraterrestrials seemed to be in an out-of-body state. I just seem to leave my physical body and communicate with whoever or whatever they are. I was trained to believe that every human being leaves their body when they are asleep or often in a trance state. My research from 1955 through 1970 and again 1979 through 1983 seems to confirm this. The skeptic may sneer, but the experience in the mind of the individual involved is just as valid as a direct physical contact.

People are definitely talking more now about UFOs. I've received some letters recently from New York, New Jersey and Pennsylvania about UFOs. People have sent me letters and I wrote back and asked them to record their entire experiences, or whatever it is that they're trying to tell me.

I would be very happy to have written-records of their experiences, but whether I get them or not is another story. These are people who are channeling. There are people who are sitting somewhere and all of a sudden see this thing and swear that they were on a UFO, and want to make sure that you don't believe they're crazy, and so forth and so on. They make me promise not to tell anybody about it, as they're confiding in me. So it's like the information that comes in (they receive or channel) about Crystal Skulls for some people, comes through their other bodies in the identical way that UFO information is coming through. I don't know if that makes any sense to you, but that's the only way I can describe it. I'm not sure I answered your questions, but your questions raise other points.

Sandra: Do you feel like you're being guided? Have you had experiences where Space Beings or a Higher Intelligence has actually said, "Go do this," or, "Go to Mexico," or "Get some people to go to certain places and do *this* because... ?" Or do you just have an inner knowingness of what it is that you need to do?

Nick: I've never personally had a UFO - Skull connection where I've received...

CHAPTER 1

Nick: Right.

Sandra: But do you feel that somewhere there is some kind of guidance going on with you?

Nick: Yes, someone, somewhere is giving me information and a great deal of knowledge. I am told many things, mostly through visions. When this happens, I believe that what I've seen and received will take place, and events will move to make it happen exactly as I have seen it. It has been this way since before my seventh birthday. At that time I was initiated and instructed by neighborhood women about some of the powers of the mind and my own relationship to crystals. These women were involved in traditional, Old World, European Wicca or witchcraft.

So I believe in a Universal Guidance or Force. But I don't hear it. I don't say like some people, "You know, what I'm hearing is, or what I'm..." For me, suddenly I just see this picture, I see a person and the scene unfolds. Now if I can just let the scene unfold and not challenge it like I've done for many many years, it would probably all function; but I don't. I become logical, I start throwing in these problems and these equations because I want it to be a certain way. Maybe that isn't the way it's supposed to be, and it will all flow [on its own]. So I say to myself, "How can it all flow anyway if it's not doing what I want it to do?" "But it is doing what I want it to do, I just don't know it-- What a big dummy!" I get in this argument with myself as it goes on. But normally it's a picture. It will come anytime during the day or night. Let's say I'll be thinking about a certain person or situation, and suddenly I see something. There are no words; I see the entire scene taking place and it's there. Then I'm the one who throws turmoil into it. When you talk to me, what happens is very simple. I inwardly see what you're saying, feeling and knowing, *and* what you're not saying, often even before the words are spoken. It's always been that way. It's always flabbergasted and puzzled me.

The reason I like to go to movies as much as possible is that it helps me to sort out problems and see things better. Often when I'm looking at a movie, suddenly there's two pictures; one inside of my mind and the other one on the screen. I walk out of the movie and the problem is completely solved. Yet, I don't know what to call this *guidance.* I wish I could say that when I hold my crystals the guidance is stronger. I wish I could say that when I did this or a certain ritual or something, it was stronger, really! It comes, it's there, it could be a moment or it could go on for long periods of time. I've had it go on for twenty or thirty minutes. I'm just sitting and there's this whole thing going on... dimensional things which transpire. In other words there has to be a guidance, whether it's from the skull or whomever.

People have told me, for instance, that they've seen me in the Crystal Skull. This was long before I ever met the Mayan Skull or before we even got to the Mitchell-Hedges Skull. People would say, "You know I saw this skull and I swear you were in this skull!" And I would say, "Oh yeah, yeah..." And that day or the next day I would see an entire scene about a skull. I would see myself involved, and think, "What is this? What am I looking at? What is someone trying to tell me? Is it my subconscious? Is it my superconscious? Is it one of my other bodies relaying information to me?" Because, the desire to be with skulls, and the desire to see skulls and get the skulls has taken me to some pretty weird places, and it has put me in some very bad physical positions. Yet this compulsion is stronger than common sense. That's the best way of saying... whatever it is.

Whether it's a guide, a teacher or one of my other bodies, it's very powerful and strong. To me, it's like a love, pure love. And you do not alter love. Things may change, but if you love, it's a movement. It may move this way and it may move that way, but it is a constant eternal thing. This guidance, this mind, this force is constant and seems to always be around me. When this happens, it seems like it has always happened. I can't remember..., since I was very young I have seen these scenes, and I didn't understand them all at this early age. My grandmother didn't understand them all. And yet today, every one of them has proven out, every single one. So, I don't know if that answers your question. You see there are no simple answers to some of the questions that you're posing here. I'm sorry but there aren't.

Sandra: Well, I know that you've gone into dangerous places to get these skulls or to be with them, but don't you always feel healthier and better when you are in the presence of the skulls? Hasn't that been your experience?

Nick: Well, yes. I have to be honest with you. As a matter of fact, all crystal makes me feel better and healthier, but the Crystal Skulls seem to magnify this. That's why the perversion of the skulls affects me so much. I think Crystal Skulls are for healing purposes and for crossing people over who need to be crossed-over. And I wouldn't be surprised if there is truth to this in some of the more ancient cultures. For example, I have heard and read in some

CHAPTER 1

ancient Tibetan information that one could use a Crystal Skull for transmigrating the soul from one body to another. Ultimately, that would be it.

I also think that the Crystal Skulls are capable of actually altering future events. I'm positive about this. And someday, I will talk about new events which I set in motion in Canada, North Carolina, New York, Connecticut and other parts of the country where I took the Mayan Skull. I think that the power of the skull would be [demonstrated] if someone could truly learn to communicate mind-to-mind with it and learn what a dimension is; whether it's light, color, sound or a combination of all of them. Once you set energy in motion from your mind, you're setting in motion a thoughtform. I actually think that the Crystal Skulls will better mankind, particularly if someday the ancient skulls are brought together.

Joshua: Do you believe there's any danger involved with the Skulls?

Nick: Recently Sandra told me that if there are twelve skulls in Tibet, then there are twelve other primitive skulls. Then she asked me whether we are stumbling into the more primitive skulls and therefore neglecting or negating those twelve positive skulls? Is there some mad plan (and I always wonder about this) that maybe there is a force just as powerful that doesn't want mankind to succeed?

Now, I get this feeling also in UFO experiences. Why are some UFO experiences, which are supposed to create pleasant educational growth on all conscious levels, causing some people so much agony or frustration? Particularly if they have had any illnesses. I've talked to a number of people who had been ill and then completely cured after UFO experiences, and others have had their sicknesses, no matter how minute, suddenly magnified tenfold. So I'm wondering, are there two forces involved? If there are additional primitive skulls, since you two and others feel that there are still twelve hidden skulls such as the Mitchell-Hedges Skull, I wonder whether they eventually will come to the surface. I don't know if this is true, but I think it is close to the truth. I keep seeing [inwardly] all the skulls together and never apart. I've made drawing after drawing about how I've seen the skulls layed-out in different temples and pyramids.

Again the problem is, as it is with UFO information, that the people in our power structure who handle and hold onto the Crystal Skulls, don't see eye-to-eye with those who share information about peace in the world. How do you

F. R. 'NICK' NOCERINO

get to the President? How do you get to the leaders of the USSR, the Emperor of Japan or other heads of governments to bring them and the skulls together?

But truly, I think the politics involving the Crystal Skulls should be very limited. They exist in the world as nonpolitical, nonreligious entities and belong in the world of spiritual activity and growth. However, people confuse religion with spirituality; I don't. ...What's the next question?

Joshua: You've already talked about the Mitchell-Hedges Skull. What information would you like to share about some of the other skulls?

Nick: One basic thing they all have in common is being stolen or let's say, "removed", from their rightful places. I think it is deplorable that some people feel this way about the Mitchell-Hedges Skull, which was a legitimate gift.

Then there is the Mayan Skull. It has an interesting history. It was stolen from a tomb in Guatemala, and worked its way north with a group of nine mentalists and their families, into the Sierra Madres area. These people are still moving through that general area. It's loaded with artifacts. What these people do is loot tombs. They have, I believe, another skull which is also a permanent [ancient] clear quartz skull. I haven't seen that one, but they claim it has a movable jaw.

The other skull that came in with the same group which brought the Mayan Skull, is the Amethyst Skull. I have seen the Amethyst Skull and it is still in San Jose, California. There are actually three Amethyst Skulls that I know about. People get confused between the skull in Marin County and the skull in San Jose, both of which are in California. The one in Marin County probably dates from nine to twelve hundred years A.D. and is very primitive looking. The one that's in San Jose (California), is a beautiful skull, although it is not the skull that was with Reis, a former president of Mexico, as some have reported. The Marin County Skull *is* the one that was with Reis in Mexico and is just a new work. It's a beautiful work, don't misunderstand me; the pictures are fine, but it doesn't project the ancient images like the other ancient Crystal Skulls do. Although I must confess, I only worked with it for five or six hours, so I don't know what its true capabilities are. Ancient quartz Crystal Skulls go back into the dimensions of time and space.

The Yucatan Skull is one of the most publicly known Crystal Skulls. It's often referred to as an Aztec Skull. Supposedly it was stolen, too. Then somehow the French got it when their troops raided these areas of Mexico. This skull was probably stolen again and then of course it was sold many times, eventually ending up in the British Collection.

CHAPTER 1

The Paris Skull, is the same sort of deal. Also called the Aztec Skull by the French, it is smaller and much more permanent (ancient) than most of our archaeologists believe. It probably was created six to seven thousand years ago, or more, and therefore its memory banks are all primitive.

If someone has a dimensional ability to work with these skulls to make each skull gather information, that's what I would recommend doing with these skulls. Somehow we must get all the skulls in one place, because the Crystal Skulls have the ability to take information and pass it to each other.

The Zulu Skull, which supposedly has a movable jaw, is as large as the Mitchell-Hedges Skull, and was called the Skull of Doom. It was highly revered. Also stolen from the Zulus. And they feared it greatly. When F. A. Mitchell-Hedges brought the Mitchell-Hedges Skull to Africa, the natives thought it was their stolen Skull of Doom. However, we have heard that this skull was not their Crystal Skull.

No one in these cultures has knowledge of the skulls anymore; mainly, I think, because the people who controlled the skulls are no longer alive. This was also the case with most of the Mexicans and people we meet in Central America. They've sought me out many times to explain to them how to use crystals and how to use the skull.

The Berlin Skull is one that the Gestapo supposedly found and brought to Berlin. The Gestapo was collecting many artifacts and icons which contained psychic power. They were for Hitler's exclusive use. This skull is also rumored to have a movable jaw. Supposedly it was in Berlin between September and November (1985), then allegedly went to Italy (possibly the Vatican) for some purpose, but it may be back in Berlin right now. The Italian Skull, I think, is the same skull as the Berlin Skull. I am almost positive of that.

The Southern France Skull, or the Skull of the Blood of Christ, is a skull that I can tell you a story about. For some reason that I don't understand, the man who was guarding this skull, thought we were the couriers for it. I didn't understand all of it at the time (during WWII) until Jaques, my traveling companion, explained to me that the man was expecting two couriers. I had crystals with me and a crystal around my neck (these I lost when my ship, the YMS-13, was sunk off the coast of France). He believed that we were the couriers because he saw the crystal around my neck and asked me some questions which I answered correctly for him. He thought we were being cautious because he knew that the Gestapo were looking for this particular skull. The Communists were taking control of many villages in France. But suddenly we had the skull, thanks to this man. It was the first Crystal Skull I had ever really touched. It was such a privilege, even for the few hours we spent with it.

I feel that this skull is somewhere in a vault right now and that this vault may be in an underground river. We tried to go back and look for it several times. As a matter of fact, the only connection I have found with this vault is with the Knights Templar's records, and several other books such as *Holy Blood, Holy Grail*. I am continually looking for clues about this skull. The church in that area, which was the landmark for me, doesn't exist anymore. So I thought there may be a new church that's there, but I don't know. Eventually I hope to find it. Supposedly it is guarded by a society called the Blood of Christ, which has no second thoughts about eliminating people who interfere with whatever it is that they're doing.

The Masai Skull is one that I've never seen, but when I traveled throughout that area, I heard a great deal of legends and many stories about it. The Masai were very fierce people and still are today. Supposedly the skull was about as big as the Paris Skull, but whether it actually is, I don't know. It was stolen.

I would say that the Paris Skull is also a replica. The Yucatan Skull I view as a less powerful or less pure skull. The Mayan Skull is a more powerful skull as clear crystals go, but the Mitchell-Hedges is the most powerful skull. It certainly is the most pure and healing skull.

The one in Peru, if my information is correct, has a movable jaw. It's a clear quartz Crystal Skull, and very large. We've always known that there was one in Peru and felt that it has never relocated or moved. We have had several groups go in (astrally project) and look for it. When I was in Peru, I couldn't find the Valley of the Dead and that was where the skull was supposed to be. I believe there is a Crystal Skull in Belize, in what I think is one of the treasure troves of the Aztecs, Incans and Mayans, in the caves which have been finally found. Supposedly, you can take the entire Carlsbad Cavern and put it in this cave and still have room to walk around; that's how gigantic it is. What I don't understand is how these caves have been there all this time in such a small country and nobody's gone in and out of them, that's all. I know some people who I hope will respond to my letter, with more information about this. Otherwise, I will write National Geographic and ask them what they know about it. And that's about all I can tell you right now.

Joshua: Is there one in Texas?

CHAPTER 1

Nick: The one in Texas *is* the Mayan Skull. It's in a vault there. If you have sixty thousand dollars, you can get it out. The one in San Mateo, California, is a newly-carved skull, done in Nepal in 1985. It's a beautiful piece of work, about as big as a softball, or maybe a little bigger. Perfectly clear, but it has no memory bank in it. In other words, you can't feel anything except the energy of the crystal. As precise a carving as this is, there are still no convex or concave optics, as there are in the ancient Crystal Skulls. The skull is too new, and there are no dimensions in it yet. It was not made from Himalayan crystal as reported; it was probably made from Calaveras crystal judging by what it looked like. It was not made by a Priest or holy man; it was made by a sculptor or artist who happened to be carving a Tibetan skull. It was a nice piece of art, but historically and energy-wise there's nothing to it. That skull was selling for $3,200 if I wanted to buy it. The people representing the skull called me back, they wanted me to make an offer. [Editors' note: Nick was never able to buy it due to lack of funds.]

Joshua: When we met Frank Dorland last September, he told us that science does not possess the technology today to recreate a Crystal Skull of the quality and perfection that we see in the Mitchell-Hedges Skull. Do you have any other information you can share on this point?

Nick: I have yet to find a sculptor who can carve me a skull as the ancient skulls were carved. I have people who will make me a skull, but they don't seem to have any idea of what that may be. They tell me they'll make it, so I'll probably just have a skull made, but they tell me right off the bat that they have no way of figuring out apexes, terminals or light formations; they'll just make a skull.

We did go to Hewlett-Packard, and a few other laboratories, with the more primitive skulls. They couldn't reproduce them. Now, there are several reasons for that. One is that the carver who made the skull didn't know anything about lapidary work, because he cut it all wrong [as far as our knowledge of how to cut crystal today]. Therefore, he did a miraculous job because the skull should have shattered, fractured or fallen apart when he was carving it. That's number one. Number two, in the laser light test and in the liquid test, you can tell that it is one piece of material. The claim has been that the Crystal Skull is a lot of pieces of material put together similar to the Hebrew fashion which they use to make magic mirrors. But this wasn't true

© F. R. 'Nick' Nocerino

In 1983, Mr. Nocerino had an opportunity to work with the Amethyst Crystal Skull. Here, he is testing the effect of various gemstones and a personal ring upon the skull.

because the skull was made from only one piece of crystal. It was a solid piece carved incorrectly, according to the scientists. They also stated that the entire facet system is completely mystifying. Also, the internal part of the skull is like someone had to get inside of the skull and put these optical systems in there. We cannot do this. Hewlett-Packard for instance; if we gave them one year, and twenty-four hours a day of labor, they might be able to come close to a skull like it, but could not guarantee that it would function in the same way as the Mitchell-Hedges or the Mayan Skulls do. So you take it from there.

Now the Amethyst Skull, which also went through Hewlett-Packard for testing, was also shown to be one piece of stone. The amethyst probably came from Brazil, because at the time that the skull was made, they were only mining amethyst out of Brazil. So there's no way that I know of, that anybody can make an ancient Crystal Skull. I sent out two blocks of crystal to be used to make a Crystal Skull. One came back unworked, and the other was shattered in the attempt. I am talking about a fairly large block of crystal I selected specifically for this purpose.

CHAPTER 1

So maybe just to be happy, I might need to have a special carved skull made for the purpose of storing my own knowledge banks in it. Also I was thinking that if I had this skull made, what I might do is let it sit through the slides we have of other ancient Crystal Skulls, hour after hour, to see if that would achieve my goal. Such a skull would have a way, as all crystal does, of duplicating information and energy.

Sandra: So that's seven, of what you would consider human-sized ones, [*Nick:* Right.] but I've been trying in my mind to see the nine you talked about. I know the story behind some of these because you've told me bits and pieces.

Nick: Well, there are two skulls that could be considered human-like but they're not, because I've seen too many since like them. I call these 'infant skulls' and they're about as big as the one I saw in San Mateo, California [the skull from Nepal] in other words. I've seen hundreds of various sizes, from marble-size to softball-size. Most of those came out of Columbia, Bolivia and Honduras.

Sandra: You say the Mitchell-Hedges Skull is the most pure, but when you talk about the Rose Quartz Skull, it sounds like that one is too. Out of all these skulls that we've talked about, what would you say is the one that you feel the closest affinity to?

Nick: The Rose Quartz Skull, if I can ever find it again. But next to that, the Mitchell-Hedges Skull, because these two seem to be identical in every way except their color; one is clear and one is rose. You know, right now I would leave my wife, my home and my children to go find that skull if I knew where to go! It's not coming through during the times I astrally project to see where the skull is and make contact. It seems that wherever it is or however it is, I'm not getting anything from it and I don't know why. I feel that it may be in an obsidian case which cloaks the skull's energy. If someone takes it out and starts working with it, then I will sense that and begin to take a look at it again. I'll even go as far as the Amazon to find it.

Joshua: Would you say that the Rose Quartz Skull is one of the thirteen key Crystal Skulls?

Nick: Yes, I would. Although in my mind, I have to be honest with you Joshua, I see all these skulls as clear quartz crystal. I have some theories about this which I'm still working on.

F. R. 'NICK' NOCERINO

Sandra: Nick, when I meditated on the Mitchell-Hedges Skull during our research trip to Canada, one of the colors that came out was rose, so maybe that would be the reason. Do you want to talk about your theories?

Nick: Well, I think it's very possible that there are other skulls of different color vibrations which are used in conjunction with the clear quartz Crystal Skulls. And I would think that there are three, maybe four colors which I would look at very closely. These colors would be green, blue, and red. I think the red falls into a category that we don't understand yet because I've examined thousands of stones from all over the world and I haven't found a red stone yet, except a ruby. I don't know of any ruby that's big enough to be carved into a human-sized skull, unless the ruby is man-made or mentally apported. And we can't tell the difference between the man-made pure crystal and a natural crystal, except for the vibratory feeling. The natural crystal has the vibration of the Earth, which you feel immediately, and the man-made one doesn't.

Yes, I would say that one of my theories, which I'm working on now, is that there are color combinations involved. Or it's very possible that people who couldn't carve other colored stones used pure colored crystal pieces, shards, spheres or whatever you want to call them, to activate the Crystal Skulls. Now there's citrine in Columbia which I think is very strong and could also have been used as a tool to carve a skull. Of course, we already have Amethyst Skulls, and this type of quartz is found all over the place. But, I think that somewhere there's a pure amethyst such as the Ural Amethyst, possibly in Brazil, not like the Mexican Amethyst which is very blocked up, blase', has all these different matrixes and isn't pure. We need to find a pure amethyst and a pure green stone with clarity to continue our color tests.

Fine, now if the tribes were unable to get the stones or lost the ability to make the skulls (by the mind or however it was made, and I'm not the only one who thinks the skulls were made by the mind), they would have automatically gone to anything else. They would have gone to jade, which is green, or certain types of agate. I've eliminated verasite and meraposite from consideration because I've never found any artifacts made from it. In other words, they would use the local availability of a particular stone, which could have been sodalite, lapis, or whatever it happened to be. For the red, they could have used rhodocrosite. I doubt it, but maybe ruby. And even rubies could have different colors. A simba ruby compared to a royal ruby is so

CHAPTER 1

different it's ridiculous. Most people don't understand that the ancients could see colors that we can't see in the stones. So that's what we look for. I observe this time and time again in homeopathic work with doctors. They're looking at it as a yellow stone, but by throwing certain lights on it, such as dark light, black light, you know, radio light, or using various mental wavelengths on it, the color changes. It's very possible the ancients could have used all clear quartz crystals, looked at them and knew each one had a specific color pattern to it. These are theories that are running around in my noggin, and I'm just throwing them at you because you asked the question. Yes, next?

Joshua: You've told us you want to discuss the Hollow Earth in your own forthcoming book. Could you elaborate on some of those theories now?

Nick: Well, my basic theory is that there are three types of life on the Earth. It's possible that people from other planets live within our planet, because they realized that catastrophes happened upon the surface of the planet. If they came here, they would have found it just as reasonable to go inside the planet to live. We have no way of actually determining what's inside our planet. There are too many legends and too many stories, particularly if we follow Admiral Byrd, Samuelson and a few other people, to dismiss the probability of beings living within the Earth. Everybody probably wouldn't be telling the same story and not be telling the truth that there is a world within a world. Now, I believe there is some sort of intelligence within our Earth, but you see I go further than that. In legends and in most of the history that I've been able to find of worlds within worlds or lifeforms in the world, there seem to be two types, one that is evil and one that is good. They seem to be in a constant turmoil and they seem to have a direct connection with extraterrestrials and UFOs.

Sometimes I think that there is a Force afoot on this planet or within the planet (for lack of a better word, the Hollow Earth), that can project itself outward (as we're learning to do now with machines) and affect sensitives and people who are having UFO contacts. Their purpose is to diminish or destroy that particular contact level. So that if there are such things as Apples or Seeds [Editors' note: Star People or extraterrestrials who incarnate into an Earth body to be of service to the planet.] and they are to be awakened, this force may cause so much agony and pain that they don't want to be awakened. I believe that there definitely is something like this occurring in the world.

F. R. 'NICK' NOCERINO

I believe there is an intelligence that is in contact with other planets. This intelligence not only is in contact with it, but actually permits the ships from other planets or other dimensions to come into the water, and take what they need from the water. I believe that the most likely bases are off the coast of Chile. Better than 80% of all UFO reports and sightings that I have looked at give these types of reports (I already have a couple hundred books about UFOs in my library). The majority of UFOs are either going into water or coming out of water. Now, it doesn't matter whether we're talking about the Great Lakes, the Bermuda Triangle, off the English Channel, or wherever. People watch these things go into water. Or, they have reported sightings of UFOs coming out of seas, lakes, etc. So yes, I believe there is a culture under the water. We have no way of understanding or communicating with it. We have no way of getting that far down. Someday when we threaten them, we will know about it. I don't know if that helps, but that's my belief.

While viewing the scenes in all the Crystal Skulls which I have worked with, I was led to research mermaids because they appeared within the skulls. I had been researching mermaids for a long time and found scattered information about them. There was a report in 1983 which stated that a body floated up along the coast of Africa. The body was intact except for one thing-- there was the upper portion of a man with a fish tail. It was short, supposedly 3-1/2 feet to 4 feet, and allegedly it was completely tattooed. This shows an intelligence! How do you tattoo your back if you're a fish? I mean, do you have an octopus come over-- how do you do that? Now following that, another body came up in the Philippines or near there. This one was slightly mutilated and nobody knew why when it was found. And again, it was half fish and half man. This year [1986] a body floated up with no head... they don't know how the head came off. The body had a complete tattoo entirely down the back of its hands, its arms and all over its back, and down to the fish part of it. This time they were nice enough to give it to a university. So now we have a tangible research project on this.

Joshua: Well, I think we should stop soon. I have two more questions.

Nick: Oh, we're going to stop? I was having fun, I haven't talked this much in a long time about what I think. Most people want information, not what I think.

Joshua: What do you believe are the true purposes of the Crystal Skulls and how do you see them interfacing with the so-called changes that appear to be

CHAPTER 1

going on with our Earth? In other words, are the skulls coming out now because the planet needs whatever it is they have to offer?

Nick: Going backwards on your questions, I don't know for sure that the Crystal Skulls are involved with the changes happening to the Earth or its environment. I whole-heartedly agree that the planet needs what they can provide. We can go further than that. I would say that if someone on the planet could understand their dimensions or their energy, and tap into them, then this would be of tremendous benefit. In other words, if we could feed the knowledge stored in the skulls into a computer or whatever device is needed, it would be invaluable for us. Just think of the information we would gain from them! I think that we would not only receive information about the present, but from the past and the future as well. You have to understand that a great many skulls are not being uncovered. When you consider the size of the planet, tribes, nations and the cultures, I feel we're being deprived of a vast amount of knowledge which the Crystal Skulls would give us. I would further say that they will help us now and in the future.

I think that the Crystal Skulls would better mankind. I believe their purpose has something to do with creating some form of continuity between peace, the controlling of the Elements and a better world. The skulls are giant computers in a very small package. They can be tapped with other stones, or with mind-power particularly, so that information can be extracted or inserted. What I don't understand is why the people who have these skulls in their possession don't realize this. This totally confuses me. Why would individuals knowingly not want to create an extended energy of crystals, where several skulls are placed together, facing each other? This arrangement will allow them to absorb each other's energies and then we can see if there are any changes. Why they haven't done this, I don't know.

Again, I think there is a hidden Force that stops the skulls from coming together at this time. I feel at times that this Force has even harmed some people I love very dearly. I don't profess to understand it completely. So far it's been incapable of doing the damage that I imagine it could do to me. I don't know what protects me. If I notice that the energy is all wrong, all I have to do is think of balancing it and it happens. I may suffer a little in-between but it doesn't last as long as it does with other people, where it prolongs itself, gets worse, and can be intensified by electronic devices such as TVs, computers, etc. I'm referring to high-frequency devices which utilize man-made crystals.

F. R. 'NICK' NOCERINO

Sandra: Do you have an opinion on whether the Skulls have a gender, male or female?

Nick: I feel that through the interaction between women and the Crystal Skulls, world peace can be achieved. I know this is a radical thing to say, particularly when they're still throwing wives into pyres [Satie] in India; parts of the world are still so primitive in terms of gender issues. You have to remember that only 20-25% of the world has allowed women their freedom and their right to use their minds.

The skulls are female; the skulls are controlled by a female energy, and I have no doubt of this. I believe that there is a male energy which interferes with the release of knowledge from the Crystal Skulls. I firmly believe that when the feminine energy on this planet awakens, all of the Crystal Skulls will manifest and come forward. I'm not just talking about perverted, primitive skulls found in the Americas, but other Crystal Skulls like the Rose Quartz Skull, the Mitchell-Hedges Skull and perhaps one that's hidden in Belize or Berlin somewhere. And then we could talk about whether there is such a thing as a Green Skull, Blue Skull or a Red Skull. As women take control of their own consciousness, these skulls will come forward. This is the best way I can express what I believe.

Joshua: You once mentioned to me that when the Mitchell-Hedges Skull was found, Mayans from all over Central and South America showed up within a matter of days. I thought perhaps you could share your theory about how these people were able to get to Lubaantun [Belize] in such a short time.

Nick: In the ancient Wicca, as well as in Tibet, and various parts of the Orient, they have what are called scanners and communicators. These are people whose only job is to sit and look at a particular location or situation as they are instructed, and report to their superior precisely what is happening. As a good example, Shirley MacLaine wrote about the Masai in one of her books about how they were able to tell her everything that she was doing, even though she was several hundred miles away. In this case, the Elders were able to merge with the warriors guarding her and see through their eyes.

Also, when I was once in Africa, I learned something very interesting while visiting with some people from the Masai Tribe. If someone in the tribe had a question or problem, the Elders would simply sit down and stare into the fire, and after a while they would receive an answer which was very accurate.

CHAPTER 1

When I talked to others afterwards, I learned that all the information that had been given by the Elders was absolutely correct.

Relating these stories to what happened in Lubaantun, I believe that knowingly or unknowingly, many of the shamans were involved down there when the skull was found. I feel that the shamans were able to simply sit down and relay a message (telepathically, with their minds) to other people, five hundred or a thousand miles away. The people who came to see the Mitchell-Hedges Skull didn't just journey from Central America; they came from all over Mexico and everywhere. Now, nowhere in any written accounts or research is there a record of any priest who sat behind the skull to control it. Normally, if you want to send out telepathic messages while in the presence of a Crystal Skull, you would sit behind it. So it's my belief that whoever did this was able to sit in front of the skull, mentally project images to all of these other shamans, whoever or wherever they were. As a person in psychic research I accept that, I believe that. I would be surprised if they didn't do that.

What is astounding is that other Mayans came a thousand miles and arrived in Lubaantun in such a short period of time. How did they do it? They certainly didn't travel through the jungles. How did they travel? Is there a direct path from one point to another point underground? For example, two groups leave the same location at the same time. Yet, one group arrives at their mutual destination days ahead of the other, even if they are both traveling at their fastest speed. How does this happen? I mean these are the things that I get into and that's where I guess I lose some of the logic, because I start thinking about an illogical approach. So what flabbergasts me so much isn't that all of these people started to know the Crystal Skull was again available; it's that they all arrived so quickly at the site where the skull was discovered!! I'm talking about jungle dangers such as condors and jaguars who attack without warning, scorpions, poisonous centipedes, etc. On the Yucatan alone I could think of twenty ways of dying very quickly, for someone who doesn't know what they're doing. But even then (in the 1920's, when the area was strictly jungle and swamp), how fast can you move through trees and bushes where you have to chop and cut to move forward? Consider that it takes three to ten years to clear a ruin just to get into it. These people came from hundreds upon hundreds of miles and showed up at the meditation center there. Why was that meditation center, which possibly held

F. R. 'NICK' NOCERINO

ten thousand or more people, still being used? Why was it the only forbidden place that members of the F. A. Mitchell-Hedges expedition were not allowed to go? You see, all these things started to come into my head. Where did these people come from? They came with women and children. This is not a trip that you take lightly, you know. How long did this go on? Natives were arriving continuously. Now you could say that after the first flow of people, some left to spread the word to others, but the fact is that all the natives stayed at the discovery site for a long time and natives still were arriving.

Joshua: Do you think there was a prophecy that the Mitchell-Hedges Crystal Skull would come up at that time?

Nick: I think the prophecy was that the skull would come back, but not that it would be rediscovered at that time.

Joshua: I'm wondering, if so many people did come from such a great distance, it must have been a long awaited celebration.

Nick: Oh it *was* a celebration; according to what Anna Mitchell-Hedges describes, yes.

Joshua: But it almost felt like it was a prophecy they had, that when this skull reappeared, then certain other things would start happening.

Nick: In his book, Mitchell-Hedges says that the most ancient artifacts are still to be found in the Bay and Cayman Islands, and that the most ancient of Mayan people may still be alive there. I asked June Kirkwood, who works at the College of Modesto Library, to locate the Bay and Cayman Islands for us. She found for us a copy of the book, *Danger, My Ally,* by F. A. Mitchell-Hedges.

When I was studying Mayan populations in the early fifties, and was a subscriber of the Encyclopedia Britannica, I would send them a question and they'd tell me how many Mayans there supposedly were in any given location, what languages they spoke and so forth. They think that the Mayans miraculously disappeared about nine hundred years ago, but there's been a large disappearance of the remaining Mayans within the last fifty years. You see, these are little things that I look at. But I don't discuss them because I don't have any sense of them yet.

F. A. Mitchell-Hedges tells us in his writings that when he went to the various Mayan islands and villages, the natives claimed to never have seen a white man before. Now, this was an area which was loaded with pirates, an area that was constantly invaded by buccaneers and lord-knows what else. If these natives had never seen outsiders, that meant that they remained hidden for some reasons or desires. They were protected by the primitive surroundings. This is evident when you read some of Mitchell-Hedges' descriptions of how his expedition wandered through the jungles searching and suddenly stumbled onto a village.

Most of the Mayan people who had outside contact would have been killed or died by the time Mitchell-Hedges' group arrived. This is based on the fact that the natives' memories and accounts of white men were not very good. Yet, these natives had memories of ancient white men who could fly by levitation, but the Mayans didn't know where they came from or returned to. This is supported by the Inquisition Manuscripts written by Junipero Serra, who was the Grand Inquisitor of the Americas. These papers talk about another civilization in Mayan territory, which was controlled by a tribe of bearded white men. This bears further examination.

Sandra: Tell us more about the ancient artifacts found in the Bay and Cayman Islands.

Nick: Well, there's supposedly a complete boy made of rock quartz crystal. It's very possible that in the same area there's a Crystal Skull. I haven't passed that over either, you know. What relationship does this pure rock quartz Crystal Boy have with the skulls? Is this some form of master stone which can be used with a Crystal Skull? In order to locate the Crystal Boy, I would have to mount an expedition that would cost a half million dollars. I would need guns to fight my way in and out, and Lord knows what else. So I don't know, but I am very very interested in someone locating that Crystal Boy. If the Crystal Boy is as ancient as Mitchell-Hedges felt it was, then imagine how incredible it would be if we found out that we couldn't carve it today. If we were able to put it through the same tests as the Crystal Skulls, wouldn't it be amazing to find out it's a similar type crystal!

Sandra: This entire field continues to be nothing but amazing! We thank you for sharing so much time and energy with us today, Nick. There's much valuable information in this interview that needs to be shared.

Nick: I hope people will find it interesting. As I've said before, visions of Crystal Skulls came to me at an early age and through the years they have been a special quest for me. Although my life has taken me along some very interesting and fulfilling paths, I have never dismissed my childhood dreams and their connection with the Crystal Skulls. They both raise many questions. Why me? What is their ultimate purpose or use? How many more are there? Where are they? How do we get them all together in one place? There are many more questions in my mind. Perhaps someone who reads this book will assist me in finding those answers I am so committed to discover.

CHAPTER 1

PHOTOGRAPHS FROM THE
1985 RESEARCH PROJECT

The following is a series of photographs from the research done with the Mitchell-Hedges Crystal Skull in Miss Mitchell-Hedges' home. Depicted in this section are various tests and techniques which were used while working with this artifact.

© F. R. 'Nick' Nocerino

Members of the Research Team from left to right: Ron Dickinson, Sandra Bowen, DaEl Walker and F. R. 'Nick' Nocerino (team leader). Widely renowned as the most famous of all known ancient Crystal Skulls, the Mitchell-Hedges Skull is considered to be the world's largest gemstone.

© F. R. 'Nick' Nocerino

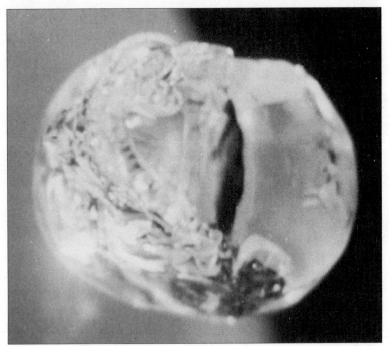

© F. R. 'Nick' Nocerino

Top: Mr. Nocerino activating the Mitchell-Hedges Crystal Skull by placing various gemstones around it in the hope of generating holographic images within the skull.

Bottom: Sample of a scene which appears within the Crystal Skull. Many people feel this is an image of Bigfoot.

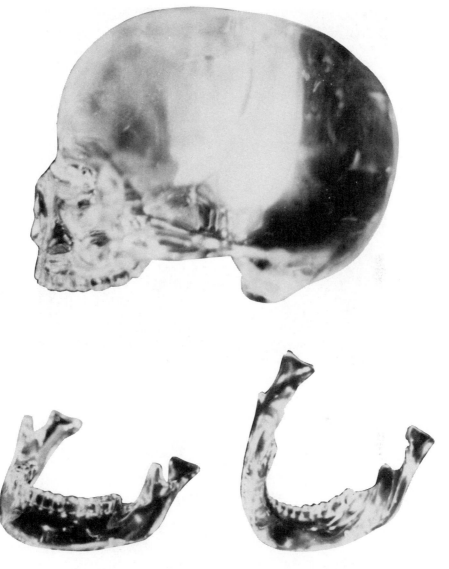

This group of pictures shows the Mitchell-Hedges Crystal Skull separated into its two components, the cranium piece (top photograph) and the detachable lower jaw (bottom left: upright view; bottom right: inverted view). Photographs © F. R. 'Nick' Nocerino

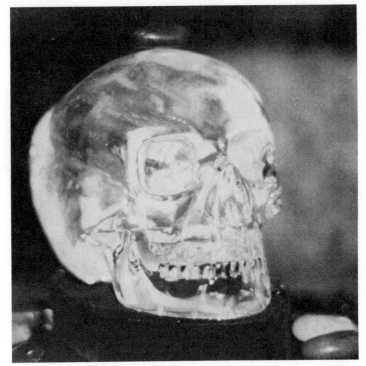

© F. R. 'Nick' Nocerino

© F. R. 'Nick' Nocerino

Top: A view of the Mitchell-Hedges Skull on its special stand during the research team's tests with gemstones.

Bottom: Here the Mitchell-Hedges Skull can be seen with candles and crystals. The researchers were interested in the effects of candlelight upon the skull.

Top: Sideview of Mitchell-Hedges Crystal Skull showing suture lines appearing in the top portion of the skull.

Bottom: Sandra Bowen working with the top part of the skull, exploring the difference in energy when the cranium is separated from the jaw.

Sandra Bowen gazing into the Mitchell-Hedges Crystal Skull in Anna Mitchell-Hedges' living room during the 1985 research project.

hortly after becoming involved with the Crystal Skulls, I had the following experience during a guided regression:

WE WERE TOLD TO RETURN TO THE LIFETIME PREVIOUS TO THIS ONE. I saw myself on the Planet Uranus. I recognized many friends from my current lifetime, as well as Light Beings who were there. We were all working around what appeared to be a gigantic pool table. There was a huge computer panel at one end. We were working at a fast pace programming the Crystal Skulls and I was aware of these Light Beings supervising us. There was joy in doing this work; I was content. Two of the beings came to me and telepathically said that I must return to the Earth. I protested. The reply was, "You are needed there to teach."

I was very rapidly placed in a tunnel; they handed me a crystal and said, "When you meet those with crystals, you will understand." I then saw myself being born, and I looked at the clock (which was a suggestion made to me while in the regression). It said 4:43 PM instead of 4:45 PM which is on my birthchart.

I was born on February 4, 1943, and it wasn't until 1978 that I knew what a crystal was. My first astrology teacher began to teach classes on crystals. We would use them for meditation, dreams, and other consciousness exercises. Two years later, she and I attended a crystal symposium in Palo Alto, California. And there I had my first connection with the Crystal Skulls in this lifetime. F. R. 'Nick' Nocerino was showing slides of the Mayan Skull which he had personally researched. Something stirred within me and I wanted to know more. My path became clear. I decided to become Nick's student and began receiving messages about the Crystal Skulls from my Space Being friends on Uranus. I am very grateful for the continuing guidance they offer me, and to Nick for the patience he has shown while answering all of my questions.

AND YES, I FINALLY DID HAVE AN OPPORTUNITY TO BE WITH A CRYSTAL SKULL on the Earth-plane. This occurred in October and November of 1985, when Nick set up a trip to Kitchener, Ontario, Canada, for a research team of four people to be with the Mitchell-Hedges Crystal Skull. Besides myself and Nick, Ron Dickinson (a member of the IBM Think Tank) and DaEl Walker (author of *The Crystal Book*) were the other members. We spent three blissful weeks with this wonderful Crystal Skull. I felt that I received a profound healing from the skull which has made me a much stronger person. We are very grateful to Anna Mitchell-Hedges for her hospitality.

In 1986 and 1987, I began to lecture with Joshua Shapiro (and Nick sometimes) about the Crystal Skulls, thus beginning to fulfill my promise to my Space Being friends. It is a wonderful feeling to see this book become a reality. I hope it opens up memory banks for the reader and helps you to find your path in this sometimes difficult Earth life.

CHAPTER 2

Crystal Skull Research

The following are my impressions and experiences while researching the Mitchell-Hedges Crystal Skull with F. R. 'Nick' Nocerino, Ron Dickinson and DaEl Walker at the home of Anna Mitchell-Hedges in Kitchener, Ontario, Canada, October 31st through November 20th, 1985.

IMAGINE MY EXCITEMENT AFTER FOUR YEARS OF DREAMING and envisioning my lifetimes working with the Crystal Skulls, sometimes one skull, at other times thirteen (this information comes from working with Nick to uncover a number of past lives through regressions), and finally being able to actually put my hands on a Crystal Skull and gaze into its eyes! We were so warmly and graciously greeted by Anna Mitchell-Hedges ("Please call me Sammy," she said) and her secretary, Cynthia. There it was, this wonderful love of my life, sitting on the coffee table smiling. "Won't you have tea?" they said. And guess where we had it? They placed cups, saucers and the teapot on the table with the Crystal Skull! We were so anxious to touch it but knew that the schedule which was previously planned had to be confirmed first. So, Nick and Cynthia discussed this while Ron and I talked to Anna about the flight, accommodations, etc. Nick and Cynthia finished the schedule; however, we didn't follow it after the first day because it continually changed, giving us more time to work with the Crystal Skull.

We returned to the hotel buzzing with excitement about what we wanted to do and how much we could accomplish with this priceless object. Thus began the ideas-- How will the Crystal Skull respond to each person; will the energy change; what effect will different colored lights have upon it, as well as sounds, crystals and other stones? Nick had his large bag containing nearly every kind of gemstone: Lapis, malachite, amethyst, you name it. Ron brought his water crystal (also called an 'en-hydro'), crystal ball, smoky quartz and various other stones. The water crystal and I became very attached to each other (Don't anyone tell Ron!). I brought three crystals which told me they wouldn't miss this opportunity for the world.

That night we didn't sleep much. The next day we bundled up, put all of the equipment into the car, including video equipment and cameras (lights,

SANDRA BOWEN

© F. R. 'Nick' Nocerino

action!) and we were on our way. There was the Crystal Skull, and this time there were no tea cups around it. Anna said, "It's all yours," and I took a deep breath as Nick said, "Ok, let's measure its energy range." He took out an aurameter and said, "It is emanating six inches out from the skull right now." Then the magic moment... "Sandra, sit down, touch it and meditate!" I sat and put my hands on each side of the skull, then I said "OM MANI PAD-ME HUM.[1]" A most beautiful rose color seemed to come out and permeate the room. Suddenly, Nick was yelling excitedly - "Look at this rod, it's going crazy!" - and out the door he went, coming back much later. "I could have kept going further down the block," he said, "but it's raining out there." We found that if we put a person in front of the skull, the energy increases 20 feet every 40 seconds. Nick also found that this was a

---

[1] This is a powerful Sanskrit mantra. Sanskrit is a sacred language developed from a "sounding" foundation. Words were shaped according to how the sound vibrations affected the human body, and therefore the spirit. "Om Mani Pad-Me Hum" is translated as "Praise to the Jewel in the Lotus."

CHAPTER 2

solid wall of energy in all directions, and at least 10-12 feet high (probably much more).

ALL I KNEW WAS THAT THIS CRYSTAL SKULL WAS TALKING TO ME. It said, "I'm very sad, for I miss my brothers and sisters [Crystal Skulls]." I then touched the front teeth and found three which were chipped. I was sad about this and I said, "It's too bad your teeth are chipped, for my memories of you are as a perfect skull." I had to admit though, that despite lying around under tons of rock for at least 24,000 years (and maybe much much longer than that), this Crystal Skull was truly blessed to be in almost perfect condition.

Ron then meditated with the Crystal Skull and we had the same results with the aurameter. I also saw [with my inner vision] him turn into a Mayan priest in full regalia-- a past life image undoubtedly. There were peacock feathers on his head, he had a gold Mayan calendar medallion around his neck, a parrot on each shoulder, suede clothes and black paint on his face.

FOR THE NEXT TWENTY DAYS WE WORKED WITH THIS MAGNIFICENT ARTIFACT. Some of the things that stand out in my mind are:

The Skull told me that purple is its favorite color and that UFOs could be seen in the back area and on its left side. It is possible that my energy resonates to purple and that is why I heard this information. When I refer to hearing the skull speak to me, it is in a telepathic mode. I hear the messages within me, rather than hearing them with my physical ears as emanating from outside.

We found in our color tests that blue, green and purple were excellent colors for calming and for bringing out very clear UFO pictures. The orange, red, yellow and hot pink seemed to bring in a great deal of activity too, especially the orange-yellow combination. DaEl and I found that this color was a wonderful sinus drainer, and one day when Ron was working for a long period of time with this color, I just had to leave and go into the kitchen! It was very intense, even more so than the red. But no matter what color we used, there was always gold appearing within the skull. In fact, the entire front part of the face would turn bright gold by shining any single color or combination of colors on the skull. It was so incredibly beautiful-- breathtaking!!

We were able to do these experiments thanks to Anna allowing us to separate her dining room table and place a piece of glass in the middle. Then because of Ron's ingenuity, using mirrors under the table and two flashlights with colored gels cut into the proper shapes to fit, with one flashlight on top of the table and one underneath, we were able to create a makeshift colorwheel. The best part of this experiment was what occurred underneath the table, not only the images appearing in the underpart of the skull, but also the reactions of Cassius and Prince Charles, Anna and Cynthia's little dogs who were fascinated by Nick lying under the table with his camera saying, "Oh look at this!", and "You won't believe that!", or "Hope I can get it!" Cynthia thoroughly enjoyed this, and Ron and I were rushing around trying to make sure everything was captured on the audio and video tape recorders. We did this on numerous occasions.

During our scrying session, we saw hundreds of UFOs in the skull. The most dramatic one, however, was the UFO we did not see during scrying, but appeared only after developing our film. Fantastic! This picture was taken from underneath the skull and the UFO appeared in the very center. [See page 66.]

Two of my favorite people who appeared in the skull were the Crystal Man and Woman. Then there was the monkey man, and the man in a turquoise robe with gold in the middle, who always appeared between the eyes or on the nose of the skull. There were also many underwater creatures, big whales, small fish or underwater caverns. In fact, when working together at this time, Ron and I often felt like we were underwater.

Because of the intensity of becoming absorbed with the multidimensional levels of pictures and energies within the skull at this time I felt myself leaving my body. I remember saying, "Ron, I'm leaving!" This is not an unusual occurrence for people who are connected to the skulls on a soul level.

We played music one day and this seemed to create cloudiness and scenes of Inner Earth people (as I call them) with scales, helmets, unusual bodies and giant animals. I was shown a scene where a boy was standing exactly in the middle of the skull as viewed from the top, and there was sort of a little narrow clear band that he appeared in, while the rest of the skull was cloudy. In front of the boy was a computer, and I heard, "We are using computers now." Then the next day he was in front of an altar, and the third day he was with a robot. "What does this mean?" I asked. It seems that the computer and religion will come together some day in our future to create a new form which will manifest as intelligent robots. To me this meant that we are extensions of

CHAPTER 2

Space Beings, and more knowledge will come out on this. Also through the Earth's changes from natural disasters, there will be more information revealed.

A MOST GLORIOUS SIGHT WERE THE MULTICOLORED IRIDESCENT PYRAMIDS, which became taller and thinner, similar to the Eiffel Tower. They were space stations from the past, I feel. In fact, I have a past-life recall of feeding the dolphins from one of these towers in Atlantis. There was a king or high priest who sat in a throne usually above the left eye, and there were mothers in rocking chairs holding their babies.

Certain gemstones seemed to bring out the colors. These were not always seen by everyone; in fact, I really don't see colors, I sense them. The lapis was very powerful when Nick placed it on top of the skull, but part of the effects could well have been related to his energy too. The Crystal Skull strongly reacted when he put green and blue stones in the eyes, red on the head and other stones around the skull in a circle. Unfortunately, it may have been too much for Nick, since he had some discomfort in the back of his head for a short time after that.

The only physical test I set up was placing three of my crystals in front of the skull to be charged, and also to observe what the skull would do. I liked using hand signals with the skull, which seemed to come naturally to me. Whenever I have envisioned the skull in the last seven years, I always see myself doing these hand signals. It seemed to me that my conversation with the skull (using the hand signals which are similar to mudras used in the practice of Tibetan Buddhism) first involves a grounding and centering signal, then activation and formation of cohesions which open up into distinct pictures. The skull throbs and purrs (at least to me) and I can sense the essence that is behind it. The only time I felt that the Crystal Skull was upset was when I covered its eyes. It said, "Please don't do that," and I realized that much is seen through those eyes, just as it is with ours. That was the only resistance I felt from the skull.

IT IS MY BELIEF THAT THIS CRYSTAL SKULL IS A REPRESENTATIVE of loving, advanced Space Beings who delivered it to the Toltecs, and it remains as their memory of these beings. Unfortunately, the Toltecs didn't always respect the inherent power of the skull. Nevertheless, after being in its presence, a person will become more aware of his/her own true essence. I have since felt more confident and it is easier for me now to listen to my heart and make decisions.

SANDRA BOWEN

We need not fear for the future of the brothers and sisters of this Crystal Skull because they will be found with encoded records underneath pyramids. Each person who is to receive pieces of information from the skulls or are called to be in their presence will do so!

Toward the end of this trip to Canada, we went to meet with some crystal healers who had visited Anna right after we had been working with the skull. They had seen our faces inside the skull, can you imagine that! So naturally, they wanted to meet us. Anna told them how to reach us at the hotel. We went to their home and they showed us an intriguing large crystal wheel (about eight feet high) which they used in their healing practice.

I WANT PEOPLE TO HAVE THE OPPORTUNITY to see the beauty of the Crystal Skulls for themselves, but not only that-- to experience the healing, calming and strengthening which I received; be it through slides, pictures or if possible in person. Anna wants this skull to be touched! Obviously this is a very special lady who understands the meaning behind it. There are no other skulls which the general public can touch and really spend quality time with.

I would also like to see more information gathered into books, comparing at least the Mayan Skull with the Mitchell-Hedges Skull, including other Crystal Skulls that are either known or generally unknown. Nick Nocerino is in the process of preparing such a book and would like to hear from others who would like to support this work. I feel that there are thirteen Crystal Skulls which belong together, but if they do not come together in my lifetime it won't matter, for who knows, maybe there are thirteen more in another dimension just waiting for me?

I want to thank Nick for arranging this wonderful trip, and Ron for being so patient with me as I kept asking which button to push, which film to use and many other questions that a beginner asks. Those machines scare me! And lastly, I want to thank my friend the Mitchell-Hedges Crystal Skull for calling me, and the Universe for making it all possible. And still the story continues...

CHAPTER 2

Hypnotic Regressions Related to the Crystal Skulls

Section 1

UFO Experiences & Regressions
(1981 - 1982)

As the introduction mentions, Nick Nocerino's 1980 lecture and slide presentation on the Crystal Skulls was a turning point in my life. As I watched each slide, I began to inwardly receive information about the Crystal Skulls. At this time I did not understand where this information was coming from, but through a series of events and many hypnotic regressions, the pieces began to fall into place.

THE FIRST KEY EVENT HAPPENED WHILE I WAS PARTICIPATING in one of Nick's many projects to clear haunted houses. Nick led a team of twenty people to clear a house located in Campo Seco, near Sonoma in northern California. This was June of 1981. On June 26, while we were at this house, my friend Terry and I saw a very large UFO in the sky, partially hidden by the trees. It looked kind of hazy but we definitely knew what it was.

Next, Nick asked three of us to stand under an oak tree on the property (which unknown to me at the time, had once been used to hang people) and go into a light trance to see what impressions we received. One person began choking, another felt like she was dying, and I left my body and encountered two beings. They told me that if I accompanied them, my life-long search to understand why I was here on the Earth would be answered. This conversation was telepathic. Since I wanted so badly to know the answer to this question, I agreed to go with them. I was experiencing and seeing these beings with my inner vision or clairvoyance.

So, while my Earth body was still standing by the tree, these beings glided me up in a column of blue light toward a gigantic UFO, the one we had seen before. The spacecraft had windows with blinking colored lights all around them. As we arrived, a ramp came out and the two beings glided me into the ship. Inside of the craft I saw a line of people standing next to what looked like a rail. I did not know any of these people. They were being led around the ship, following the rail to a podium where one being was standing. As

SANDRA BOWEN

each person stood in front of this being, a light-encoded number was scanned from their right hand. When it came my turn, just as the being was ready to read my number, he stopped and said, "This one is different." I was guided to two other beings who seemed to be waiting for me.

This is all I remember, since at this point I heard Nick's voice calling all of us to return to our bodies and come out of the trance. I just didn't want to go back, and it was with great difficulty that I did so. Soon after this, I began to receive messages and information about the Crystal Skulls, and especially when new skulls were going to show up. I inwardly heard that I should share this information with Nick, and that either a new Crystal Skull would surface, or new information related to some activity about a Crystal Skull would be received very soon after I talked with him. I found this to be strange because at this point, I had never personally seen one of the ancient Crystal Skulls.

SHORTLY THEREAFTER, ON MARCH 1, 1982, I had one of the most incredible experiences, which introduced profound changes in my life. At this time, there had been numerous reports in the news about a very large cloud which was just hanging in the stratosphere, hovering over the western part of the United States all the way out to Hawaii. To this day, no satisfactory explanation has been given. Anyway, on this day we had a power blackout in my area of Pinole, California. During the blackout I psychically saw two purple rays of light entering my shoulders from above. I doubled over in pain and didn't know what to do. I wanted to call Nick, but he was out of town on business, so the thought occurred to me to contact Chuck, his close associate who had been with us at Campo Seco. The problem was, I didn't know where he lived or his phone number. So something gently pushed me into my car and just like in Shirley MacLaine's TV mini-series, the car drove itself as I felt an invisible presence making my hands turn the wheel. And before I knew it, the car stopped and parked right in front of Chuck's house.

Chuck let me in, asked what was wrong and I explained my predicament. He told me that there had been a number of people in Pinole calling in and reporting close encounters with UFOs. Then he asked me to sit down and he psychically scanned me. He saw two Space Beings around me and he told me that since the ray was purple (which is a high spiritual color), I need not be concerned. He also said that I was aware of their names, and as soon as he did so, I knew their names were Akbar and Josephat. I later learned that they were stationed on Uranus, but came from Andromeda and were able to spiritually project to the Earth and communicate with me. Chuck told me to

CHAPTER 2

go home and that sometimes messages can be recorded if you just let a tape recorder run. When I got home, I turned on three tape recorders and they all jammed. So I decided to do some automatic writing and see if they would choose to communicate with me in that manner. What basically was written through me was that I was ready to begin teaching about the Crystal Skulls and UFOs. They also gave me some personal advice on how to do this and placed an etheric solar cross in my right hand. They said I could use this whenever I needed to communicate with them.

WELL, WITH ALL THESE STRANGE THINGS HAPPENING, the information I was receiving about the Crystal Skulls and now these two Space Beings, I figured I had better do something to find out what was going on! When Nick returned home, I asked him and he agreed to do a hypnotic regression on my UFO experience at Campo Seco. I intuitively felt it had something to do with this connection with Akbar and Josephat.

On March 14, Nick regressed me and I was able to obtain total recall of the whole experience. Continuing from where I left off earlier, the two beings who were waiting for me were Akbar and Josephat. They appeared to me as vibrating outlines of colored lights whose shapes consisted of somewhat pointed heads, long arms and hands, and they glided rather than walked.

Akbar and Josephat took me into another room and told me that before I chose to incarnate on the Earth in this lifetime, I agreed as part of my life's mission to help share information about the Crystal Skulls and to bring out the knowledge contained within them. They said that there was a vast plan involving many other people who were on the Earth to do the same, and that at the right time this plan would go into action and I would participate. At this time I had no idea what they were talking about, but Akbar and Josephat told me [all of this was done telepathically] that they had brought me to their ship to remind me of my commitment to this plan, and that when the Crystal Skulls were activated, I would know exactly what to do. I was also informed that they would be with me every step of the way, offering guidance and suggestions on what to do, where to go and who to work with.

Then I was told that in order to prepare me for this work, they would have to put me through various healing processes to open up my chakras [psychic energy centers] and align my body vibration. These techniques involved a machine that moved over my reclining body and shined multi-colored laser beams on me. I was in a great deal of pain during most of the procedures, but the two beings did what they could to alleviate this by laying their hands upon

SANDRA BOWEN

© F. R. 'Nick' Nocerino

A holographic image of a UFO appearing within the Mitchell-Hedges Crystal Skull.

me. A third being held two crystal balls (one smoky, one clear) which had a hypnotic effect upon me and calmed my system. Throughout the whole process I completely trusted them.

I was taken deep down into the lower levels of the craft and we used a glass elevator to get there. They brought me to an amber cave or chamber filled with crystals. Also in this chamber was a clear Crystal Skull that looked very similar to the Mitchell-Hedges Crystal Skull in shape and size. They told me that this skull was used to communicate with the Inner Earth Beings and it had never physically been on Earth. They said the skull had been brought from the etheric plane and would eventually be given to the Inner Earth people in Arizona. They used this skull to awaken other people like myself who had volunteered to work with the Crystal Skulls on the Earth level, when they would bring these people on-board the spacecraft. The skull was also connected to the computers on the ship and was having information from the craft placed into its memory banks.

Also while in this chamber they handed me a device which looked like a crystal flute. It had little holes in it. There was a sapphire at the top and at its bottom were blue and yellow feathers. Different colored beams of light came out of each of the holes. They showed me that in order to regulate the beams, you just lightly blow into it and place your fingers on the holes and this will produce whatever colored beams you want to come out from the end of the flute. Somehow this flute has the ability to activate the molecular structure of people, of dimensions and of other objects. The crystal flute makes it possible to create perfection, the ultimate in terms of awareness, consciousness, total health, knowledge and creativity. Whatever one wishes to create, can be achieved with this instrument. They said that I would not be able to take it with me, but when the time was right, I would have it again. Lastly, they told me that the flute was related to the Crystal Skulls and especially to a master stone, which activates and controls the Crystal Skulls. They said that when I would be around a Crystal Skull, I would immediately know how to use this crystal flute.

I would like to digress for a moment and add to this last point that when Nick had the Mayan Skull for three months of research, they tried an experiment with Peruvian Whistles. One of the tests which is done is to see how each Crystal Skull will react to various stimuli, such as color, light and sound. There seems to be a certain combination of sounds or colors that will activate the Crystal Skulls. Nick had Steven Halpern, a past student and pioneer of New Age Music, blow on the Peruvian Whistle while in the presence of the Mayan Skull. The result was that Steven's leg was slightly burned and a woman present received a burn on her arm. A redness remained on them for several days. In other words, these Crystal Skulls are not to be played with! Unless you have the proper code, the energy generated can be uncontrollable.

After these traumatic events with the Space Beings, I was placed into a large tank containing a strange solution, and given something to drink which tasted like chocolate cherry. They also beamed a blue light upon me and I lapsed into a state of profound relaxation. Finally, when Akbar and Josephat had finished with me, they put me on a vehicle which reminded me of an Amtrak train, but it was totally transparent, and I just zoomed out and literally floated on air. Before I could blink an eye, I was back in my body. There were no fond farewells or goodbyes, just a feeling that I had been given all that I needed to know.

SANDRA BOWEN

Section 2

In Tibet With
the Crystal Skulls

In conjunction with my UFO experiences, I was attending a weekly regression class that Nick had organized in the beginning of 1982. His goal with the class was to explore our past lives and see if we could regain the ability to speak the language of that lifetime. We were told to go back to whatever lifetime was having the most affect upon us now. Whenever I went into this regression I would find myself going back to Tibet and working with many Crystal Skulls. I found out that I have had many past lifetimes when I worked with and protected the Crystal Skulls. What I would like to do in this section is share some of my most profound experiences related to the Crystal Skulls. Since I am very clairvoyant, when I go into my past lives I see them in vivid detail. I feel this type of information is important because it can give us clues as to how the Crystal Skulls were implemented and how they can be used now to help mankind.

MOST OF THE TIME I WOULD GO TO THE SAME LIFETIME IN TIBET, which I have received was approximately 435 A.D. Although there were other lifetimes in Tibet when I did work with Crystal Skulls, this one seemed to be the most important and the one paralleling very closely what is happening to me in this lifetime.

In this particular Tibetan lifetime I was a woman who had great knowledge of astrology, as well as the Crystal Skulls. My official title was Keeper of the Crystal Skulls. There were only five or six other individuals who had such a title. The group of people I lived with worked in a monastic community, which I feel may have been the Potala located in Lhasa, Tibet. Only the keepers were permitted to go into the underground caverns beneath the monastery (where the Crystal Skulls were stored for safekeeping) and bring them out.

IN THIS LIFETIME I SAW THAT THERE WAS A GROUP of thirteen clear quartz Crystal Skulls, similar to the Mitchell-Hedges Skull and something else called a master stone. The master stone was of a material similar to soapstone, very soft to the touch, but it also had a feeling of possibly being of extraterrestrial origin. It stood about five feet tall and was dome-shaped or curved at the top, straight along its side and the bottom was flat. It had two handles in the shape of

CHAPTER 2

curved snakes, which one held onto to rotate this stone which was situated on a dais. There was also some type of writing on the master stone.

There were many different patterns I would use for laying out the thirteen Crystal Skulls in front of the master stone when I would work with them. For example, sometimes I would use four skulls in the front in a straight line, and nine skulls behind them. Other times I would just form a semicircle with the skulls all in the front. The pattern of skulls with the master stone was determined by my purpose in using the skulls.

As I turned the master stone this way or that, it would activate the Crystal Skulls. What I saw as the skulls became activated was that different colored rays of light would emanate out of each skull and these rays of light would all meet at the top of the cave to form what appeared to be a pyramid. Some of the colors I remember seeing included red, blue, green, yellow, purple, pink, gold, silver, etc.-- really the whole spectrum of light. When I activated the skulls in this way, the main purpose was to communicate with extraterrestrials who were acting as guardians of the Crystal Skulls, as well as guides and teachers for my people. And this also explains why there were very few keepers, because most of my people at this time, were not developed enough in their spiritual awareness to understand the nature or capabilities of these special skulls. The people who were the keepers were all very advanced souls who had worked with the Crystal Skulls in many past lives.

THERE WAS ALWAYS GREAT DANGER CONNECTED WITH THE CRYSTAL SKULLS. This is why we had to be careful when we brought them out and why they were hidden in the underground secret chambers in which only the keepers knew how to move about without getting lost. The monks and priests of the monastery acted as guards at the door to the caves, but this was their only function. There was another group of people who knew of the skulls and wanted to have them for their own personal power games, so we always had to be alert. To protect the Crystal Skulls, they were kept in obsidian boxes (obsidian blocks all energy emanations of an object), three to a box. There was a special ritual we performed when taking the skulls out of the boxes, or when placing them back in and returning them to the caves.

One of my favorite uses of the skulls was in conjunction with educating and helping the youth in spiritual development. When children reached three years of age, I would prepare an astrology chart for them. I remember working with a young boy of twelve who was sitting before me on a high stool and I was across from him at a table, sitting with his astrology chart in front of me and one of the Crystal Skulls I had brought up from the caves. Then I placed different colored stones on the skull to activate it and it sent out various colored light rays to his chakras, to help him open up these energy centers of his body.

Another special memory was of the very large crystal on the top floor of the monastery. It was the size of a circular water bed, and had a metal railing around it. Each morning, people at the monastery would go to this crystal and with their arms outstretched and palms out, they would communicate with the crystal and silently say a prayer or mantra. It was a form of being charged-up in preparation for each new day.

ONE TIME I SAW MYSELF TAKE FIVE OR SIX OF THE CRYSTAL SKULLS into one of the great halls of the monastery where yoga was practiced at times. On the floor of this hall were all kind of markings, such as circles, squares, stars, and so on. I would position a Crystal Skull on certain places of the floor over specific markings, and just sit in the center of the skulls. I then would activate the skulls in this pattern and receive wonderful information and knowledge from them.

One of the things that surprised and fascinated Nick during the regressions were the hand signals I would make while in a slight trance. As a matter of fact, at times both my friend Therese and I would simultaneously make identical hand signals. What was occurring from my perspective as I was reliving my lifetime in Tibet, was that I was working with a Crystal Skull and would use hand signals to activate the skulls. Thus as I mentioned earlier about my research with the Mitchell-Hedges Skull, whenever I am with a Crystal Skull, whether in the physical or in my mind, I immediately communicate with it using these hand signals. When the two Space Beings, Akbar and Josephat, communicate with me, they use similar hand signals. Also the society in this Tibetan lifetime communicated with hand signals. There were certain hand signals related to the Crystal Skulls which only the keepers knew, sort of like a foreign language.

As you can see, color played an extremely important role in that life and perhaps explains why I am a color consultant right now. The Tibetans had an incredible understanding of the effects of color on a person's body, whether seen visually (e.g.-- looking at a painting or piece of beautiful artwork) or experienced vibrationally in the clothing and gemstones they wore. The

CHAPTER 2

colored rays of light which emanated from the skulls were activated in a specific way to help an individual with a particular problem. We knew how each color should be used in an appropriate manner. But only the keepers knew how to activate the various colored rays from the Crystal Skulls.

Section 3

Master LI

IN OUR DEDICATION WE MENTION MASTER LI. It's time to explain our connection to this great man. During my regressions to Tibet, I first encountered him. Master LI was the teacher of the Dalai Lama in Tibet, around four hundred A.D. (sic). He would sit in a corner and observe, never saying much unless he disagreed with the Dalai Lama. He would also communicate with others telepathically and by hand signals. In appearance, Master LI was very old. The coloring of his face was a deep brown, with oriental eyes, and a gray-white beard almost down to the top of his legs. He also had a mustache and sideburns. Master LI had long thin fragile fingers, a brilliant golden aura around him and he wore a Tibetan style hat.

Master LI is very interested in having the information shared about the Crystal Skulls, as the thirteen Crystal Skulls were in Tibet at this time. He has appeared in one way or another to almost all the members of the publishing team.

IN THIS PAST LIFE REGRESSION, I RECOGNIZED NICK AS THE DALAI LAMA. Even though I was traveling in time going back to Tibet, Master LI would tell me that in the future, Nick and I should try to write a book about the Crystal Skulls because Master LI could see the importance of the Crystal Skulls in our current times. He said the skulls would help to open people's memory banks of knowledge and wisdom gained in past lives. After this first contact with Master LI, I would feel his presence around me and always see him around Nick.

Master LI was considered a very holy man. When he was young, he went into the mountains and spent many years in silence. After he returned, he came as a Master or what some might regard as a Christed Being.

Master LI had a staff with a small Crystal Skull on top and there were snakes etched into the wood in the shape of the caduceus (two snakes intertwined). He was such a holy man that people would always bring him gifts and he had

Master LI
(The Master, as he psychically appeared to Ms. Kokorich)

his own special area in the hall where the Dalai Lama sat, lined with his pillows to sit in a meditative posture.

ALSO, JOSHUA WAS INVOLVED IN THIS PAST LIFE TOO. When we first met at a UFO lecture he was giving in Oakland, California, I remembered him very clearly. He even has the same walk as he had then! When the Dalai Lama (Nick) died, he (Joshua) and I worked with the Crystal Skulls to help educate the people, as we are again doing now. And as Joshua became more interested in the Crystal Skulls [1985], I could see Master LI appearing around him too. Although he doesn't hear him as directly as I do, Master LI has made his presence known to him. Joshua told me that every time he would type the word "Light" on the computer, without thinking of what he was typing, the letters L and I would always be capitalized. And this was before he understood about Master LI.

When we met our book designer and co-publisher, Li Greiner, Joshua became convinced of the existence of Master LI. This happened one afternoon in August of 1987, when we were filling an order for the preliminary version of the Crystal Skull book at Field's Bookstore of San Francisco. As we were talking with the bookstore owner, he pointed at Li and said that he purchased their last copy of Richard Garvin's book, *The Crystal Skull*. Joshua discovered from Li's business card that he spelled his name in the same way as Master LI. A few days later during a phone conversation, when Li told Joshua that Master LI had contacted him many years ago as an inner teacher (and suggested that he change his name from Lee to Li), the coincidences became too pronounced and Joshua really became convinced! Joshua is one of those people who likes to challenge the invisible helpers, because he feels that it is important to discern who one is working with. This is wise, but being an Aries he sometimes takes it too far!

SANDRA BOWEN

Joshua Shapiro is comparing the energies carried by a few of the smaller ancient skulls (which Mr. Nocerino has collected in his many travels) with the human sized skulls he has seen.

ntil 1983 I had very little interest in crystals and no real knowledge of their many spiritual uses. But that year an April visit to a bookstore in San Jose, California, changed all that. My friend Ruth and I went to the Ram Metaphysical Bookstore to deliver an order of my first published book, *Journeys of an Aquarian Age Networker*. While there, Francoise, the store owner, unexpectedly pulled out some pictures of an Amethyst Skull. The skull had been brought from Mexico to San Jose, California, sometime in December of 1982. Francoise said the agent for this Crystal Skull placed it in the hands of a local art dealer in order to sell it.

I immediately sensed something important was happening, as though it were a privilege to see these photographs. I was tickled when Francoise gave me a copy of one of the photos.

THE FOLLOWING MONTH OUR MUTUAL FRIEND STEVE MEHLER was able to arrange a showing of the skull at the art gallery in San Jose where the skull was being kept. Steve was trying to help sell the skull for the owner [See interview with Steve Mehler in Chapter 4]. He had been contacted by the agent for the

Amethyst Skull. This agent had met Steve previously when the Mayan Skull was brought to the Rosicrucian Museum where Steve worked as a researcher. Steve had an opportunity to work with this skull.

Steve invited Ruth and me to attend this showing. I immediately sensed that the skull would have a profound effect upon my life. Thereafter, I became quite interested in crystals and met many crystal teachers. I shared the picture Francoise had given me at any impromptu lectures on networking I gave at that time.

I HAD NO OTHER ENCOUNTERS WITH CRYSTAL SKULLS UNTIL I MET SANDRA BOWEN at an informal UFO lecture I was giving in Oakland, California in April of 1985. During the lecture we recognized each other (on a soul level), and she told me I had worked with her in a past life in Tibet with thirteen Crystal Skulls. Prior to her sharing this information, I had not mentioned my experience with the Amethyst Skull, so I knew this was a special connection. Within three days, I moved into her home!

Through Sandra I met her teacher, F. R. 'Nick' Nocerino, who had personally seen nine human-sized Crystal Skulls in his travels. Through contact with Nick, I was able to go to two crystal conferences (in Dallas, May of 1986; and San Francisco, June of 1986) and personally be with the Mitchell-Hedges Skull.

In December of 1985, Sandra and I decided to begin a series of lectures on the UFO/Crystal Skull Connection. We lectured throughout Northern and Southern California, as well as giving a lecture at the Rocky Mountain UFO Conference, sponsored by Dr. Leo Sprinkle (in Laramie, Wyoming in July of 1986). We shared slides (provided by Nick) and videos we had collected along the way. Concurrently, Nick continued to lecture about the Crystal Skulls.

In the Summer and Fall of 1986, Sandra and I began to collect information for an expanded version of our UFO book, *UFOs, Space Brothers and the Aquarian Age*. Our initial plan was to include a chapter about how the Crystal Skulls are connected to UFOs. We collected so much information, that we discussed with Nick the idea of working with him to do a separate book about the Crystal Skulls. In February of 1987, the first version of our book, *Mysteries of the Crystal Skulls Revealed*, was printed.

MY NEXT GOAL IS TO SPEND EXTENSIVE TIME WITH ONE OR MORE CRYSTAL SKULLS and be involved with a research team to continue studying them and their interaction

CHAPTER 3

with human energy. I also hope to be able to create a video that will show the various holographic images which appear in the Crystal Skulls, as well as continue to make books available about the Crystal Skulls and how these ancient tools can be used to create harmony and peace in our world.

 ## The Amethyst Crystal Skull

I DISTINCTLY REMEMBER MY REACTION TO THE PICTURES OF THE AMETHYST SKULL, during my important visit to Francoise's Ram Metaphysical Bookstore. It was as if a shock hit my entire system. It was not that the skull was uncomfortable to look at-- it touched me inwardly, very deeply. I thought perhaps this was a remembrance of working with this skull before, or having contact with it. I also remember hearing myself say, "This skull shouldn't be out yet!" I cannot say why I thought that. All I can relate is that something happened to me, something changed inside me after seeing the pictures. It was as if this had been set-up long ago with the idea that when I was ready, the part familiar with the Crystal Skulls would awaken. But inwardly I kept asking, "Why me?"

The thought occurred to me, as I looked at the Amethyst Skull, that it somehow represented one of the many outer signs that the transformation into the Aquarian Age (or the Golden Age) is really happening now! Even though I was just looking at a picture of the Crystal Skull, I felt that it was as powerful as the real skull itself. Francoise told us that they had another batch of pictures they took, but somehow these mysteriously disappeared and the photo developing company could not find their negatives. This is just one of many strange stories that surrounded the Amethyst Skull, as if there is some sort of protective energy field around it, and only those who are supposed to see or experience it do so.

THIS PARTICULAR SKULL IS MADE OUT OF PURE AMETHYST CRYSTAL, of a very deep dark purple. Steve Mehler told me that this skull had been taken to the Hewlett-Packard research laboratories, and they were not sure how the skull could have been created, even if the skull's creator(s) had possessed an advanced technology similar to our own. The crystal itself has a marbled effect with patches of different shades of purple here and there. There are a number of thin light-purple wavy lines (called sutures) which go across the top part of the skull and down the front of the face.

JOSHUA SHAPIRO

© Francoise Beaudoin

A frontal view of the Amethyst Crystal Skull photographed in daylight when Steve Mehler had this Crystal Skull for five days of personal research.

Steve also had the Crystal Skull in his home for five days; he invited many well-known crystal researchers, as well as psychics and healers, to see the skull and experience it. Steve still has tape recordings of all of these sessions.

I gathered some of the impressions received about the Amethyst Crystal Skull from local residents [San Jose] who were psychically sensitive and had been in the presence of it. Many spoke of great wisdom stored within it, as well as memories of events in history which have occurred in the presence of the Amethyst Skull. Many intuitively felt or received visions that such Crystal Skulls were used during the time of Atlantis, the Mayans or perhaps even earlier. My friend Ruth psychically saw that in Atlantis they would place jewels in the eye sockets (probably other crystals) to activate the skull. It then would light up and either communicate telepathically or actually speak in words with the head priest. The priest (or whoever was permitted to work with the skull in this way) could obtain universal knowledge and wisdom directly from the skull. She also saw that the Crystal Skull had some kind of a metal helmet that it wore.

I SAW THE AMETHYST SKULL DURING A SPECIAL SHOWING of the skull for a potential buyer at an art gallery in San Jose. The Amethyst Skull was kept in a vault at the gallery and the owner brought out the skull wrapped in a cloth. About ten

CHAPTER 3

people sat around a table with the skull. Most of the time I was very quiet, just sitting there and trying to experience the energy or vibration of it.

As I tapped into the energy of the skull, I felt a living being, a vibrant consciousness that was sleeping, yet awake enough to know we were there. Many of us felt a loving vibration and great power. I did have a chance to actually touch the skull and I felt a stream of energy move from the skull to my right hand, up through my arm and stop at the top of my shoulder. Somehow I feel that a permanent bond was made at this time. Today, whenever I think of the Amethyst Skull, I immediately inwardly see it sitting over my right shoulder, suspended in space. A few times, I have felt as if this skull has been placed over my head as if my brain is being programmed with the knowledge from this skull. So one does not always have to be in the physical presence of a Crystal Skull to work with one. To this day, I sense it is one of the main forces that guides and protects me on my spiritual/networking journeys.

One result of seeing the Amethyst Skull was that I began drawing many people into my life who were involved with crystals. I feel that the Amethyst Skull was my trigger to get in touch with my past lifetimes when I worked with crystals. Numerous people have told me that they remember me from Atlantis, which was one of the civilizations most active in the use of crystals. Also, if someone had told me back in 1983 that I would be involved with a book about the Crystal Skulls, I would have laughed. As I look back over the years, the signs were clear that this was part of the work I came here to do.

AS TIME GOES ON WE WILL UNDERSTAND MORE ABOUT THESE CRYSTAL SKULLS. But for now, I see them as physical, natural tools which can connect us to the spiritual realms and the spiritual beings who are assisting our movement into the fast-approaching Golden Age. They can be activated at any moment by the appropriate vibration, giving us wisdom and knowledge of the ancients.

JOSHUA SHAPIRO

The Magical Mitchell-Hedges Crystal Skull

Section 1
Preliminary Events to Seeing
the Mitchell-Hedges Skull

The next part of my chapter will relate my experiences leading up to being in the presence of the very famous Mitchell-Hedges Skull. For now, I would like to briefly summarize several events and insights which prepared me for this meeting with an old friend.

After meeting Nick in April of 1985, I had the opportunity to study some of the existing information on the Mayan Skull. Nick shared pictures with me, as well as many videos taken of this Crystal Skull. Watching the videos, I learned how to (scry) look for pictures and images within a Crystal Skull.

IN NOVEMBER OF 1985, NICK AND SANDRA WERE IN CANADA researching the Mitchell-Hedges Skull. About this time the second book about the Crystal Skulls came out: *The Skull Speaks*, by the Anna Mitchell-Hedges Research and Exploration Association. When I read the book, many inner openings or remembrances occurred within me. It was as if I had stepped into another dimension and now needed to integrate this level of knowledge.

Also at this time, I was at home in Pinole working on creating a UFO book *(UFOs, Space Brothers and the Aquarian Age)*. Whenever I spontaneously felt moved, I meditated on pictures of the Mitchell-Hedges Skull (in the Garvin book) while I sat in front of my computer and typed about all sorts of inner visions and physical sensations that I experienced.

It's impractical to include all the writing that I did, but there were a few key experiences. On one occasion I remember inwardly seeing a young boy sitting in a field, gazing into a Crystal Skull. I could not tell if the boy was me, or if this scene was from the past or had happened in another world. In this place anyone could borrow a Crystal Skull from a library of knowledge (implying that there were several skulls) and just go into nature and have their own personal experience with it, receiving great wisdom and knowledge telepathically from the skull.

CHAPTER 3

On another day, my inner visions revealed different Crystal Skulls, throughout North and South America, that were linking up somehow. These included the Mitchell-Hedges Skull in Canada, the Amethyst Skull in San Jose, California, some unknown skulls in the Yucatan and the skull reported to be in Peru, with each of these four groups representing one of the four directions. Inwardly, I saw beams of light connecting these Crystal Skulls. The energy around me at this time was so intense that I felt very close to passing out.

Another very different experience occurred while gazing at a photograph of the Mitchell-Hedges Skull. Right in front of my eyes, I saw the skull changing shape and moving. To this day I am not sure whether I had moved into an altered state of consciousness, or whether the picture was actually dancing in the physical.

Whenever I transcribed my experiences while working with the pictures, I would have many physical sensations. For example, I would feel pressure (or the sensation of being touched) in different places such as the neck, head, arms or legs. Most of the time, it would only be one side of my body or the other. Also there were sensations of coolness, heat and tingling. Since beginning my search into spiritual and metaphysical studies, I have always had these things happen and have become used to it. However, in this case it was happening so rapidly and shifting very fast. My theory is that I was having my vibrational frequency altered so that later in the following year, when I met the Mitchell-Hedges Skull, I would be ready to receive whatever information or energy the skull would give.

When Nick and Sandra returned, I naturally had a chance to see the photographs and slides they had taken of the Mitchell-Hedges Skull during their research. The pictures were fantastic, and it really helped that I had already had an opportunity to scry with the photos and videos of the Mayan Skull. I also discovered that some of my experiences correlated with things that happened in Canada. For example, when we closely compared notes, we found that generally whenever I had particularly noted a surge of energy, usually the research team had been working with the Mitchell-Hedges Skull.

Of course, the Mitchell-Hedges Crystal Skull had performed with much greater results than the Mayan Skull. The holographic images within the Mitchell-Hedges Skull were sharper, more distinct and vivid. The test with colored light on the Mitchell-Hedges Skull produced vibrant colors, and the skull felt more calming and peaceful. As you will see in Sandra's chapter (Chapter 2), a clear image of a UFO appears in this skull.

FROM DECEMBER, 1985, THROUGH FEBRUARY, 1986, Sandra and I lectured about UFOs and the Crystal Skulls. It was through these lectures that I really began to develop a gift for seeing the pictures which form inside of the Crystal Skulls. After one views slides of the Crystal Skulls on a number of occasions (we gave about ten lectures in this three month period), scrying becomes almost a natural ability requiring little effort. Plus, one gets a sense of the fabulous ability that these Crystal Skulls have for storing images of events in time. And still to this day, no one is quite sure how the skulls do this.

Section 2

Crystal Skull Report

This report was submitted for the Crystal Skull Seminar held at "Shared Visions" in Berkeley, California during April, 1986. It was conducted by the Society of Crystal Skulls International. All the members of the 1985 research team which went to Canada to work with the Mitchell-Hedges Crystal Skull were in attendance. In addition, I am including personal insights and theories which this report gave me an opportunity to share from prior experiences with the Crystal Skulls. This was based upon my study of photographs/slides of various Crystal Skulls shown by Mr. Nocerino and the interviews which Sandra and I conducted for the preliminary version of our Crystal Skull book.

THIS TWO-DAY SEMINAR WAS THE FIRST TIME THAT ALL THE RESEARCHERS who went to Canada were able to collectively share their experiences. The lecture was well-attended. For the first time, the research team presented to the public two different picture package sets of the Mitchell-Hedges Skull, showing the results of the various tests they had performed.

As with other Crystal Skull lectures, most of the people attending were able to see pictures and images within all the Crystal Skulls presented in the slides (Mitchell-Hedges, Mayan, Paris, and several Amethyst Skulls). In fact, just prior to this event I received an interesting inner vision. I saw a person's face appear in a Crystal Skull. This was not just a holographic image moving within the skull, but it was an image of a living person or being, who was using this skull as a monitor screen to talk with someone. I later learned that the researchers present had similar experiences in working with a Crystal Skull.

CHAPTER 3

DURING THE LECTURE, THE LEVEL OF ENERGY IN THE ROOM BECAME QUITE INTENSE for me and a few of the others as well! So intense that several people reported fighting off a drowsiness through various parts of the lecture, unable to consciously handle the information or energy broadcast. For myself, there was some dizziness and a great deal of pain and pressure on my neck and shoulders. My feeling is that either the skulls trigger submerged memories and bring forth an enormous amount of energy, or we as a group were tapping into the vibrations recorded within the skulls of their misuse by people in the past.

While viewing the slides of various Crystal Skulls, I could see (in my mind's eye) energy beams of light hitting certain points on my shoulders, and these areas became very tight. Unfortunately, I have not yet developed my inner sight or clairvoyance to the degree where I am able to say what color these rays of light were. In times past, when I have been in similar intense energy fields, I usually find it takes several days or a week to fully integrate all vibrations, as my muscles are sore and my body is sluggish. It feels as though I had a vigorous workout of various exercises.

I have found that when my body is exposed to these higher vibrations, it has a tendency to shake (it feels like an earthquake), and different blocks, negativity or imbalances will come out. In any case, I found that after both days I was on 'overload.' Perhaps I needed to use some system of grounding before entering such an intense energy vortex.

ONE OF THE QUESTIONS I HAVE HAD FOR SOME TIME concerns the purpose served by actively scrying or looking for images within a crystal. Apparently, searching for the pictures in the skulls draws one into the energy of the skull, making it easy to merge with it. Now as far as I know, most other crystals which have images appearing within them (that can be seen by the physical eyes) do not do so to the fantastic degree observed in the Crystal Skulls. Even at this seminar, not only did many in attendance see these pictures, but the images came to life and started moving around and changing before our very eyes. I understand from talking with Sandra and Nick that when they were with the Mitchell-Hedges Skull in Canada, these changes occurred very quickly, as though watching a movie.

One observation I had, based upon the comments (shouted out enthusiastically) of others at the conference was that each person seemed to see the same type of images or subject matter from slide to slide: UFOs, dragons, strange creatures or faces, various scenes (caves, underwater), buildings/structures, etc. Also, different people would focus or be drawn into

JOSHUA SHAPIRO

different sections of the Crystal Skulls (such as the nose, eyes, chin, teeth, cheekbone, temple, forehead, etc.). Some people saw an image in the entire skull, others would see a picture on top of a picture, and on and on. This suggests that how an individual perceives the images inside of the skull might describe the type of person they are and what particular inner senses they had developed. In Garvin's book, Frank Dorland discusses this idea, describing the skull as a mirror reflecting aspects of each gazer's conscious or subconscious mind. This could be a piece of the answer we are seeking about the powers of the Crystal Skulls, but I have a feeling there is much more to it. So, what can be the true purpose served by the skulls changing and sharing pictures, when many times what one sees makes absolutely no sense, or one has no idea how to relate to these perceptions?

When I have made contact with the Mitchell-Hedges Skull through the pictures or slides, it seemed as if the skull (or the consciousness which works through the skull and controls the energy within it) ties into the gazer's unique vibration and works with the gazer in whatever way is needed most. This seems to occur whether the person is consciously aware of it or not. With this particular skull, I felt healing and love accompanied by calm and peace.

ANOTHER THEORY I HAVE ABOUT THE HOLOGRAPHIC IMAGES comes from a few ideas that popped into my head while I was listening (with Sandra) to some of the taped conversations made by the research team while they were in Canada. I trust this spontaneous source of information. It usually produces useful insights. One of these insights was that each of the skulls is connected to some sort of Master Skull or master computer in another dimension. The master computer can instantly tap into the living records of any individual working with a skull on Earth. Once this activation takes place, the master computer sends images to the Crystal Skull which are flashed back for the viewer. This telepathic information draws from several dimensional levels which are appropriate to that individual's spiritual evolution.

So, to summarize, it is clear that the slides and photographs are actually an extension of the skulls' energies. Thus, the co-authors of this book feel it is important to share information on the Crystal Skulls in any form possible.

NOW, THE NEXT QUESTION WOULD BE WHO CONTROLS THE MASTER COMPUTER? Is it on 'automatic' following some Universal Laws or Codes programmed many millennia ago by some race so advanced that we cannot comprehend them?

CHAPTER 3

Or are there actual beings who work the computer from other levels of space or dimensions?

During an interview with Andrija Puharich at the Star People Conference held in Los Angeles, in April of 1983, he described a similar situation when relating his experiences with Uri Geller regarding UFOs. They received messages from a race called HUVA or HOOVA (this is supposedly where the word Jehovah or God comes from, he stated). This race told them it was acting as a Guardian Force for our planet. They had programmed their computers and spacecrafts millions of years ago to handle different situations as they occurred on the Earth, as our world strived to advance in its planetary evolution. Actually the messages they received came from a computer known as HOOVA.

Another clue on how the Crystal Skulls may work in sharing their information with us comes through our research into the UFO / Crystal Skull connection. One of our channelers, Michael Kant, stated that the Crystal Skulls operate in a similar manner as the crystal helmets used aboard spacecrafts to bring knowledge and wisdom directly into the brain centers of Space Beings. He said that the crystal helmets are connected to a master computer or databank containing this information. It has been suggested that just as information can be entered (programmed) or removed from the crystal helmets, so too can the Intelligence, which works or acts through the Crystal Skulls, insert, take out or hide information that is kept in the skulls, depending upon who is in the presence of the skulls and what their intentions are. This would serve as a protective mechanism insuring that no information could be pulled from the skull and misused by unauthorized Earthpeople. In these cases, what could occur is that either the viewer's mind-probe would be blocked, or the individual(s) might receive some type of electromagnetic shock or feedback causing some temporary discomfort.

Again, a personal experience which ties in with the crystal helmet occurred while I was meditating on the pictures of the Mitchell-Hedges Skull in the book, *The Crystal Skull,* by Richard Garvin, while the team was in Canada with this skull. I felt intuitively as if a helmet were placed around my head. I felt myself receiving some type of information which I believe was helpful when I actually was in the presence of the Mitchell-Hedges Skull. Perhaps this programming was to help this very report or the book which you now hold in your hands.

But, to answer the question of who is in charge of the activity or energies we see in the skull: they must be some very advanced beings possessing technology and wisdom beyond anything we are familiar with.

Now that I have explored all these different possibilities, let's go back to the original question, "Why be so concerned with the pictures and images inside of the skull?"

QUOTING FROM NICK'S MANY LECTURES OR PRIVATE CONVERSATIONS, "The Mitchell-Hedges Skull has a mind of its own!" The lecturers at the Crystal Skull Seminar all agreed that with this particular Crystal Skull, no matter which activation procedure was used, even if the same process was repeated, different results usually occurred. Of course, for the scientists who like controlled experiments with verifiable and reproducible results, this will create a big headache.

I think it is safe to conclude that the Crystal Skulls draw one into making contact with them. The gazer's vibration activates the skull on some level, which then sends back energy appropriate to the observer that helps to further open a person's chakras, removes memory-veils of knowledge contained in a person's consciousness, etc. Maybe we can say that any form of energy or vibration creates a response in the skulls, but that the type and magnitude of response can be totally unpredictable.

I think that another purpose for scrying Crystal Skulls is that they present alternative realities to our minds. It can cause one to look far beyond conventional explanations of physical and universal laws. This gives credibility to the notion that whatever we can imagine must actually exist somewhere, even if it is on a dimension which we do not know! If the human brain were used at 100% efficiency, then perhaps the Mitchell-Hedges Skull would be a model for the expression of its ultimate perfection.

WE ON EARTH NO DOUBT NEED MUCH EDUCATION on taming and controlling the powerful gift of our human minds. The Crystal Skulls give evidence of this too, as well as evidence of other dimensions. For example, I found the Paris Skull to be one of the most primitive-looking. While viewing slides of this skull, I did not receive the same peaceful feeling as with the Mitchell-Hedges Skull. The skull had a heavy-laden energy, full of violence and sadness. Looking directly into its eyes I felt a great, cold sadness about our human history of brutality and disrespect for our home, Mother Earth. My feeling is that at the time of the creation of this skull, it was a very loving stone, a perfect piece of work. As people began to misuse it in human sacrifices and tried to use its power for destruction, the physical form of the skull began reflecting this. Thus the skull changed from one of total beauty to a disheveled piece of crystal attempting to look like a human skull. For me this was a graphic example of what the power of our thoughts can do when directed in a so-called negative mode.

At these Berkeley lectures, Nick introduced the concept of laying grids on pictures of the skulls to better focus on a particular portion when looking for images. Nick suggested placing a grid overlay of boxes (which can be 2,4,8,16,... in number) over the picture of a Crystal Skull and then looking for the images within each box. He demonstrated with the slides how to use these grid patterns.

WHEN I FIRST BEGAN TO SCRY PHOTOGRAPHS, SLIDES OR VIDEOS of the Crystal Skulls, I found that my eyes would automatically look at particular sections, as if I had received this training in other lifetimes. Sometimes I feel as if I don't have control, as if I am literally pulled towards gazing at something. I interpret this as my Higher Self guiding me to look at an image when I am not thinking about anything in particular or when my mind is blank.

Scrying with pictures of the Mitchell-Hedges Skull at Nick's home prior to this seminar, I got another insight concerning the skull's ability to act as a doorway to other dimensions where space and time are meaningless. In these pictures, one sees multiple images of the people working around the skull or with the skull itself. In some of these pictures, the photograph splits and on one side of the picture are objects and people who were not in the room when the shot was taken.

Other aspects of these dimensional phenomena in the skull are: 1) the appearance of what I can only call 'windows' in the skull, or strange slanted geometric planes or patterns that spontaneously appeared; 2) in several of the pictures taken of the Mitchell-Hedges Skull, the skull's ability to project outside of itself, by having the colors (which came out during their color tests) appear on the photographs beyond or in front of the skull. Again, the research team was not sure how the skull did these things, but we could say there is much more to the Mitchell-Hedges Skull than what meets the eye!

In addition to just using my physical eyes to see the images within the skull, sometimes my inner vision would work in tandem. I would dimly see an outline of an image or scene, but I would require my mind's eye to clarify

JOSHUA SHAPIRO

exactly what I was seeing. Sometimes I could just feel the vibration of the holographic picture and would instantly know what I was perceiving. At other times I would become curious, and if I was permitted by the Source which was projecting these images into the Crystal Skull, I could follow the vibration of the picture and feel the essence of its creator.

At the Berkeley seminar, Ron Dickinson shared with us one of his personal visions from his meditation with the Mitchell-Hedges Crystal Skull. I saw his experience quite clearly as he described it. He saw some type of control room with monitors on a wall, except each monitor was made out of quartz crystal. There was what looked like a Mayan priest facing this wall of monitors, and each monitor was displaying a different scene from various parts of this world or possibly other worlds. This room reminded me very much of the control rooms we see on news broadcasts, or similar to the center of a strategic military base as we see in the movies.

ANOTHER IDEA WHICH CAME OUT AT THE WEEKEND SEMINAR dealt with Nick's feelings that the creators of all the Crystal Skulls were a vastly superior race of beings who very possibly are still on or within the Earth and have been here for a long time (possibly hundreds of thousands, or millions of years). I had a very strong affinity with this theory. Nick also felt that the AMHREA book, *The Skull Speaks,* seems to support a similar theory.

When I visualized this race or attempted to make contact, I saw an energy beam off my right side and in front of me that appears to be a silver/blue/white color. As I went inward to touch the beam, my right ear felt as if someone were speaking to me and it tingled, but I couldn't quite make out any words; as if my ear were in another dimension. What I felt/heard intuitively was that in the near future our Earth is going to see almost daily changes (accidents or Earth-changes). The emergence of the Crystal Skulls is another attempt to remind humanity not to misuse the resources of the planet. The skulls are here to assist us in recreating a planetary harmony and balance, and to guide us to wisdom/information/technologies which can help! Thus comes the need for books or printed information to explore various explanations about the nature of the skulls and how they relate to the emerging Aquarian Age.

It is my feeling in support of this theory, that while the group was in Canada, they were assisting in a process on the physical level to help reactivate the skulls. Since that time there have been rumors of other Crystal Skulls being found, which may be linked to the activation of the Mitchell-

CHAPTER 3

Hedges Skull. I feel that more skulls are now being released since we need their powerful energy. I also feel, that all the members of the research team in Canada worked with the Mitchell-Hedges Skull as Mayans in a past life and that they had then promised to help share information on the Crystal Skulls at some future time.

The Guardian Race which Nick described seems to contact us when they choose to and when we are prepared for such contact. They will intuitively call those individuals to come into the presence of the Crystal Skulls and impart to them the necessary knowledge to help with their own transformation. This Race is the force which has opened doors to allow researchers to work with the known Crystal Skulls, or decided when other skulls will surface. They are the ones who, in the proper timing, will bring the appropriate resources together to educate our race about the Crystal Skulls, Crystal Technologies and Universal Wisdom.

Section 3

First International Crystal Congress
(Held in Dallas, TX, May 2-4, 1986)

I flew to Dallas for my first crystal conference, with Nick and his wife Khrys, Sandra, Ron and Neoma (a student of Nick's). I was drawn to attend because the Mitchell-Hedges Skull would be on display. I also had the opportunity to support the Society of Crystal Skulls, International by helping them sell their Crystal Skull photo packages, as well as some of the New Age books we had published up to that point.

Prior to attending this crystal conference, I had a strong intuition to listen to a taped interview that Sandra and I did with Michael Kant. It felt like preparatory work prior to seeing the Mitchell-Hedges Skull. As you will read in the transcripts of our conversation (see Chapter 5), Michael claimed that the Mitchell-Hedges Skull was created by the mind power of seven Atlantean Priests who transformed the human skull of an Atlantean Priestess named Shee-thee-tra into a Crystal Skull. One of the other main reasons I listened to the interview was to hear the correct pronunciation of the priestess' name so I could use it while in the skull's presence.

Thursday evening, May 1, in Dallas, I had my first encounter with the Mitchell-Hedges Skull. In fact, I had the distinct impression that it snuck up on me! As I was introduced to Anna Mitchell-Hedges, I failed to notice the skull sitting on the table to my immediate right. When Sandra pointed it out to me, I literally jumped back, letting out a yelp of excitement. After viewing many of the slides and pictures of this Crystal Skull taken by the research team, I was so sure I would psychically sense it if the skull was nearby, but I didn't. As I slowly approached, I was in such awe I could not touch it. I was trying to remember what I used to do in past lives when I worked with the Crystal Skulls.

The conference gave me just the opportunity I had been looking for to study the skull up close. I noticed the very detailed and fine craftsmanship, which to me closely paralleled the anatomy of a human skull of bone. From a distance, it had the appearance of being made out of clear plastic, but once I touched the skull, I knew it was crystal. During the Berkeley lecture just prior to this conference, DaEl Walker mentioned that when there was no activity around the skull, it was clear as glass. However, whenever I had a chance to be near the skull, it was never totally clear. There were always some type of specks or lines within it. For the most part, to my dismay, I did not physically see very many of the beautiful images and pictures I had seen in the slides from the research done previously. I expected to see something grand take place; however, we must remember, there are very precise ways of activating these holographic images. Whatever the consciousness which activates the images within the skull *is*, it only does so when it is appropriate, not when we humans think the skull should do some type of show for us.

One false impression I had of this skull was that somehow the jaw connected to the top piece and interlocked, even though it is a separate piece. As I discovered, the cranium just sits on top of the jaw. Anna Mitchell-Hedges has a special stand with pegs which hold the jaw in place through the two small holes on the underpart of the jaw. I feel that these holes were drilled by one of the civilizations which had the skull and they were not there when it was originally created. Another part of the skull that you really can't see from pictures are the open-style cheekbones, like small handles on each side of the face. This was new to me.

ANOTHER SURPRISE I HAD FROM MY FIRST MEETING WITH THE SKULL, was that I was not assaulted by a tremendously powerful energy from it. I was especially astonished when I later checked with Sandra as we retired to our hotel room, and found out that she was experiencing a great deal of energy from the skull. Slowly the conclusion came to me that somehow this Crystal Skull has the ability to conduct multiple contacts with people around it, and each

CHAPTER 3

connection can be totally different. The skull was starting me off slowly, thus enabling us to get acquainted. Since Sandra had spent three weeks with the skull previously, it seemed to be that their connection was continuing where it left off.

However, the effects of the skull eventually hit me before I went to sleep that night. I couldn't stop talking to Sandra about my observations and a few other insights which were literally flooding my consciousness. Although I don't remember most of it now, one of the recurring effects the skull had on me was a great amount of energy to talk to people. It was often difficult for me to stop.

I had great difficulty falling asleep the next two nights because the Crystal Skull was resting only a few hundred feet from us in another room of the hotel. I felt surrounded and uplifted by incredible energies which felt very cool to me. I have come to understand that this represents how my body reacts to balanced energy. In front of me, I saw flashes of different colored lights and odd geometric shapes which I could not identify. All of this was happening regardless of whether my eyes were open or closed. As I gazed at the mirror in the room, the effect seemed to amplify. I inwardly asked what was happening and saw in my mind's eye incredible Light and Love emanating in all directions. I experienced it as a great healing.

After attending DaEl's lecture, I watched Anna Mitchell-Hedges set up the skull for display, and a little bit later I finally touched the skull. I was drawn first to touch the front teeth, which Sandra mentioned were chipped. What was interesting about the two chipped teeth I touched was that they formed a symmetry, one on either side of the very front or center tooth.

At one point in the conference, after returning from the cable TV show which Nick, Sandra, DaEl, Ron and I did about Crystal Skulls, Crystals and UFOs, Anna Mitchell-Hedges asked me if I would watch the skull while she went back to her hotel room. It was quite an honor that she intuitively trusted me. But more than that, I was beginning to understand that I had a role in educating people about the Crystal Skulls. From my three close visits (the first meeting, sitting next to the skull in DaEl's lecture and the request to watch over the skull), I felt like the skull was telling me that I would be involved and help share information about Crystal Skulls. From these experiences I inwardly knew that I had worked with these skulls in past lives, serving as a protector for them. When I gazed into the Mitchell-Hedges Skull's eyes, I also felt pulled into an incredible and infinite flow of love from within it.

JOSHUA SHAPIRO

ONE OF THE FIRST PATTERNS I DID SEE WITHIN THE SKULL (and which has shown up in the photographs and slides from the Canada trip) was the way the skull would divide into two hemispheres when viewed from the top. Sandra then pointed out a "Crystal Lady with wings" in the center, which I was also able to see. In addition, there appeared to be slanted geometric planes and a few streaks or criss-crossed lines (sutures) within the skull, but not too many specific images.

One thing I did learn from this experience about scrying with Crystal Skulls, especially ones as clear as this, was that the reflections of objects in the skull's vicinity can be easily seen (like plants, part of the building, cars from the nearby highway, etc.). Since this crystal is not a flat smooth surface (it has bumps and different layers, as it is almost exactly like our own human skull), it was difficult to peer within the skull. It was almost like trying to see through thick glass. It was easier for me to see images or shapes from farther away than close up.

Another observation I made about scrying is that cameras (photo or TV/video) seem to be more sensitive to the energy emanating from the skull, and on many occasions will pick up pictures we cannot see with our eyes. A clear example of this involved looking at the local TV interview done with Nick and Anna Mitchell-Hedges, which we were able to record. On this videotape you can really see some interesting images in the skull.

WHEN I HELD THE SKULL BY ITS SIDES (OR TEMPLES) AND MEDITATED, I felt like I was tapping into an infinite energy source. Later on I noticed an inner strength starting to emerge, more confidence to speak out to others, leaving caution to the wind. Since I believe this Crystal Skull is a communication and recording device to other realms and dimensions (spacecraft too), I looked squarely into its eyes (where I feel most of the recording of information is done), and inwardly asked: "I want a truly conscious UFO Encounter, P l e a s e . . . !" I am sure the message was received. Now, whether anything will happen or not will be another story. But I believe it's possible to let your imagination open up and have fun with these ancient objects, as long as you remain respectful. And by the way, Ladies and Gentlemen up there, if you want a volunteer for that kind of story, I'm sure ready and willing.

In conversations with Nick and Sandra about their research in Canada, they told me that there was a great deal of activity which happened in the underpart of the skull, but unfortunately we could not see that area due to the stand upon which the skull was mounted while on display at the conference.

CHAPTER 3

My general hunch was that since there were so many people around the skull, it just couldn't be activated like in Canada where only a small group worked with it, focusing on specific goals each day.

Anna Mitchell-Hedges was a delightful and joyous person. I thoroughly enjoyed listening to her stories and watching her interaction with those around the skull. She is truly a reflection of the healing and joy of the skull. What an interesting life she has led through the places she has visited and the wonderful people she has met in conjunction with this beautiful skull (some say the skull smiles a lot)! I mentioned to Anna how much patience she has to be willing to sit with the Crystal Skull, hour after hour while it is on display. She told me that when a person loves to do something, as she does in sharing the skull with others, it requires no patience at all. And how well I understood her words. In the short time I was with the skull, I felt profound and positive changes begin in my life.

A BRIEF COMPARISON OF THE TWO ANCIENT CRYSTAL SKULLS I have been with might be useful. The Amethyst Crystal Skull is not as human-looking as the Mitchell-Hedges Skull. It is interesting to note that when I saw the Amethyst Skull for the first time, it too felt like it was very quiet and not too active. I did feel there had been quite a bit of misuse with it and that somehow the skull had retained this type energy. With the Mitchell-Hedges Skull, I felt absolutely no negativity in any way, just a totally loving and healing crystal. The Amethyst Skull seems to be more compact and doesn't feel like it can channel the wide range of energies that the Mitchell-Hedges Skull is able to.

The Crystal Skulls have been known to appear clearly in peoples' inner vision. When I intensely focused upon photographs of the Mitchell-Hedges Skull before I went to Dallas, it appeared in my mind's eye in front of me, about two to three feet away and off to my left side. After the Dallas Conference, this inner image became much sharper and shifted slightly towards the right. I feel that I can now make inner contact with the Mitchell-Hedges Skull at any time.

THE DAY BEFORE WE LEFT FOR TEXAS, I was helping to reorganize the furniture in the main office where I work. While moving a typewriter, I scraped my left wrist against the wall. I noticed that during the conference, the healing process of my wrist seemed to be accelerated about two to three times its normal rate.

JOSHUA SHAPIRO

Upon returning home to Pinole, California, I still felt the so-called side-effects of the skull. I noticed my emotions would keep going from one extreme to another; from joy and laughter, to absolute depression and anger. When I finally sat down to write this report the first time, this condition had restabilized and I felt lighter and more peaceful. While in Texas, I kept hearing from within that this trip was accelerating my inner channels to be more open as a healer, and that my inner vision and intuition will become more developed. This is one of the associated effects one finds with people who have had physical contact with the Crystal Skulls.

SUNDAY, MAY 4 AND TUESDAY/WEDNESDAY, MAY 6/7: We had returned from the conference, and I was suddenly quite depressed. There were several strong earthquakes around the world during these dates. I thought perhaps my mood reflected an increased sensitivity to the vibrations of the Earth following the days with the wonderful Crystal Skull.

Other changes I have noticed since the Dallas Crystal Congress: my singing voice has become stronger since this trip; I have more strength to speak my mind, a feeling of inner power throughout my entire being, and a balancing of my masculine/feminine polarities. The conclusion I make on these shifts or changes is that when one moves into a very powerful vibration (whether it is an energy vortex in a certain location on the Earth, such as Mt. Shasta, California, or Sedona, Arizona[1], or in this case, a Crystal Skull), one becomes transformed and revitalized, with a cleansing of negativity or nonharmonious vibrations.

I have an inner sense that my life is taking a totally new and exciting direction, as if the old patterns are literally being shaken out to make room for

---

[1-]Mt. Shasta is a mountain located in Northern California, about an hour north of Redding. This area is very wooded and is considered a holy site by the Native American Indians as well as many involved in the New Age. People feel it is a high energy vortex with an etheric city above it, and a crystalline city underneath the mountain with tunnels leading to the Inner Earth. There are many reports of UFO sightings in this vicinity.

Sedona is located in Northwestern Arizona, about two hours north of Flagstaff. This city sprouted up when people spontaneously started to move there and it is a center for the arts and tourism. In this location there are four major energy vortexes and also many reports of UFO sightings, especially near what is called Bell Rock.

CHAPTER 3

the new. This could be described as an inner earthquake, as the new loving vibration that was planted by the Crystal Skull starts cleaning house. After struggling a long time to ground myself and participate in more group situations, this has now become easier. It is easier for me to relax more and take one day at a time, instead of feeling pressure about future events or having uncertainties about what is to come.

Summing up this section, I would say the time is right for the Crystal Skulls to take their proper place in our society as receptacles of interdimensional universal knowledge. I feel that this is what they were originally intended to be used for. The Crystal Skulls activate the divine presence within us; they mirror back to us who we truly are, eternal spirit, Light Beings. By experiencing the different Crystal Skulls that are available at this time, we see a reflection of our existence on the Earth, going from the more primitive-looking skulls such as the Paris Skull, to the beauty and perfection of the Mitchell-Hedges Skull (or perhaps the Rose Quartz Skull which Nick has seen). I feel that within these receptacles is vital information about the current transition our planet is going through into the Age of Aquarius, a Golden Age.

Section 4
The Crystal Congress
(San Francisco, CA, June, 1986)

In the opening ceremonies for this conference, the Mitchell-Hedges Skull was displayed right near the podium where Nick gave the opening speech. Sandra and I were sitting about forty feet away and we could feel its power. It was so strong I could not focus on the speakers. I kept feeling myself being pulled into the Crystal Skull. And as I sat there, I had a vision of Mayan natives kneeling in prayer in front of it.

We had a booth at this conference where we sold books and Nick's picture packets of the Mitchell-Hedges Skull. On Saturday afternoon during one of our breaks, Sandra and I went over to see the Crystal Skull. We did a short prayer with the skull and then she left, but I couldn't leave. I felt a loving energy surrounding me and I knew I wasn't supposed to go. So I stayed a few minutes, asking the skull, "How do you create the images within yourself, when you are so clear to begin with?" Then I inwardly heard, "Watch," and I saw an etheric copy of the skull move out and float above it. Then I heard, "Now look at the skull and see what you feel." I looked at it and felt that it was empty, as if it had been transformed to ordinary rock quartz crystal and

JOSHUA SHAPIRO

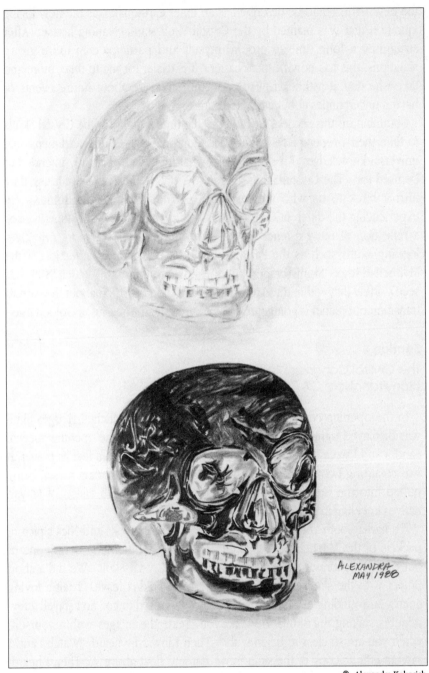

" I saw an etheric copy of the skull move out and float above it... "

was no longer special. As a substance, crystal is the best conduit for the high level energies passing through it, and the skull shape draws immediate attention. But it is an *external* consciousness which is in control of the skull and works through it.

THE OTHER MESSAGE WHICH I RECEIVED was also in-line with my question. I saw little bubbles forming inside the skull and shifting ever so slightly. It was so subtle that if you weren't watching this precise spot in the skull, you would never have seen it. I was seeing the crystal change its form right in front of my eyes. Then I heard, "You see, we can instantaneously re-model this crystal at will. To describe it to you in a way you would understand, think of it as if we could change the crystal to a liquid and mold it." So, the Mitchell-Hedges Skull had indeed answered my questions and given me an experience I shall never forget.

When I left the table that the skull was on, I felt a tremendous feeling of joy. I loved everybody and felt very elated. Imagine what would happen if we could get several Crystal Skulls together, generating a vibration like this. Maybe they could immediately eliminate all negativity in our world. Also, as I reflect upon this experience, I recall that while I was gazing at the skull and having this short conversation or communication, I was oblivious to the entire world.

ANOTHER EXPERIENCE AT THIS CONFERENCE was seeing twenty or so carved, contemporary crystal skulls which were for sale at a booth across from ours. First, it was a thrill to see *any* crystal skulls (the human-sized ones are the most rare) and now here was a table full of them! The person who was selling these skulls was Damien Quinn of Talisman Trading Co. They ranged in size from that of a golfball to a softball. Of course each of these skulls was one-piece and very beautiful (in my opinion), but they were not nearly as close a copy of a human-shaped skull as the ancient Crystal Skulls are. When I felt the energy of these small carved skulls (or projected into them), most seemed to be empty, however the larger rose quartz skull was charged with some type of energy. Nick got a chance to take pictures of all these carved skulls, and in some of our later lectures in 1986, we were able to share slides with people. All of these skulls were carved by a twenty-one year-old Brazilian (of Portuguese-Italian ancestry) who is a master carver in quartz and a descendant in a long line of stone carvers. [See Photogallery.]

JOSHUA SHAPIRO

It is my hope to eventually acquire a human-sized carved skull so we can demonstrate at our lectures how the ancients worked with Crystal Skulls. It will also be interesting to see, if this is permissible, how a Crystal Skull such as the Mitchell-Hedges Skull would program some of these carved skulls. Besides this Brazilian carver, there are other carvers in Mexico, South America and Germany, as well as one out of Nepal who is supposed to do excellent work. The interest in carved crystal skulls has greatly increased in the United States and there is a great demand for them. If you are interested in purchasing a carved crystal skull, refer to our Crystal Skull Resource Section (Appendix D).

 ## Additional Experiences and Update

I would like to include in this last section of my chapter, a few other interesting experiences which have happened to us as we progressed in our research with the Crystal Skulls, including both the preliminary and revised editions of this book. The time period which will be referenced is July of 1986 through November of 1987.

ACCORDING TO NICK, SANDRA WAS THE FIRST PERSON to link the Crystal Skulls with UFOs. Consequently, Sandra and I wrote to Dr. Leo Sprinkle about attending his annual UFO conference in Laramie, Wyoming (July of 1986), to present information about the Crystal Skulls. Although he had a full lineup of speakers, he was able to fit our lecture into the schedule. We also showed videotapes about the Crystal Skulls. We received a warm response from the UFO researchers, contactees and abductees who attended, and made many new friends. Some people were so fascinated that they went to the conference in Denver the following month to actually see the Mitchell-Hedges Skull which was on display.

In August, Sandra and I delivered some of our UFO books to the metaphysical bookstore in San Anselmo, California. While we were talking (as mentioned before), we came up with the idea of adding a chapter to our UFO book which would include the connection with the Crystal Skulls. To facilitate this project we decided to rent a computer, and did so in September. There were so many requests for information about the Crystal Skulls that we decided to write a separate book.

We began to transcribe the interview we had with Nick at the beginning of the year, and the interview we had with Michael Kant the previous year. We decided that rather than continue spending money on a rental computer, we would buy one. Our friend Larry Byram, helped us to purchase a Macintosh computer and let us use his laserprinter. Once we were committed to the book, we began to get many inner suggestions about who to interview and how to put a preliminary book together. So for about four months (from September to January) I went to work, transcribed tapes at lunch, came home and disappeared into my office to work on the book. Our goal was to have a book ready in time for the Whole Life Expo in Los Angeles, in February of 1987, as this area of the country had been the most interested in the Crystal Skulls.

After collecting and organizing all the information, there was additional support from our friend and business partner, Jeff Cohen, who helped with editing, re-writing and planning. Then Nick gave an outline and provided photographs for the book. We received a few illustrations from local artists.

AT THE WHOLE LIFE EXPO WE SOLD ABOUT SIXTY BOOKS. Sandra and I lectured to over a thousand people. The largest group we had spoken to previously had been about seventy people at Dr. Sprinkle's conference. We were overwhelmed by this response and had a wonderful time. Nick also did a workshop about the Crystal Skulls at the Expo.

Prior to the publication of this version of the Crystal Skull book, we had sold about nine hundred copies of the preliminary version. We did very little advertising, although we did have an article that appeared about the Crystal Skulls in the August issue of one of the finest UFO magazines in print, "California UFO" (out of Santa Monica, California; Vicki Cooper & Sherie Stark, editors). This article produced an enthusiastic response from people all over the country. Slowly but surely, the book started to be sold in several New Age bookstores in other states.

ONE OF THE MOST DRAMATIC RESPONSES TO THE BOOK came from Kathy Grimshaw. Kathy was literally guided to our book at Paper Ships, a bookstore in Marin County. For many years, she had been working with an amethyst crystal ball and psychically saw three Crystal Skulls inside of it. So naturally, she wanted to find information about these Crystal Skulls. When she wrote to us about her experiences, I felt it was important to contact her immediately. Soon she joined us to share information about the Crystal Skulls. In conversations with Kathy, Sandra learned that she had been accessing the Mitchell-Hedges Skull through her amethyst ball. Her meticulous records coincided identically with the images seen by the research team in Canada.

One day she placed her crystal ball and another clear crystal on top of the preliminary version (which has a picture of the Mitchell-Hedges Skull on the cover). After a few hours, she came back to the book and noticed that there was a hole burned through the cover and that the first ten pages had been singed. There was no sunlight hitting the crystals, so Kathy believes that the interaction of her crystals working with the cover picture of the skull caused this. She now uses these crystals for healing and considers them to be very powerful.

Another woman from Washington State, was writing a book about Atlantis and bought a copy of our book. After she read portions of the channeled information, she wrote to us and said that the channels were discussing, detail for detail, the very information she had written in her book. This is a common response we have received, as many others have had their own experiences echoed in this way. Many people have reported that after reading our book they had openings in their consciousness. This sometimes included physical sensations (tingling) all over the body, as well as a feeling that their head was exploding with information.

After the preliminary book was published, Nick told us that he heard about many new human-sized Crystal Skulls that had come out. However, in most of these cases the owners have not been willing to release information about them. Since many Crystal Skulls are priceless and unreproducible objects, these owners are concerned about the security of their possessions.

IT SEEMS THAT WHATEVER WAS NECESSARY TO COMPLETE the current version of this book was made available to us. There are invisible helpers who bring these resources into play. Long ago, when I began to investigate and share New Age or metaphysical information, it took a great deal of energy and hard work. Now, possibly due to the Harmonic Convergence (August, 1987), the doors are opening up and it is fun to do this work. If my guidance is correct, things should get more interesting as we move into the rest of 1988 and the next decade. I believe that there will be more Crystal Skulls released by the Higher Guardian Forces, and I hope that we can include more information in a future

CHAPTER 3

book about research done with ancient Crystal Skulls. The ancient tools like the Crystal Skulls are finally emerging and it appears that a whole new level of reality is about to break forth.

JOSHUA SHAPIRO

Crystal Skull Researcher, Steve Mehler, with the Amethyst Crystal Skull

CHAPTER 4

teve Mehler has Master of Arts Degrees in Social and Natural Sciences with Specialty Areas in Prehistory and Ancient History, and Human Ecology/Environments; and a Bachelor of Arts Degree in Physiology and Anatomy. He was a Research Assistant at San Jose State University, on a grant-funded project in the field of Prehistory and Ancient History, focusing on Goddess religions and Egyptology. He worked at an archaeological excavation of a Neanderthal site in southwestern France, employed by the well-known French Prehistorian, Professor Francois Bordes. Steve was a Staff Research Director and Scientist for the Rosicrucian Order (AMORC) in San Jose, California, and was involved in all phases of metaphysical and parapsychological research. Steve had the opportunity to do psychic research with the Mayan Skull in 1980, and with the Amethyst Skull in 1983.

INTERVIEW WITH STEVE MEHLER

The following interview conducted by co-authors Sandra Bowen and Joshua Shapiro in San Jose, California, in October of 1986, relates Steve's experiences with the Amethyst and Mayan Crystal Skulls.

Joshua: You've been involved in researching two Crystal Skulls: the Amethyst Crystal Skull (which is still in San Jose, California) and the Mayan Skull. Let's discuss the information you collected while in contact with these skulls. First, when did you see these crystal artifacts?

Steve: Well, maybe we should start at the beginning. In November, 1979, I was working in the Research Department at the Rosicrucian Order, AMORC, here in San Jose [California], when I was approached. Actually, the Research Department was approached by a man with some photographs. He wanted us to comment on them. So they brought the photographs to my attention, since I have some background in Prehistory and Archaeology. The photographs were of the Mayan Crystal Skull. Now, at that time I knew very little about these items. Being a scientist interested in Prehistory, I had heard about these things, maybe even seen a photograph in a book, but I knew very little about the skulls.

However, we studied the photographs and did some psychometry work on them. We were told that the man who was representing these items was an agent for a Mayan priest. He promised that he could bring the actual skull in for us to work with. So that was arranged in January of 1980.

We organized a whole day of psychometry, with one session in the morning and one in the afternoon. The afternoon session featured Dr. Marcel Vogel, who claimed to have had many years of expertise in crystallography. These were very interesting sessions. I recorded them both on audiotape and also did a written report on them. That was my first experience.

Joshua: Is there more about your connection to the Mayan priest or his agent?

Steve: I became friendly with this agent for the Mayan priest. He promised to bring the Mayan Skull in again. We had another session with it and it was given to me personally to work with for a weekend with very interesting results.

CHAPTER 4

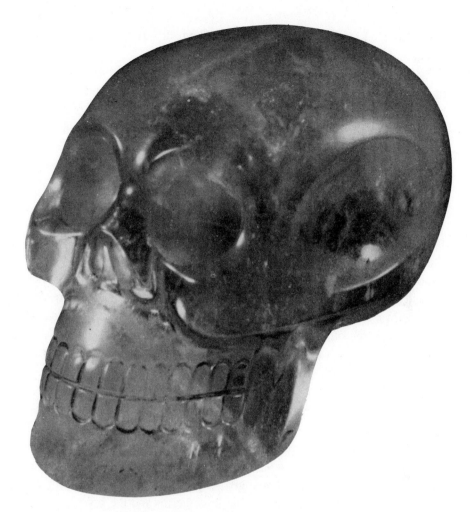

The Mayan Crystal Skull   © F. R. 'Nick' Nocerino

To summarize, the psychometry sessions basically corroborated each other; the skull was declared to be the same as a computer or library, able to store information from the mind, to be released (as Vogel said) by breath or by sound. Information could be released to anyone who tapped into it. We also felt (I had a couple of sessions later on with the priest, and he corroborated) that the Mayan Skull was used for healing.

So I then got involved with these two people, the priest and his agent. Unfortunately it didn't turn out as well as I would have liked. They were interested in selling this item. So a lot of time was spent trying to set up sales with people who might be interested, but in between I did some interesting

STEVE MEHLER

work with it. I found the skull to be fascinating. It was definitely a storage bank of information.

My last contact with the Mayan Crystal Skull was March of 1980. We were then told that it had disappeared from the area. I have since found out that it was put on loan to a lawyer in Texas and that's the last I've heard of it. Our contact degenerated because they were more interested in selling it than in the psychic or scientific research. So, I didn't hear from them for awhile.

Now to go on to the next item. I left Rosicrucian Park and was no longer involved with the Research Department; however, I stayed in contact with the man who was the agent. I then got involved with him a couple of years later, in another business operation. In the course of that business venture (which failed), he told me that he had been involved with the priest again and that there was another skull. Would I be interested? -- Certainly!! Now, this happened in November of 1982. So I went to his house and there was another Crystal Skull. He told me it was amethyst, though I had never heard there was an Amethyst Skull. According to all the literature, there was the Mitchell-Hedges Skull, the other skull that's in the British Museum, and this one (the Mayan Skull), which are all clear quartz. There was no mention of an Amethyst Skull in any literature, or in any psychometry done with other Crystal Skulls.

I got involved with the Amethyst Skull, again for the same personal reasons, but the agent wanted to have it sold. We made contacts; that's why I contacted F. R. 'Nick' Nocerino. Nick had a session with this skull. Marcel Vogel had another session with this skull, and the Amethyst Skull was given to me for a week. In that week I arranged for groups of various people [to see the skull], through my contacts with the Rosicrucians and the psychic/crystal people I knew. I arranged as many as twenty or thirty different psychometry sessions with the Amethyst Skull. For me, that was to be the most extraordinary skull of them all. Of the two I've experienced, I had much more affinity to the Amethyst Skull. It was a tremendous thing. I felt it was older than the Mayan Skull.

Again, to summarize the psychometry material, the Amethyst Skull was made by the same process (as the Mayan Skull), and we can go into more detail about the manufacturing later. But, it was also an energy/information storage receptacle. Vogel felt that the Mayan Crystal Skull was a language decoder, that it had the ability to translate ancient languages into modern thought. People could use it as a computer in that respect. We felt more with

CHAPTER 4

the Amethyst Skull that it was just a general energy transfer device, a storage unit of tremendous amounts of information.

Based on our psychometry sessions we felt that the Amethyst Skull is the older of the two Crystal Skulls. In fact, the priest told us that the amethyst was not grown on this planet. It might have been shaped into a skull on this planet, but the crystal is not from this planet. If you wanted to associate a civilization with it, I'd say Atlantis-- I'd say it's at least 20,000, 50,000 or 100,000 years old. *When* it was shaped into a skull, I can't give an accurate estimate, but it's very ancient, and many many different civilizations have handled it. It's gone through Atlantis, Egypt, ...people felt it was in the hands of Alexander the Great; there's even a story that one of the reasons the Crusaders went to the Middle East was to get this Crystal Skull, as well as the search for the Holy Grail. This Crystal Skull was involved with the Rosicrucians in the Middle Ages and with the Knights Templar.

According to the agent, the last time the Amethyst Skull emerged was as a paperweight on the desk of the Mexican dictator, Porferio Diaz, in 1910. [Editors' note: we have no confirmation of this.] It then disappeared, and later reappeared in the hands of the Mayan priests, got passed down, and now it's here. But it seems to be a catalyst in many great civilizations for thousands and thousands of years. Another item of information we felt came through was that this Amethyst Skull is a trigger for the other skulls.

In psychometry we came to the conclusion that there are maybe twelve skulls, a rose quartz one, a smoky quartz, a lapis, a clear amethyst one (which Nick was looking for) and several more. We feel that there is a circle of twelve skulls, and maybe this one [amethyst] sits in the middle as the thirteenth and triggers all of them. A woman had a vision of this and actually drew a picture of all of them. There was even an opal skull, which would be an incredible thing because opal is very hard to carve. I have no way of saying yes or no on these ideas or impressions. I feel there *are* more [skulls]. We also feel that all of these Crystal Skulls are supposed to be here [in the United States], and that more will come out. I have lost contact with the priest and I had a sort of falling out with these people, which I'd rather not go into. Again, there seemed to be greed involved, and that's why they've lost control of the Amethyst Skull now!

Joshua: Thus, based upon your work with these two skulls, what would you say is the purpose of these Crystal Skulls? You said they are computers, but how were they utilized and how will they be used in the future?

STEVE MEHLER

© Francoise Beaudoin

Steve Mehler psychically linking into the inner depths of the Amethyst Skull.

Steve: Well, they seem to be coming from higher intelligences, whether they are extraterrestrial or interdimensional. There seem to be "beings" attached to these skulls, which may not necessarily be from another planet, but may be occupying this space, just in a different dimension. They seem to be here to aid humanity, as a catalyst to speed up evolution. In other words, the information which can be tapped into from these skulls is endless. I would like to work with them continuously because the information coming out is incredible. The skulls are here because humanity is at a critical age right now. We're at the point where we're going into the so-called New Age. There's so much interest in psychic things, and a tremendous interest in crystals, crystal technology and applications. The skulls are here to aid those who can connect with and contact them.

There definitely seem to be "beings" involved, I could show you drawings of them. The "beings" which have been drawn fit into alleged extraterrestrial fourth encounters. They are very similar; it's amazing, all the correlations involved. We definitely had the feeling of "presences" involved, that something was overseeing [us when we were working with the skulls]. The skulls themselves seemed to be personalities, to be beings, yet there seemed to be other things outside them connected as well. There was always the feeling (as you mentioned about the Mitchell-Hedges Skull) of the Amethyst

CHAPTER 4

Skull being very loving and gentle, because it has the particular qualities of amethyst itself, which is a healing and gently balancing stone, and the skull seemed to do just that.

A brief anecdote-- Amethyst means "without drunkenness" in Greek. The Greeks named the stone this because they believed that amethyst would take away hangovers and drunkenness. A perfect story to go along with that is about a woman who has some fame as the "Earthquake Lady," Clarissa Bernhardt, known for predicting earthquakes. She came in and had a session with the skull. The man she's now married to came along and he had a bad hangover. After ten minutes of handling the Amethyst Skull, he reported that his hangover was totally gone. And he didn't know that this is a property of amethyst.

A lot of healing went on with the skull. The Amethyst Skull seemed to have the ability to draw out illnesses and bring them to a head. It brought on healing crises, which *could* be seen as doing harm, and people could misinterpret what was happening and say it was causing problems. But it caused a crisis in a situation and then effected a healing. So the skulls are definitely here to aid us, there's no doubt; and again I would say there are other intelligences involved in control of the skulls. The priest told me specifically there is a higher presence involved in controlling the skulls.

Joshua: This seems to correspond with what is written in the book, *Quartz Crystals, A Celestial Point of View,* by Lavandar, which talks about a Crystal Brotherhood (existing in various portions of the Galaxy) that has knowledge of doorways to various dimensions in Space. The skulls may serve as these interdimensional link-ups. My feeling is that the Mitchell-Hedges Skull represents some kind of a higher level development (if this is the correct term). I'm not clear yet on exactly how the Mayan and the Amethyst Skulls were created. Now, we feel that the clear quartz skulls that are in the museums in London, England and Paris, France, were probably an attempt to reproduce a Crystal Skull such as the Mitchell-Hedges, and they may have been carved.

Steve: Maybe. I think just the smaller ones were carved by the Aztecs, but as the priest told me, the Mayans did not carve any of them.

Joshua: Right, we believe the Amethyst and Mayan Skulls were not carved; they are too smooth. Frank Dorland said to us once that he could take the

British Skull and personally finish it so that it would look very nice and so forth. But in the case of the Mitchell-Hedges Skull with its movable jaw, no one seems to know how the creators duplicated a human jaw in crystal so precisely. There's another spiritual channel we've talked to about this skull, who also said that they were able to duplicate almost everything just by carving, but they couldn't reproduce the jaw.

Steve: I can only speak about the skulls I've been involved with, and I have only a superficial knowledge of the Mitchell-Hedges Skull. However, through talking with Marcel Vogel and with others who have experienced it, there was a lot done with the Mitchell-Hedges Skull! The Mayans did many dark things; there were a lot of scare tactics used with the Mitchell-Hedges Skull to keep people in line, etc., so it has a checkered history. There's no doubt of its power, from the photographs he showed me; as Dorland said in the book, *The Crystal Skull,* it's full of thousands of prisms, which can make tremendous lighting effects!

Joshua: Yes, because it's totally clear; before they [the research team that went to Canada] started working with it, the skull was totally clear. Nick said that one had to psychically fog it to see things. He said that with the two you have worked with, they were already fogged up, and you had to clear them first before you could see images/pictures through scrying.

Steve: Exactly, and the Mayan Crystal Skull does clear the more it works with someone who's attuned to it. The funny thing about the Amethyst Skull is that though it seems to be opaque, it does change color when affected by human consciousness. The Amethyst Skull is slightly different in manufacture, in that it's probably from two pieces that were fused together, while the others seemed to be from solid pieces of quartz. The Amethyst Skull was made from a cluster, so there are two sides which are distinctly different. One side is a different color than the other, and they would change colors. There's a suture line that goes right through the top which seems to divide it in half.

Joshua: One of the things that I've experienced as a difference between the two skulls I have seen in person is that the Amethyst Skull also seems to have recorded a lot of the violence and greed which was occurring around it. I feel that energy is still in the Amethyst Skull. I find the same thing when I view slides of the Mayan Skull; whereas the Mitchell-Hedges Skull doesn't seem to retain this type of energy.

CHAPTER 4

Steve: That's funny because the Mitchell-Hedges Skull has the worst reputation of them all as "The Skull of Doom!" Supposedly people died around it... from accidents. Even Mitchell-Hedges himself said attempts were made on his life while he had the skull, so it has that dubious reputation.

Joshua: Perhaps it is because the Mitchell-Hedges Skull is more powerful?

Steve: Or perhaps it's been in the West too long, which can pollute it. But I could add something about the feeling of the Amethyst Skull. That feeling seems to be an initial one. The same thing happened with Clarissa Bernhardt. When she first started working with the Amethyst Skull (she had worked with the Mayan Crystal Skull before), she said it didn't seem as friendly. But that seemed to be the initial response with it. As you connect with the skull, the deeper things involved with it seem to come out. Now, the priest explained to us that at some point a seal was put on the Amethyst Skull, so that it could not be used for evil or harmful purposes. I'm sure it was used prior to that for negative dark-side power. But the more one connects with the Amethyst Skull, if one has involvement for a long period of time, the more one feels tremendous powers of love, warmth, healing and similar reactions. I had it in my possession for a week; it was incredible what was coming out to me.

Joshua: What differences did you notice in your life during that week?

Steve: All sorts of events seemed to happen; again these things can be misinterpreted. There were events that could be said to have caused harm; people seem to pass away in your life when you're involved with these things. My mother passed away right after I was involved with the Amethyst Skull. The man who was the agent associated with the Mayan Skull, said that when he first got it his brother died in an automobile accident. So a lot of times people connect these 'calamities' as being involved with the skulls; it could just be coincidence. But a lot of powerful events do happen in your life after contact with the ancient Crystal Skulls. I've said to people that I wouldn't want to own these things. I'd love to have access to the Amethyst Skull to work with it, but I wouldn't want to own it.

Joshua: Did you notice whether your inner awareness or psychic gifts were heightened?

Steve: Oh yes, that's for sure. Even someone claiming not to be psychic, not to be involved with any mystical/metaphysical things, suddenly starts having psychic events in their life. The Amethyst Skull, even more than the Mayan Crystal Skull, opens all your chakras and allows a lot of things to come out. I have precognitive abilities, and with the Amethyst Skull they were heightened greatly and intensified. People who are psychic were able to have tremendous visions, were able to see pictures of civilizations. I have numerous reports and accounts of people who saw specific events in the past.

Joshua: Would you say, based upon your own experiences and those of others who were able to see the skull, that your life was changed in a positive way?

Steve: Yes, as I said originally, when I first [in 1979] got involved in this, I really was not that aware of Crystal Skulls or even just regular crystals. I had an interest in crystals, but no real knowledge of past cultural uses of crystals and how they're being used today. Now I have more knowledge. I have no doubt that these skulls opened it all up. I know I was a Crystal Engineer in the past. People said I was a Crystal Scientist in Atlantis. These are things I might have scoffed at seven years ago.

Joshua: The same thing happened to me. I had no interest in crystals whatsoever, and then after I saw the Amethyst Skull, suddenly crystals started coming into my life.

Steve: Your interest then was mainly about UFOs and now you've been able to make the connection; there definitely is a connection with so-called higher intelligences. Everything seems to be related to these entities... Now I have tremendous knowledge of how crystals were used in Atlantis, in Egypt, by the Mayans, the Olmec, et al. Due to this, my interest in Prehistory has been intensified.

I can talk at length about prehistorical uses of crystals. But the modern uses are just as fascinating. People don't realize the uses of crystal today in our computers, our timepieces or radios, etc. So many people aren't yet aware of all the many ways that crystals can be used for healing. I have come in contact with so many healers who use crystals. The crystal technology of the past is now coming up to merge with the technology of today. It will be the technology of the future.

It's also amazing, all the different types of stones from lapis, to jade, to smoky, to clear or citrine, all of the different effects that the various ones have.

CHAPTER 4

The difference between amethyst and clear quartz supposedly is traces of manganese, which gives it the purple color. But there is much more to it than that. Amethyst is much different than clear quartz in vibrational properties and effects.

If I were to compare the two skulls that I worked with, the Mayan Crystal Skull was of a much higher energy. If you gave it energy, you would become immediately wired. It could raise your vibrations. I think that was its use as far as healing goes. But it also was scarier; it scared more people, it was much more active. Although you could get that negative feeling from the Amethyst Skull at first perhaps, it then had a calming effect. It was much quieter and the vibration was much more balanced; it would balance one's vibration. Of course, the people who would work with it did connect with it. The more I would work with the Amethyst Skull, the more I became attached to it. Francoise Beaudoin [Steve's friend and owner of the Ram Metaphysical Bookstore, who also had this Crystal Skull in her home for one night] felt the same way. And in fact, we felt we were connected to it in past lives.

Joshua: Well I'm sure you were. What we're learning is that you do not try to find the skulls, they find you. [*Steve:* Exactly, there's no doubt about it.] And that's how I felt when I had a chance to see the Amethyst Skull.

Steve: As far as we know factually, there were only four known, full-sized Crystal Skulls. But like I said, we had more than one occasion for people that weren't present at each other's sessions to corroborate each other. Many people said that there are twelve skulls, that there were all these different other types. I talked to Nick about that and he felt that it was true. Other people also told me that there was a *clear* Amethyst skull. Marcel Vogel felt there was a twin amethyst to the one in San Jose, California, and that there's yet another amethyst skull. Some people have said that they've psychically seen a Rose Quartz Skull, a Smoky Quartz Skull, an Opal one, and a Jade Skull, which is incredible. [*Joshua:* Jade or Emerald?] Yes, this could be, but I've heard them say jade... to make up twelve different colored skulls. It's real interesting.

Joshua: One of our channelers, Michael Kant, talks about thirteen main Crystal Skulls in Tibet, which are not necessarily on the physical level. They are more etheric than physical, and they are helping to broadcast the higher teachings and higher knowledge. He says that these thirteen main skulls were taken to Orion after Atlantis was destroyed. Then they were brought back to the Earth, perhaps to Egypt.

Steve: You just triggered something interesting. When we asked the priest where the skulls came from, where the Brotherhood is that's involved with them, he said Orion.

Joshua: Did he? As a matter of fact, Michael mentioned Orion as the place where the Unicorns and the Blue Madras of the Inner Earth come from. Are you familiar with that? [*Steve:* I'm familiar with the story of the Blue Race.] What have you heard about them?

Steve: Well, supposedly there was a more highly developed race which evolved in Lemuria, then disappeared; but there are still traces of this race.

Joshua: One of the main reasons we are writing this book is to look at the possibility of a connection between UFOs and Crystal Skulls. In the slides which Nick shows in his lectures (or those we have shared in our own lectures), people see UFOs in the Mayan Skull and in the Mitchell-Hedges Skull; such as the picture we showed you prior to this interview. Spacecraft have also been clearly seen in slides of the Paris Skull and in the British Skull. With the Amethyst Skull, we don't have any pictures with UFOs because the skull is so dark.

Steve: Well, I've received pictures from people who have made drawings of "beings" which are connected with the skulls. [*Joshua:* With the Amethyst Skull you mean?] Yes, and with the Mayan Skull.

Joshua: That is one of the things you also see in the Mitchell-Hedges Skull; you see extraterrestrial beings. They look like what contactees have drawn.

Steve: Well the reason that I say this is-- Are you familiar with the book, *The Andreasson Affair?*[1]

Joshua: Yes.

Steve: The beings that are shown [in that book] are the same as the beings depicted in one of the drawings about the skulls. I'll show you the drawing and you'll be able to see that immediately. [Steve opens a folder of drawings by people who worked with these two skulls.]

---

[1] *The Andreasson Affair,* Raymond Fowler. New York. Bantam. 1980.

CHAPTER 4

This fascimile illustration was the vision of Michael Campbell (1949-1983). While working with the Mayan Skull, he saw three beings using the energy of their minds to change a round crystal block into a Crystal Skull. The energy beams coming out of their Third Eyes were a gold color. The beings stood 16 feet tall with mantles around their necks. Their black eyes felt very innocent and gentle to Michael. There are three pyramids in the background with crystals atop.

Joshua: My feeling from the appearance of the beings shown in the drawing is that they are like androids, sent by Space Beings or higher intelligences because the Earth is too dangerous for them to do their work directly. Thus they send these so-called servants instead.

Steve: Also, supposedly their vibrations are too high (because we are of a lower vibration in these dense bodies), so they can't necessarily communicate on our level. So that's why these interdimensional beings have been contacting us.

Joshua: Yes, it looks very similar. Oh, I see now; in this picture he is seeing three beings with energy beams coming out from their Third Eyes which are hitting a block of quartz and transforming it into a Crystal Skull.

STEVE MEHLER

Steve: Right. That's an actual representation of a way in which the manufacture of the skulls could have been done.

Joshua: Through the process of the mind?

Steve: They are using the Third Eye, through the process of the mind. Here's another picture[2], showing a physical means of manufacturing too, besides a psychic manufacturing. This process seems to be the overall consensus of those who believe these two skulls were physically formed-- that they were made with water pressure. Now, the shaping was done by hand with only the use of a grit or polish such as sand; no high-tech was involved. The skulls were formed by the use of great concentration of the mind, a kickwheel and a lot of water pressure. Primarily, the timeframe had to be at least Lemuria. Some people felt that with some of the more recent skulls, that maybe it was during the time of Atlantis. But most people placed these forms as far back as Lemuria.[3]

The skulls were made in a high ultraviolet type atmosphere, not the type which we have on the planet today. The sun's rays were shooting a pure ultraviolet light down; this was involved with the shaping too. ...Now, with this drawing[2], the man saw that a lot of these dimensional beings were involved. So, in other words, it could have been a physical maker in a dense body on this planet who was being guided by the higher beings during the time that the manufacturing was being done.

Joshua: This is one of the theories which Sandra talks about-- that if the extraterrestrials did not specifically bring the skull here, then they inwardly guided receptive individuals about how to make them.

Steve: Yes and that feeling is shared by others. In fact, there is one man who really connected to this theory because he is a sculptor. His name is Dale Jordan, and he did his crystal work with Marcel Vogel. He is now the Curator at the Rosicrucian Egyptian Museum [in San Jose, CA]. Dale is a very high being. He psychometrized both of these skulls for me, and he really wanted

---

[2]·This picture not shown. It is Dale Jordan's drawing of a machine shaping a skull.

[3]·Lemuria was a large continent located in the Pacific Ocean which is said to have existed anywhere from 50,000 to 200,000 years ago. Supposedly, the stone figures on Easter Island are remnants of this civilization.

CHAPTER 4

to connect with the means of manufacture, being a sculptor himself. In fact if you go by Rosicrucian Park now, you'll see the new statue he made of Tutmose III. Dale did an excellent job on that.

He said that he connected with one really high being and was being guided through this process of water pressure, spinning the crystal, and operating a pulley system with a kickwheel, while using a lot of mental concentration and being aided by higher forces. He really felt that he connected with the skull's maker, and that's how he felt it was done; spinning, a lot of spinning and shaping by hand. Vogel said it was done by polishing with a grit. He got more into physical manufacturing.

Joshua: Was there anyone working with the skulls who channeled that lasers might have been used during the polishing process?

Steve: Yes, lasers were used at that time, but not the way we use them today. A laser involves the high excitation of crystals [or gases] by an energy source. So yes, there probably were other crystals that were involved in the shaping of the Crystal Skulls; there could have been some type of a laser effect. I'm convinced that in Atlantis they used some type of lasers, so that's no problem for me.

Joshua: Do you have permission to use these drawings?

Steve: Yes, but Michael Campbell's would be difficult for me to let go. You could have a facsimile drawing made of it. Michael Campbell has passed on to a higher plane. He had a very interesting psychometry session [with the Mayan Skull], but I can't release his material at this time. What's noteworthy is that his drawing is quite similar to the one that Betty Andreasson drew of her UFO experience. Actually, Michael was the person who gave me the book, *The Andreasson Affair.*

Joshua: Michael must have had either conscious or subconscious contact with Space Beings.

Steve: I'm sure he did. Michael saw them; he was actually with them. In fact, he got into a lot of problems in his psychometry. Michael saw a scene of Lemuria where there was a battle of "beings," a certain type of war involving crystals. He saw these "beings" as the original Man (Adamic), before humans occupied the dense bodies that they are now in. They were very gentle, peaceful, loving and unaware of things. Michael saw another negative force

STEVE MEHLER

that came in and tried to destroy them. These people didn't understand death as we do, so they were destroyed by the Force. Michael started to have some emotional problems in reaction to his psychometry; he connected with it very personally. He said that the beings [depicted in his drawing with the Crystal Skull] were the benevolent (not negative) ones.

Joshua: Did he connect it with pyramids too?

Steve: Yes. Michael saw pyramids in Lemuria in his psychometry. He saw all the scenes taking place in Lemuria.

We had psychometry dates that the Mayan Crystal Skull was at least 20,000 years old. The Amethyst Skull was even older. Maybe it was carved, but why was it shaped into a *skull?* Many people have different ideas about this. I personally believe that they were shaped into skulls on this planet. I have no problem with what the priest told me that the amethyst crystal was not grown on this planet, and that the Amethyst Skull perhaps was shaped in Lemuria. My personal feeling is that the Amethyst Crystal Skull is much older than the Mayan Crystal Skull, and it was used as a model, that perhaps the others were copied from at a later time.

Joshua: Yes, that's a good question that I'm sure a lot of people are going to ask. When one looks at the known skulls, why do they have different shapes? You see, one theory is that perhaps there were different races of Man and the Crystal Skulls are representing the various skulls of these races.

Steve: Francoise had this belief that it was extraterrestrial. She saw the back of the skull was very developed as the cerebellum. My undergraduate degree is in Physiology and Anatomy, so I have a very strong anatomical background. And I agree, it is actually fully developed, but there was no cerebral cortex. It's really not ET because that wasn't the way this skull was shaped. But Francoise was thinking it was modeled from an extraterrestrial being.

My feeling is that's not true. The skulls are all symbolic. They weren't anatomically correct, except for the Mitchell-Hedges Skull, which is very much like the human skull with a detachable jaw and a full cerebral cortex. These other Crystal Skulls were shaped only for symbolic reasons; they weren't actually modeled after any living being because there's no forehead. There would be no intelligence as we would know it because there's no cerebral cortex.

CHAPTER 4

Joshua: That's a good point to consider.

Steve: I never felt that they were modeled after humans, except for the Mitchell-Hedges Skull. The specific reason why the Mitchell-Hedges Skull may be so different than the others *is* because it was modeled from a human skull.

Joshua: ...Unless it actually *was* a human skull that was changed into crystal. [*Steve:* Which is quite possible.] This is what Michael Kant claims.

Sandra: This makes sense too. Do you feel that the Amethyst Skull is the only one which is masculine?

Steve: No, it didn't feel masculine to me, no. [*Sandra:* In terms of shape?] No, not in any kind of terms. I said it was symbolic. This skull had a more neuter feel to it, it had both masculine and feminine energy. While with the Mayan Skull, people called it a she, they had definite feminine impressions of it. I don't think it was shaped based on any living model, at least any human model that was ever on this planet.

Sandra: I've only seen one skull.

Steve: The Mitchell-Hedges Skull.

Sandra: Right. I've just heard that all of them (in terms of shape when they have been analyzed) are feminine skulls, except for the Amethyst Skull being masculine.

Steve: Again, to be anatomically correct, not at all. The skulls seem to be coming from higher intelligences, whether they are extraterrestrial or interdimensional. A skull is found, and anthropologists or physical anthropologists would say that it's a male or a female skull. But believe me, that's not steadfast because it can be that there are many female skulls with very thick bone which could be mistaken for male skulls when taken out of the ground; and the same mistake could be made about a lot of male skulls which have very thin bone. The skull is not a good determinant for gender. When scientists find a skeleton, they usually go more by the pelvis and by the ribs, etc., to find out if it's male or female. The skull really is not highly accurate alone; solely having a skull to say that the being was a male or female is insufficient. No, I never felt any of that, that this skull was either male or female.

STEVE MEHLER

Sandra: What kind of beings did you see within?

Steve: I got a feeling about the beings who control the skull, that we couldn't call them masculine or feminine, that they're androgynous.

Sandra: And they look like these in the picture?

Steve: Yes, oh yes. More than one person who has been involved with both the Mayan Crystal Skull and the Amethyst Skull has drawn that face. That's why I feel that the same Brotherhood, the same beings, are involved with all the skulls. But I had a definite feeling that they were not extraterrestrial; because of how they moved around, they were interdimensional. They had apparently existed on this planet with us at the same time, however, if you're working with Crystal Skulls or high energy items like crystals which can raise your vibrations, you can see or experience these beings. So this means that the beings are not necessarily from another planet; they exist alongside us. People said the beings were Lemurians who came down into dense bodies. In the book, *Secrets of the Andes,* by Brother Philip, he calls them the Elders, or the ELs. They have conquered matter, energy, space and time; they have left this timeframe, but one of the ways they do contact us is through the Crystal Skulls.

Joshua: In other words, they are looking for doorways where we can meet them halfway?

Steve: Yes, definitely. The crystals are part of that. I have no problem believing you when you say that the Mitchell-Hedges Skull could have actually been a living being whose skull was crystallized. To me crystals are keys from higher intelligences to lower intelligences.

Joshua: The structure of quartz crystals incorporates a six-pointed star pattern. Within any six-pointed star you can infinitely draw other six-pointed stars. So to me this implies that a quartz crystal acts as a doorway which connects to other dimensions. The crystal's form is a physical projection of these dimensions and crystals are our tools to access them.

Steve: Sure. A major difference between crystals and us is that we are carbon-based creatures and they're silicon-based creatures. There's no doubt, we felt that these [Crystal Skulls] were living beings. People really connected with them. I felt so close to the Amethyst Skull, I actually felt I knew it. This wasn't merely an inorganic mineral of an unusual form.

CHAPTER 4

Sandra: I had the same experience with the Mitchell-Hedges Skull. I remembered a life I had as a Mayan working with it.

Steve: Yes, that's the way I feel with the Amethyst Skull. I know I did too.

Sandra: Did you have UFO experiences before you saw the skulls?

Steve: Yes, I've had them. I have UFO experiences that go back to my youth, which I just kept to myself and never even talked about. When I was eight years old growing up in New York City, I saw unexplainable lights; I had a first encounter. Never spoke about it to anybody. In 1975, in Santa Cruz, I had an experience; and so as these things have come up more and more, now I talk about them.

Sandra: What kind of experience did you have in 1975?

Steve: One night, I saw an orange light that expanded and contracted, moved and hovered as I was looking out a window. I lived in Santa Cruz on Soquel Avenue. I first thought there was an explosion somewhere and there was a fire downtown. I didn't hear any fire engines and didn't see anybody responding to it. It seemed to just be a couple hundred feet off the ground and it expanded, glowed, moved, and then just totally disappeared. It wasn't until I had read J. Allen Hynek's books a couple of years later, that I realized that this was a recurring event that a lot of people had seen.

Sandra: How about the childhood experience you mentioned?

Steve: When I was eight years old, I was on the top of my apartment house in the Bronx, New York. I saw a formation of lights flying, which I first thought were just airplanes. Then they made a tremendous turn, a 90° turn, and came back to hover. I had the awareness at that time that they were not airplanes, they were something else. But I never spoke about it to anybody until just the last couple of years. I haven't had any increase in such sightings since I became involved with the skulls; just more of an increase in knowledge of things, an awareness of higher intelligences and all the information about UFOs that has come my way. When I worked at the Rosicrucian Order, they didn't want to get involved with the subject of UFOs at all. That was a taboo subject to them. And this is common; many groups don't want to discuss UFOs.

Sandra: Do you feel that now you have some kind of direct communication with the Beings?

STEVE MEHLER

Steve: Well, the priest told us that if you get involved, you get initiated into the Brotherhood when you work with the skulls. So yes, I'm in contact with these same things. Once you're in, you're not getting out. You can't go backwards. There definitely was a feeling of initiation in working with these Crystal Skulls, that I became part of the group. Other people have felt the same way. People who have had a psychometry session with the skulls hugged me, thanked me, and kissed me when they left; and people have all felt connected. Everyone that has been involved with the Crystal Skulls feels this bond rejoining. It doesn't make any difference whether you ever see the skull again.

Sandra & Joshua: Right.

Steve: All my crystals here have been charged with the energy of the Crystal Skulls; I feel totally connected to the skulls.

Joshua: We are finding that there is a greater interest in Crystal Skulls now. Do you agree?

Steve: There is a definite increase in interest, you're right. I could sit and talk about these things for days. I mean, there's just an incredible amount of information that was released. There seemed to be an ability of these skulls to tap into various areas that correspond to different functions of the brain, and you get information dealing with that. In other words, if you put your fingers to the skull's eyes and meditate, you see a lot of visual things. If you go back to the area corresponding to the auditory centers of the brain, you hear things, etc. As you meditate on the various areas of the skulls, you can get information which corresponds to the functions of the brain associated with that area. So they are definitely programmed that way. It's incredible!

Sandra: Were you familiar with anyone who used hand signals for activation when working with the skulls?

Steve: No, we mainly activated them through breath, through sound. The priest did an experiment with it where he didn't do anything with hand signals, but he did activate the skull through psychic ability.

Sandra: In my regressions when I've been with the Mitchell-Hedges Skull, I automatically go into a whole series of hand-signals which actually activate the skull. My feeling is that the beings which work with me use them as their

CHAPTER 4

language, and so I am communicating with these beings as well as with the skull.

Steve: I definitely agree with what Vogel said about the skull being a language decoder, because this Mayan priest didn't speak English and I don't speak Spanish. [*Sandra:* Right.] I had a session with the Mayan priest and his interpreter. When I asked a question, it had to be translated into Spanish to get an answer. One time when I questioned the priest, he turned to answer me in Spanish and I knew what he said. Then the translation came through and I said, "That's not what he said, he said such and such." And the translator said, "I thought you don't speak Spanish!" ...He put the message right into my brain!

Sandra: Yes, the priest did the same thing with me. Nick had him over to his home for dinner. We were talking about all my experiences related to the skulls, and my energy problems because of them. And then when I went home that night, he came to me [astrally] and talked to me in Spanish. He did a healing on me and I talked back to him in Spanish. I don't speak any Spanish [*Steve:* Right, it's amazing!!] and it was really wonderful to communicate.

Steve: Yes, the priest has [astrally] visited me many times, and he has visited Francoise too. We both felt very connected to him. I still don't understand what his connection was with this other person [the agent], because then the greed got involved. They were so insistent on selling these artifacts. Why, I begged? We had set up our own Crystal Skull research group. I formulated a whole structure and they were going to let me borrow the Crystal Skull. We were going to work with it and give lectures with it. I would have given them a rental fee for it and so on, but the greed involved was too much; at first they wanted $100,000, then $200,000, then they wanted a million dollars! This was the price they were asking for these artifacts, a million dollars. He would have sold the Mayan Crystal Skull to the Rosicrucian Order for $200,000 if they had raised the funds. But the Imperator of the Rosicrucian Order wanted to have nothing to do with the skull because he just didn't see it as a verifiable artifact- it couldn't be documented. The priest and the agent were offering to exhibit the Mayan Crystal Skull in the Rosicrucian Egyptian Museum for free, and the Imperator turned it down. There was so much greed involved, and it was so inconsistent-- the price constantly rising for no reason. This is why I had to back out.

STEVE MEHLER

I just wanted them to loan me the skull and we would have done incredible things. We could have worked with healers and all types of people. People only wanted ten minute sessions with the skull, just to meditate with it and then go on their way. Whatever work they were doing would be increased and improved. But the greed was just too much. That's why they've lost control of both the skulls. [*Sandra:* I agree with that.] But the skulls will eventually be with the right people they are supposed to be with.

There are so many stories I could tell you about when we tried to sell it. We had a deal almost closed with a very wealthy woman in England. The agent gave me possession of the Mayan Skull so that I could verify it, gave my phone number to a woman so she could call me and confirm that I was a legitimate scientist who had worked with these artifacts. Just when the deal was supposed to go down, we stopped hearing from this woman. They made inquiries and called, but this woman totally disappeared from the face of the Earth; there was no trace of her and no way to track her down. There are a lot of stories like that; deals that were almost closed, people who said, "Oh yeah, here is a millionaire who will buy this item!" Boom... no contact, no continuation.

Joshua: It's almost as if somebody is in charge and wherever the skulls must be, they will be.

Steve: It disturbs me personally, because I get impatient that these items are just sitting in vaults. You know, like the one in the British Museum, the one that's in the lawyer's hands in Texas [Mayan Skull], and this one [the Amethyst Skull] which has just been sitting in a vault in downtown San Jose for three years. [Editors' Note: As of the publication of this book, the gallery has been closed and the Amethyst Skull is in private hands.] It is not interacting with people and it's said to be covered with silk and trappings. There is so much that could be done with these things educationally.

Joshua: What connection do the two Crystal Skulls now have with the Mayan priest and his agent?

Steve: They lost both skulls by just putting a loan on them. For $10,000 they let go of the Mayan Crystal Skull. There was so much greed that I finally could not personally deal with them anymore. I was also disappointed with the priest. He knew where I was at, and he knew where Francoise was located. We had sort of made a bond with him; he promised he would get back to us with more things. It's been years and I haven't heard from him. For awhile I

CHAPTER 4

had many sessions with the priest, a lot of great information. He told me a great deal about the Mayans, the Olmecs, etc., ...wonderful stuff. We had a good rapport. He claimed he was feeding his whole village, and that the reason they were trying to sell these items was that he was supporting a whole Mayan village in Mexico. His people were poor, they were starving. That's why he was ordered by the Higher Brotherhood to come to America to deal these items to the right people who were wealthy and could use them the right way. But it didn't seem like that was what was happening. They seemed interested in just anybody with the wealth to pay for the artifacts. And, you know, to say these items were worth a million dollars-- it's really so arbitrary. These skulls are priceless to me.

Sandra: I don't see how anybody could try to sell them, when they know their healing and spiritual value.

Steve: Right! Just in meditating quietly with these skulls incredible things can happen...

Joshua: Did the priest mention where the Mayans came from?

Steve: Well, he mentioned more conventional stuff, not exactly where they came from. He said that they were an older people, prehistoric. Also, he talked a lot about the Olmecs, which I was very interested in because the Olmecs taught the Mayans everything. The Olmecs were much older than the Mayans. He didn't specifically say where they came from, but he said that the Mayans, the Olmecs, the Incas and the Egyptians had contacts with the Higher Brotherhood, with higher intelligences.

Sandra: What about the Toltecs, do you know much about them?

Steve: I know different things about the Toltecs. There's a whole Toltec philosophy of Don Juan in Carlos Castaneda's books, but what is taught in Anthropology about the Toltecs was that they were a late Indian tribe, very warlike and aggressive. They conquered the Aztecs and the Mayans at the end of their civilization, and they were the last Mayan groups. But they practiced many black arts, a lot of controlling and manipulative things. Now, Don Juan's story of the Toltecs is much different. He claims they are a much more ancient source of a shamanistic group that wasn't all dark. The priest took a map of all the Mayan sites and he showed me which were dark, those which were bad and should be avoided, and those which were good to be around. He pointed to Chichen Itza, all the sites in the Yucatan, and he said to stay away from them because the Toltecs there had charged all of those sites negatively. But then he talked about where the Mayan Crystal Skull came from-- Copan. He talked about Copan, Tikal and Palenque, which are the three main sites. They were the great sites of Light and crystal research, especially at Tikal. The Mayan priest claimed the Mayan Skull was found in Copan in 1912.

Sandra: The reason I asked about the Toltecs is because when I was channeling with the Mitchell-Hedges Skull, I received that they were a group that had done things with this skull.

Steve: This is the map he used to show me. Copan is in Honduras. He said that all the sites up here, Chichen Itza, Myapan and Uxmal, were charged negatively because of the Toltecs who had taken over the Mayans at this point. In fact, blood sacrifices were done and they used the skulls for negative power trips. But of all the sites here, especially in Oaxaca and Tabasco, (this is where the Olmec were) these were all positive ones. Tikal, Copan and Palenque make a right triangle, and those are the three main sites.

Sandra: Could you elaborate on the history of the Mayan Skull?

Steve: I was told how this skull was discovered. There was a plague around 1910 that was wiping out Mayan villages and the priests all gathered together. They did a very powerful ceremony and prayed to their Higher Brotherhood to help them. Then some Mayan priests were hired to help with the British excavation and when they overturned a stone altar at Copan, there was the skull. They didn't tell the archaeologists; they took it home to the village and cured the plague. And that's how it got passed down.

Joshua: Did they say anything about whether the Amethyst Skull was at the same site?

Steve: No, the priest was vague about where the Amethyst Skull had actually come from. Again, the agent stated that it was used as a paperweight for Diaz. When Diaz lost power, it returned to the right hands. The priest just said it was handed down through the generations of the priests, and that's a long time. He didn't know exactly what site it could have come from; he said it was from Oaxaca originally.

Joshua: Did he explain how he was able to take possession of these skulls?

Steve: Yes! He was vague though. He wouldn't be specific, but he said it was because of his initiation into both the Mayan and the Aztec Brotherhoods. He

CHAPTER 4

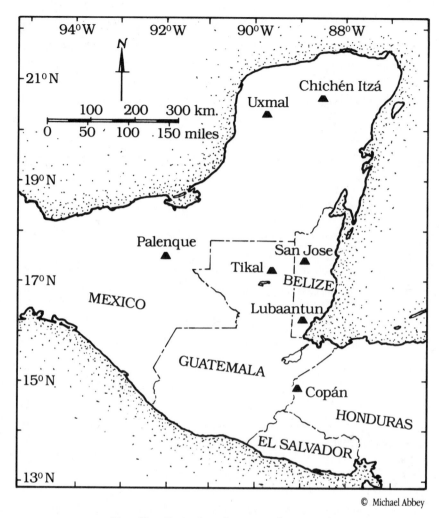

© Michael Abbey

*Map of key sites in Central America where several
of the ancient Crystal Skulls have been found.*

said that he was part of a certain priesthood which has the knowledge about the location of a hidden cache that was passed down, and he's supposedly been given the authorization to release these items.

Joshua: Do you feel that saying he wanted to sell the skulls was a ruse? In other words, do you think that he had some other reason for bringing the skulls here?

Steve: That's an interesting question. We felt really connected to him and that his motives were pure, but I think that there was something with this other

STEVE MEHLER

individual, the agent who he was connected with-- that the priest was putting him through a series of tests. I think it was correct that they did need money to feed the village and that people were starving, but that was only a partial reason. There was something involved with this agent who had been a priest (he told us) in a past life, had failed and needed to go through certain tests in this lifetime. So I believe that the priest's motives were complex. Some motives were for money, some were to get these items to us, which he was told to do by the Brotherhood. In fact, he was told to bring the skull to the Rosicrucian Order specifically.

Joshua: And he didn't know who he was going to meet there?

Steve: He was just told that they would know how to use it. "Take it to the Rosicrucians." Then he said that he was told the Amethyst Skull should come to Francoise and me. He *said* he was "told" these things, but I feel that the greed factor was partially what was involved.

Joshua: Do you have any feeling or sense that somehow you will be involved with some kind of a group or organization which will have the Amethyst Skull, or literally be a guardian for it?

Steve: I dreamed of it. [*Joshua:* How about during the period when you were working with it.] Yes, I felt that I was supposed to be doing this work. I was supposed to be a scientist working with these skulls. Not owning them, but having access to them, yes.

Joshua: Nick says he knows a few people who are willing to buy these skulls and have even put out offers. We are very interested in any stories about the skulls. It's like suddenly they are receiving absolutely no response to any of their numerous offers, as if someone just turned this whole process off. And these are people that really have the money to buy them. So Nick said that the next time I talk to the owner at the gallery (where the Amethyst Skull was stored), I should ask him how much they are asking for the Amethyst Skull. There's supposedly a man who already has paid money for it, but somehow it's not working out. I guess this is par for the course.

Steve: I know. I could tell you, I had numerous accounts like that working with both skulls, trying to set up deals. He used me as a scientific ally-- I mean I was the Archaeologist, I could verify things, and so on. I read the Hewlett-Packard reports of their tests with the Crystal Skulls.

CHAPTER 4

Joshua: What were the results of these tests?

Steve: They could not determine how the Mitchell-Hedges Crystal Skull was made. I believe that they made the same conclusion about the Amethyst Skull and the Mayan Skull. The scientists said that there wasn't any indication of hydraulic or high pressure tools used. All three skulls were "carved" against their natural axis, which means that if you were to hit it with a hydraulic tool, it would shatter into many pieces. Hewlett-Packard had no idea how the skulls were made, but *they* even said that the skulls are much older than they had previously estimated. They believed that the skulls are older than the Aztec or Mayan civilizations. All the scientists agreed that the skulls are very old and that they couldn't have been created by modern means of manufacturing.

Joshua: Now, the archaeologists believe that the Mayans (I guess the Aztecs and the Incas too) didn't use a lot of crystal. Is that true?

Steve: No, they are more or less agreeing now that they did use crystals, but you know they put labels on things. For instance, archaeologists have called some of these skulls Aztec or Mayan. [*Joshua:* Right.] So they said that they believe the Indians carved them, but they have no idea how. They don't give the Indians credit enough to have had the technology to do so, but they just label the skulls 'Aztec' or 'Mayan.' They have to accept the fact that the Mayans were incredible carvers of jade and that the Aztecs employed certain Indian groups known as the Zapotecs and the Mixtecs, who were great artisians. They did a lot of jade carving and so they were recognized as great artisians. It is known that they used crystals. But, academic anthropologists don't know why, and archaeologists don't know how, because most of the scientists don't have any understanding of the metaphysical uses of crystal.

However, Nick's research teams in 1979-80 called that skull a Mayan Crystal Skull because that's what the anthropologists would do-- they would say yes, it was found in Copan, so it must have been made by the Mayans, and so we'll call it the Mayan Skull, or the Aztec Skull, or this or that. The Mitchell-Hedges Skull has been classified by some archaeologists as being carved by the Aztecs, and being just a couple of hundred years old, even though Hewlett-Packard won't say anything. I don't believe that the Aztecs or Mayans carved any of the ancient human-sized Crystal Skulls. The Hewlett-Packard scientists put the skull in alcohol baths and they did weight and light polarization tests and so forth. The skulls were all carved from one single piece of crystal, although the Amethyst Skull may be different, as it seemed to be a cluster that was molded together. But the way it was molded together cannot be duplicated by modern techniques.

Joshua: Do you know if Hewlett-Packard did any other tests with color, light or sound on the skulls?

Steve: I don't know if they did, but we did at the Rosicrucian Research Department. We did tests with laser light and with ultraviolet light on the Mayan Skull.

Joshua: What kind of results did you get when you used the different colors?

Steve: Similar to the Mitchell-Hedges Skull, but not as fine. If you hit the Mayan Crystal Skull with a beam coming from the side, it comes out through the Third Eye. So it's prismatically set to do this. Lighting sometimes comes out in different areas, like through the eyes. There are built-in prisms that will refract and reflect light in different ways. The Amethyst Skull being opaque, of course, showed less effects since light doesn't go through it. It glowed in the dark though. All the skulls glow in the dark, they all have their own aura. The Mayan Skull has a blue-green aura, and the Amethyst Skull has a purple to blue-green spectrum to its aura. If you can adjust your eyes and meditate with a Crystal Skull in absolute darkness, after a while you will see them glowing-- they do glow. You will see this after you work with them. They are just like generators and they energize the more you work with them.

Joshua: When the team worked with the Mitchell-Hedges Skull, they observed colors coming out of it that should not have been there, because they weren't shining those particular colored lights upon the skull. Especially gold light; they said it came out all the time. Did you see that with these skulls? I guess we can only talk about the Mayan Skull, because the Amethyst Skull is such a dark purple.

Steve: Just its own aura... I mean the aura colors we saw shouldn't have been there [based upon the colors we put into the skull]; we shouldn't have seen the color blue-green, but that's what indeed came out.

Joshua: Did the colors ever come out in a specific area of the Mayan Skull or was it just as you're saying, that these prisms reflected the light in a certain direction or position in the skull?

CHAPTER 4

Steve: Just in the Third Eye. With the Mayan Crystal Skull, wherever you hit a side with white light, it would emerge as colored light through the Third Eye, sometimes as purple.

Joshua: So what you're saying is that somehow the skull is processing the light so you see something in the Third Eye.

Steve: Yes, that's a psychic vibration, there's no doubt. You know the purple spectrum is the highest visible vibrational range.

Joshua: Has anyone told you about having a direct communication with these Crystal Skulls?

Steve: Yes, people would say the skulls were talking to them in their minds. In essence that's what I felt it was doing; like if you asked a question in meditation, and you put your hands on the skull, the answer would come into your mind. Now, I'm not sure whether it was their own voice or they were actually hearing a voice speaking out. When Michael Campbell psychometrized the Mayan Skull, he came up with a language; he was actually starting to speak in Mayan. I transcribed it, but I have never translated what he said. He came up with a whole series of phrases in Mayan.

Joshua: The first time I saw the Amethyst and the Mitchell-Hedges Skulls, I felt like they were quietly observing me.

Steve: There's a time of attunement that has to happen with these skulls and after a while you connect with them. There is a period when certain people will get initial reactions to these skulls, but these aren't the deeper reactions which would come out later. It takes time to get to know the skulls, just like with people.

Joshua: Some people are lucky if they get to see one Crystal Skull in their whole life. I've seen two and I know there are others. Even just through the pictures, one can get to know the skulls. How do you feel about this?

Steve: I was totally amazed that there was an Amethyst skull. When I had seen the Mayan Skull and then it disappeared from our lives, I said fine, I'm a better person for having experienced it. What I found is that it's important to go beyond just observing the skulls-- I found that every single person, whether they had connections with them or not, would feel something upon touching them. I had people who were not into metaphysical and mystical things or crystals, put their hands on top of the Amethyst Skull and say, "Wow, I can feel it!" Every single person who was involved with Crystal Skulls and held or touched them, definitely felt something. So there is a reaction. I believe that was how they programmed the skulls; to attune with the human vibrations, like turning on a switch.

Joshua: If these skulls could speak through you after working with them, what messages would you say that they would want to share with other people?

Steve: Well, the conclusion which I came to was just one phase of my understanding of these skulls, that they are solid physical proof that what we call God, what we call higher intelligences, exist. There is more than just the human intelligence. It could be human, but of a higher intelligence than Earthlings. A single message that a lot people received was that 'Love is the answer,' that 'Things will turn out right in the end;' positive messages (a lot of people said), one sentence phrases. The greatest feeling that I felt from them was a tremendous affirmation of why I became involved in all these things, in metaphysics and mysticism-- that here was solid physical proof! This wasn't just other people telling me of their experiences, other encounters, etc. I was getting a direct message that, 'Hey, this is proof, this is it. There is something more!' And that when we get to know these skulls, we're going upwards. It was a positive message to me, totally positive that these skulls were sent here to benefit us, to aid us, to let us know that there is God, higher intelligences, higher beings.

Joshua: Now, let's pretend just for a moment: you have possession of a Crystal Skull for an unlimited amount of time. What kind of research would you do on a Crystal Skull if you had one under these conditions?

Steve: Healing was one of the primary things I felt I wanted to use them for. I would contact (and I have those contacts) a lot of people who do massage work, body work and counseling, to let them have sessions with the skull-- just meditating with it or holding it to raise their own energies to improve their healing work. Then I would work with gathering the knowledge, and with transcribing some of the information. I feel that the most functional thing that they could be used for now is healing, to really heal people. I mean, I could see people throwing away their crutches like they do in these, you know, faith

CHAPTER 4

healings, and I'm serious. But I think that exposure to the skulls can change a person's self-image. The Crystal Skulls could cure cancer, AIDS and many other diseases if used properly. So healing would be my primary function for using the skulls because I have a medical background too; then for knowledge, pure knowledge. After that, asking them questions and writing down the answers. Writing books of knowledge from the skulls.

I could work day and night. That was the problem, I didn't sleep! I stayed up all night with these other people coming through, day and night. I had people visiting like there was a revolving door here.

Joshua: And you never got tired or fell apart?

Steve: No, and I stopped eating. You settle for burn-out after a while. Eventually, I had to take the Amethyst Skull, wrap it in silk, put it back in the case and let it sit for a while because I was burning-out. But I worked four days straight like that, almost without sleeping or eating. I couldn't sleep at night, so I had to put it away. When I put the skull away, put *it* to sleep, then *I* could sleep.

Joshua: I had a similar reaction when I tried to go to sleep while the Mitchell-Hedges Skull was in the same motel. Normally, when I go to sleep I am out immediately.

Steve: Yes, me too, but with the skulls around I couldn't sleep. I had both skulls in this house, so I'm sure the vibration of the house has been raised because of that. Another interesting thing which I also should add is that when I had the Mayan Skull in my possession, my friend Shasta and others claimed they saw a UFO go over Rosicrucian Park, right over the Park. There was an increase in sightings in this area at the time that we were working with the skull. Like you asked before, *I* didn't have an increase of UFO type experiences, but other people did.

Joshua: Ok, so what you're saying is that as one works with the Crystal Skulls to activate them, they can trigger an opening for spacecraft to come through into our world. It almost sounds like an invitation or a directional light beam which they can use to more easily locate us.

Steve: I agree. It also raises your energy to the point where you can work with these beings. They may be here all the time like I said; they may be here interdimensionally and we just can't see them. But then peoples' vibrations raise up and suddenly they have the contacts. People have dreams where beings come to them and talk with them, whereas before they saw the skull they didn't have such dreams. And I've felt a decrease in my dreams since the Amethyst Skull has been locked in the vault of the art gallery.

Joshua: When you were working with either of these skulls, did you ever have any feeling that somehow they were perhaps connected to a crystal helmet?

Steve: No, a mask. [*Joshua:* A crystal mask?] Yes. The priest talked about a lot of other things, including a full-sized crystal man, a six-foot long crystal Mayan priest. He also talked about a crystal mask which he was eventually going to bring for us to see. The priest said the masks were much more powerful than the skulls because only someone of a higher vibration could work with them. He claimed that when the mask was placed over one's face, the energy of the cosmos goes right in through you. But if the person putting on the mask was not at the necessary level of advancement or attunement, he or she would die, burn-up or disintegrate.

Joshua: The book, *Initiation,* by Elisabeth Haich, talks about a scepter made out of copper and gold. It could conduct these higher energies, and if somebody was to touch the scepter or even be in its presence when it was activated, the person would be instantly disintegrated.

The crystal Mayan Priest is very interesting to me. This ties into what Michael Kant talks about; that underneath the ruins in Peru there are Crystal People. The priests used the power of their minds to change the chemical matrix in the bones of the subject into crystal. The chemical matrices or lattices in the bones were the building blocks to copy, and with these they had a stored vibrational record of everything that the person knew. These people would crystallize a person's skeleton after death, rather than creating a statue or painting to commemorate the person as we do today.

Steve: Do you know the part in *The Andreasson Affair* where Betty Andreasson was supposedly taken to the Middle World? She was taken to a crystalline city; the buildings were made of crystal.

Joshua: This is what some people believe the Inner Earth is like; that they have crystalline cities. Whether it's true or not, the essence is that this information does exist and is getting ready to come out. The Crystal Skulls are

CHAPTER 4

almost a signal of this in many ways because mankind can only be allowed to have what it can work with and understand.

Steve: We've done things with pictures of the skulls in meditation circles and a lot of things happen. While viewing pictures of the Amethyst Skull and Mayan Skull, we saw scenes of Mayan ceremonies, caves, jungles, other crystals, dancing, etc. All of us had previously been with the Crystal Skulls in person, and the psychic impressions from our meditations with pictures of the skulls were similar to those experienced and recorded during sessions with the actual skulls.

Joshua: This is the reason why the pictures of the Crystal Skulls have been released. In our understanding, these skulls can only be in one place at one time, yet through the images which carry a portion of their energies, the skulls can be in many places simultaneously. The skulls, or the beings which work through them, seem to be able to connect with photographs and videotapes filmed of the skulls.

Steve: Yes, I'd like to see the Crystal Skulls brought together because that's what I feel is supposed to happen. All the Crystal Skulls actually work off one another.

Joshua: Yes, that's what most of us feel, but there is a timing involved so we will see what happens.

ADDENDUM: The following is a theory that Marcel Vogel shared with Steve. This was presented at the close of the interview.

Joshua: Could you explain the Lattice Defect Theory?

Steve: Quartz is silicon dioxide. This is a silicon atom bonded to two oxygen atoms. Vogel claims (and I know this from my chemistry background-- that's why it made so much sense to me) that there are times when there can be a defect in the lattice of the crystal. There can be a silicon dioxide molecule with the silicon atom missing, leaving an empty bond there. So he claims that the empty space where the atom would be, could be occupied by the energy of the mind, pulsed human thought. Someone concentrating could pulse a thought into the crystal and it would be stored there. He says that due to

STEVE MEHLER

defects in the lattice of crystals, information can be stored. Putting it into computer language, he said there were billions and billions of bits of information that could be stored. So that's how he claimed the Crystal Skulls could be used as computers, as a reference library which could store information using pulsed thought from a human mind. Vogel demonstrated how this is done through breath control and pulsing the thought-energy into the crystal, and it made sense to me.

Vogel talked about billions of stored bits of information in this Lattice Defect Theory. And he also talked about the means of manufacturing the skulls, which he called Concoidal Fracturing. He claimed that the skulls were broken, split, fractured and then fused together through thought, human mental energy. He claimed that he could duplicate the skulls, that he could make a Mayan Crystal Skull and an Amethyst Skull. I gained a lot of information about crystals and Crystal Skulls from Vogel because he worked with all four of the Crystal Skulls, as Nick has-- The Mitchell-Hedges Skull, the Crystal Skull in the British Museum, the Mayan Skull and the Amethyst Skull. Nick Nocerino and Marcel Vogel are the only people I know who have worked with four Crystal Skulls, so that makes them very valuable resources. But I would say that Nick Nocerino is the pre-eminent researcher in the field. He has over forty years of research into the Crystal Skulls. Nobody has done as much work about them as he has. I enjoyed working with him.

CHAPTER 4

PART II
PHOTOGALLERY

ANCIENT CRYSTAL SKULLS
MITCHELL-HEDGES CRYSTAL SKULL
BRITISH CRYSTAL SKULL
MAYAN CRYSTAL SKULL
AMETHYST CRYSTAL SKULL

COMPARISON
ILLUSTRATIONS

CONTEMPORARY CARVED
CRYSTAL SKULLS

Mitchell-Hedges Crystal Skull

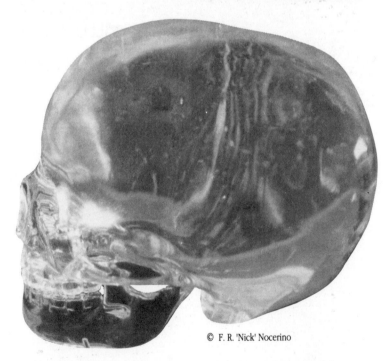

Top: Three-quarter view (Note the reflection of the skull in the glass plate underneath.)

Bottom: Side view showing more features of the jaw (Note the various sutures towards the back of the skull.)

British Crystal Skull

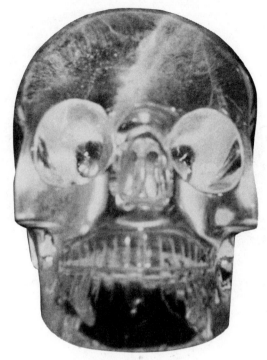

© John Shimwell

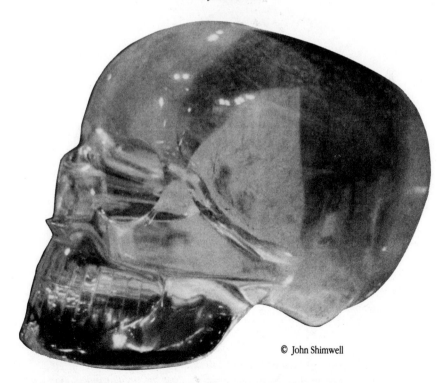

© John Shimwell

Front view (top) and side view (bottom) photographed through the glass case in which this skull is exhibited in the Museum of Man in London, England.

Mayan Crystal Skull

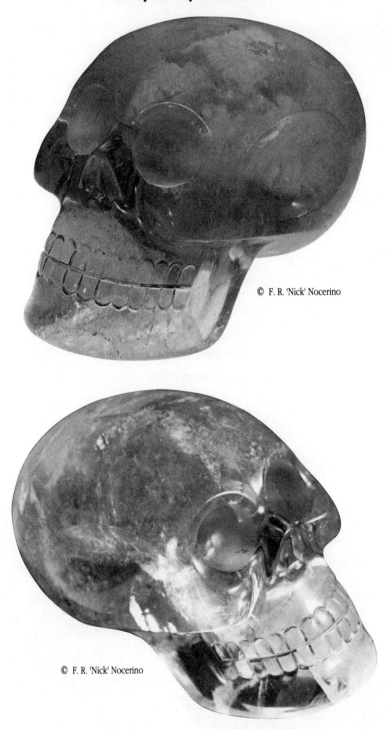

© F. R. 'Nick' Nocerino

© F. R. 'Nick' Nocerino

*Three-quarter profiles of the Crystal Skull photographed during Mr.
Nocerino's four months of extensive research. Note the circular indentation
in the temple (top picture) and the style of the jaw and teeth.*

Amethyst Crystal Skull

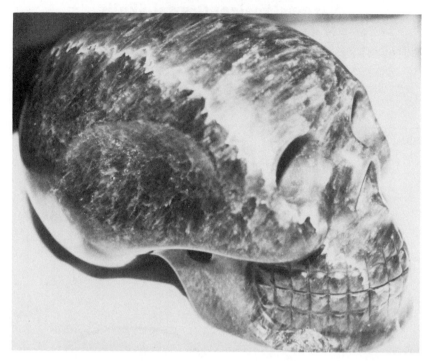

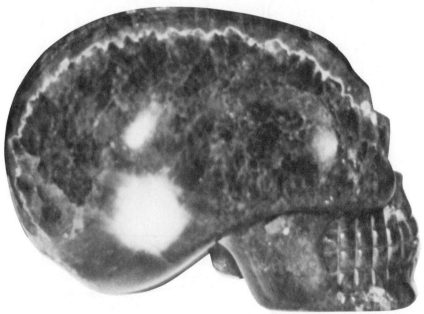

Top: Three-quarter profile taken during Mr. Nocerino's session with the skull, showing the circular indentation in the temple and the suture line which spans from the jaw to the back of the cranium.

Bottom: A side profile of the skull with another view of the suture line. The large white spot (back portion) is the matrix where the seed crystal began to grow.

Schematic Comparison of
Various Ancient Crystal Skulls
(Front and side profiles, scaled to size)

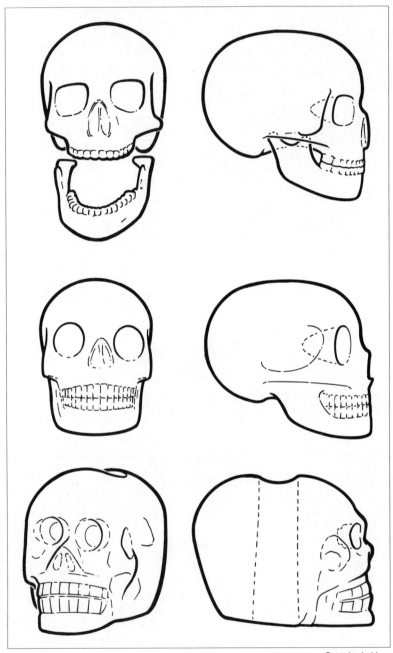

© Michael Abbey

Top to Bottom: The Mitchell-Hedges Skull, the British Skull and the Paris Skull. The Mitchell-Hedges Skull is different from the others presented, because the jaw is a separate piece. The Paris Skull's style and cut of crystal is similar to smaller Aztec skulls that have been found and has a hole cut into it from the top.

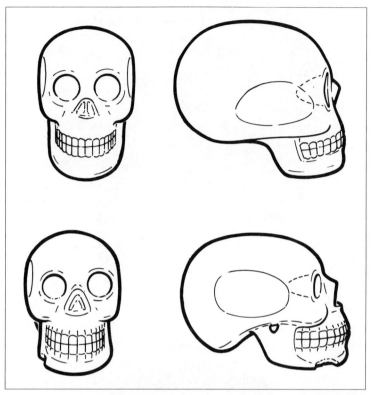

Here we see the Mayan Skull (top) and the Amethyst Skull (bottom). Note the similarity in shape and size. With these Crystal Skulls we find a different style of modeling, including cranial elongation and ovoid indentations.

Contemporary Carved Crystal Skulls

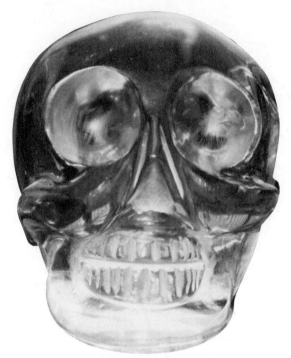

© F. R. 'Nick' Nocerino

© F. R. 'Nick' Nocerino

*A front (top) and side view (bottom) of carved skulls made in 1986 by
Brazilian carvers and brought to the U.S. by Talisman Trading.*

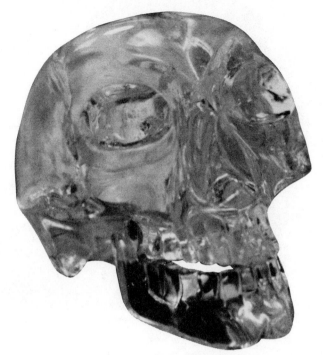

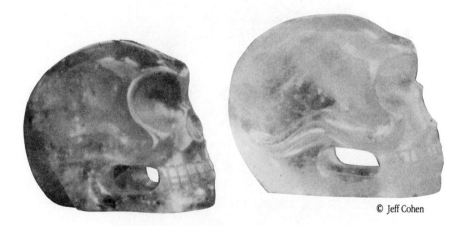

Top: A differently shaped carved skull; more alien-looking with a somewhat pointed and open jaw. This work was commissioned by Talisman Trading.

Bottom: Another style of recently carved skulls, more human-looking with spherical openings between the jaw and top part of the skull. This style is becoming more common. These particular skulls belong to co-editor, Jeff Cohen.

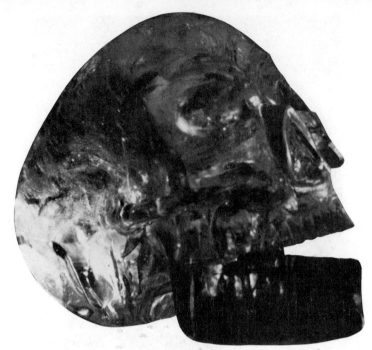

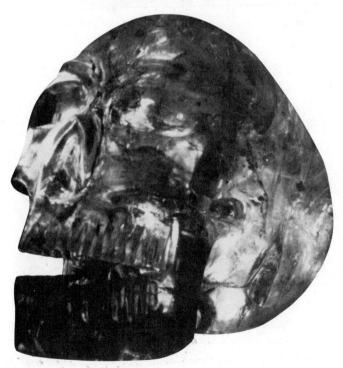

A contemporary crystal skull deliberately carved with the mouth open; brought to the U.S. by Talisman Trading.

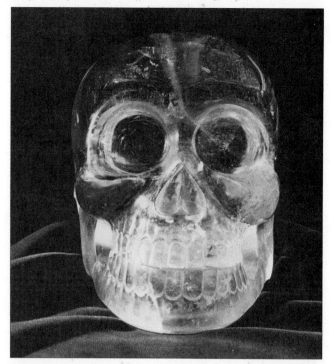

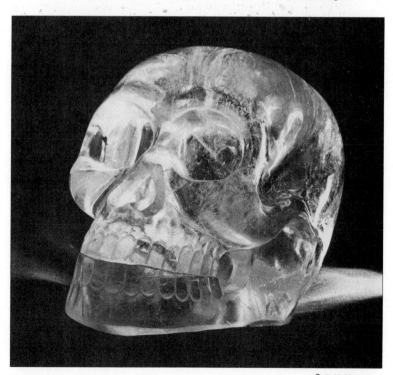

This carved skull was commissioned by R. H. Youngman, who selected a piece of quartz from Brazil. The carver took over two hundred hours, using many special hand-fashioned tools. The skull was finished by polishing it with diamond. It weighs 7.57 kg (about 17 lbs).

PART III
CHANNELS

JON KLIMO
MICHAEL KANT
SANDRA BOWEN
NEVILLE ROWE

JON KLIMO
INTRODUCTION TO
CHANNELING

on Klimo is a former Rutgers University Professor, who holds degrees from Brown University and has designed, administered and taught in doctoral programs in education and psychology. Currently living in Berkeley, he is a core faculty member, helping to train counselors and clinical psychologists, at Rosebridge Graduate School in Walnut Creek, California. He is the author of the book *Channeling: Investigations on Receiving Information from Paranormal Sources*, published in the Fall of 1987 by Jeremy P. Tarcher. It has been acclaimed as *the* definitive study of the phenomenon of channeling. Jon is working on many other writing projects, as well as continuing to teach and lecture. His work reflects an interdisciplinary attempt to combine the study of consciousness, cognition, creative alternative science and metaphysics in a true "Unified Field Theory."

"CHANNELING" IS THE MOST RECENT TERM for a phenomenon that has existed throughout history and in all cultures. Someone capable of this phenomenon today is called a channel (sometimes, a channeler). Past names for a channel have included medium, visionary, mystic, seer, soothsayer, oracle, prophet, shaman, and psychic. But one thing is common among all of these names. They all refer to fellow human beings who have information or energy that comes to or through them from some other level of reality than the physical as we currently understand it, and from beyond the self as defined by mainstream psychology.

Such a process presupposes that we on Earth exist within a much larger "house of many mansions"-- a multidimensional reality with its other precincts inhabited and occasionally heard from by us. It also presupposes that who we think we are-- the self, personality, or identity familiar to us in the physical and psychological mirror-- is not all that there is to us; that we are much more translucently open to the give and take with other informing energies, with minds alien to our earthbound ones, and with larger Mind or Spirit. The membrane separating humans from each other and from others elsewhere in the cosmos is capable of being much more permeable than we have been led to believe by our current science. Our scope is wider than we have been limited to practicing in our day-to-day consensus reality.

TYPES OF CHANNELING RANGE FROM FULL-TRANCE channeling of specific, identifiable non-physical entities, to personal creative intuition and artistic inspiration which taps a more diffuse, impersonal source that also seems to transcend one's normal self and usual earthbound limitations. In the case of trance channeling (the most publicized kind today), the channel reportedly goes unconscious in order to step aside or vacate the physical body to allow an extradimensional being or presence to operate through it with speech or other communicating behavior. Material can be received in the extremely altered states of normal sleep and dreams.

Channeling can also be a more conscious process of being present in awareness but having trains of thought telepathically enter one's head that seem to not originate within oneself. Or one can consciously hear sub-vocal verbal messages with the mind's ear and repeat them to others or write them down. Visual information can also be received clairvoyantly with the mind's eye. Through the process of automatic writing or the Ouija Board, one can be fully conscious yet have one's hand operating beyond conscious control,

INTRODUCTION TO CHANNELING

being used by another to write, type, or spell out messages. Inspirational speaking and writing are additional terms for a somewhat subtler, more conscious version of having a kind of thought or language flow from beyond oneself superimposed upon one's own discourse.

Whatever way channeled information is received and conveyed, it is said to emanate from extradimensional beings who range across a wide spectrum. Some are human, some are not. The non-human kind range from God or the universal Mind, to angels, non-human spirit guides, Nature or Cosmic Spirits, and extraterrestrials, who are often called "Space Beings" or "Space Brothers." The majority of this latter kind of channeled source say that they have both cognitively/technologically and spiritually evolved to a higher physical or non-physical dimension of reality, with the ability to be able to alter the vibrational frequency or density of their bodies and their "flying saucers" or "UFOs" to interact on occasion with us of normal consciousness on our current earthly level of reality.

Other kinds of channeled sources include discarnate human spirits not unlike us, except that they no longer operate with physical bodies as their learning vehicles. But just to have survived physical death-- as we all do, according to the channeled literature-- does not mean instant omniscience. One could contact the spirit of an "Ascended Master" such as Jesus, or an Einstein or Plato, but one might also get a Hitler or some recent mentally-ill suicide deciding to impersonate Jesus or actually thinking he's Einstein. However, the literature tells us that, as part of what is called Universal Law, "Like attracts like." If, going into the channeling enterprise, you practice an open-minded dedication to your own growth and self-knowledge, and maintain clarity of spiritual intention on behalf of the largest good for all, if you minimize doubt and fear and maximize being of loving service, and if you ask for channeled contact that will further such, you are not likely to be matched up with a kind of metaphysical "blind date" that is out of step with your own desires and intentions.

ONE CONCERN WITH REGARD TO CHANNELING (whether one becomes a channel oneself or merely is a consumer of what is supposedly channeled through someone else), is that we be responsible to our own best selves and to the best of each other-- on behalf of the unity of the Supreme Being that is our common source and identity. Also, that we not demote ourselves and our own resources and best intuition just because we happen to be currently

JON KLIMO

operating on a physical level of reality. We each have our own inner connection to the Universal Truth. So we are told by the channeled sources themselves. Undue attachment to knowledge, guidance, or charisma outside of ourselves, irrespective of the level of reality inhabited by its source-- save for the very highest and most spiritual-- turns our backs on the potential that we are each our own channel, and that the Kingdom is within, or by way of the innerness of each of us. Such self-denial and dependence on others can be problematic and counterproductive to our own and our species development. The best of the channeled sources tell us not to overly depend upon them for information and guidance, but to become channels of the love and wisdom of our one common Source. Toward that Source are all individuals and all species, across all dimensions of being, little by little, returning.

December, 1987
Berkeley, California

The Mandala of thirteen clear Crystal Skulls underneath the Potala in Tibet, as channeled by Michael Kant. Note the two Stars of David, each formed by one group of six skulls, and the Master Skull located in the center. In this artist's depiction, you see swirling energy being activated by the Mandala, sending out key harmonic frequencies of Light to our planet.

CHAPTER 5

Michael Kant is a conscious channel who has experienced many contacts with various spiritual beings, including extraterrestrials, angels and those of the Solar Hierarchy. He had two conscious UFO experiences where he was taken aboard spacecraft. For his first contact, Michael was greeted by beings from the Pleiades and given a tour of our Solar System and the Inner Earth. During his second contact, Michael was taken aboard 'The Dove,' the spacecraft associated with the spirit of Jesus (known on this level as Sananda), and was given additional information related to the transformation of our world into a new level in the Aquarian Age. Michael is a teacher of Cosmic Sciences and is able to read 'Fire Letters,' a universal meta-symbolic language. He is interested in Atlantean and Sacred Sciences, crystals, UFOs and Light-based Technologies. Michael is also in contact with many other New Age teachers worldwide.

Early Contact with Michael Kant

ABOUT THE SAME TIME JOSHUA ENCOUNTERED PICTURES of the Amethyst Crystal Skull in a San Jose bookstore (April, 1983), he began receiving a number of letters from Michael Kant. He had read Joshua's first book, *Journeys of an Aquarian Age Networker*, and through his inner guidance was told to make this contact. Joshua usually received one letter per month from Michael discussing what he was up to, and sometimes Joshua wasn't too sure what Michael was writing about. It appeared that whatever the source of his information, it dealt with higher spiritual truths and the Light Universes, or what we might call interdimensional heavens. In any case, Joshua felt it was important to collect and store this information, as he intuitively knew that Michael was receiving some key material related to the transformation occurring on our planet.

As Sandra and Joshua became more involved with the Crystal Skulls, they began to look more closely at some of Michael's letters and sure enough, he was talking about various subject areas which were directly related to their research. So they decided it might be interesting to interview Michael and see what kinds of answers he would provide to questions about the Crystal Skulls.

Thus, in this part of the book, we would like to share with you portions of his early letters. Also, since Michael deals with some fairly advanced spiritual concepts and universal terminology, we would suggest that the reader consult our Glossary if there is a question about any of Michael's wording. A great deal of his terminology is similar to what is used in J. J. Hurtak's book, *The Keys of Enoch.*

WE HAD A CHANCE TO INTERVIEW MICHAEL ON THREE OCCASIONS. Just after Sandra and Nick returned from their research trip to Canada to work with the Mitchell-Hedges Skull in November of 1985, an interview was scheduled for the early part of December. However, through a mix-up we stopped by his apartment on the wrong day. So that it was not a wasted trip, we left a series of questions for Michael [See the next section for a portion of this list]. Shortly thereafter, we received Michael's answers and rescheduled our first interview for December 27, 1985. The second interview was in November of 1986, and was arranged to clarify some points made in the first interview. We tape-

CHAPTER 5

recorded all interviews and portions of the transcripts from these sessions appear later in the chapter. The final interview occurred on Halloween, 1987, where we explored new material.

The co-authors have found Michael's information to be informative and intriguing. Below is a sample of the material which Joshua received from two of the first correspondences sent by Michael. Hopefully, it will give you an idea of what he is like:

LETTER, JUNE 4, 1983 -- "Our relationship on Atlantis was an important one. Being in the College of Priests, we worked closely with the thirteen skulls of crystal. The Crystal Skulls came from another dimension originally and could actually communicate like people. They serve in the same capacity as Chronomonitors." [Editors' note: Galactic devices used to observe and police the universe, which provide planetary data to the Space Beings.]

LETTER, MAY 20, 1983 -- "Our paths have crossed before, when we were working in Atlantis with crystals such as the Amethyst Skull. Originally the Earth was a crystalline planet, as are all the higher dimensional planets. Before the fall of the Earth into the Kali Yuga[1], you could literally see the center of the Earth. During the time of Atlantis, crystals were produced through mind projection from the ethers, apports from higher dimensions and spacecraft, and during the latter days of Atlantis with lasers and alchemy. The Crystal Skulls found in Mexico were an example of the laser-treated skulls (including the Mitchell-Hedges Crystal Skull)."

"Originally the Great Pyramid was built about 40,000 B.C. by people from Aldebaran located near the Pleiades. Other pyramids soon followed to help energize and stabilize the Earth. Crystal Skulls, Crystal Tablets and many ancient Crystal Temples were always placed in key areas of the harmonic grid system."

---

[1] The Hindu name given to a series of prophecies grouped in seven year cycles. These cycles collectively explain how the Earth will return to the higher dimensions, the original state the planet was in.

MICHAEL KANT

FIRST SERIES OF QUESTIONS ASKED ABOUT THE CRYSTAL SKULLS

The following is a portion of a series of questions we left at Michael's door prior to our first in-person interview. The answers to these questions helped shape the types of questions that were asked approximately two weeks later. The abundant use of capitalization throughout (including the questions, which Michael corrected) is indicative of Michael's unique style of writing and has been retained as such. This brief section should be helpful to the reader and guide him/her into the interview portions.

❑ What is the origin of the Mitchell-Hedges Crystal Skull?

This famous Crystal Skull was originally in one of the thirteen healing temples of Atlantis. The Crystal Skull is that of the female priestess 'Shee-thee-tra,' [Editors' note: Sandra received 'Sha-tree-tra', with the "r" rolled, when she was at Mt. Shasta for the Gathering of Light held by ASSK, August, 1986.] who was killed during one of the last earthquakes on Atlantis. It was transformed into crystal through the crystal art form of <u>Morphocrystallic Transformation.</u>

❑ What are the 'Key Years for Planetary Changes' and timing of 'Key Planetary Events'?

Planetary changes and events don't have a cosmic clock for their beginning or end and depend on the change in consciousness of the Planetary Evolution and Intelligence as they ascend Jacob's Ladder of Light.[2] <u>The sense of time one experiences in daily life is actually based on the flow of sodium ions in the Biocrystalline Body of Light.</u>

❑ Will Key Light-Workers be brought together in a stronger Network of Light than presently is the case?

Key Light-Workers are even now being brought together and in the near future will form Communities of Light at Key locations along the Twelve Crystalline Fields of Light that surround the Earth. Under the direction of the

---

[2]-Jacob's Ladder of Light-- A spiraling energy grid which links the Earth to the dimensions of Light in the constellation of Orion.

CHAPTER 5

Jerusalem Command this will take place at areas where Pyramids of Light, Etheric Temples and Light Ships land.

❏ What exactly are the Crystal Skulls and your experience with them?

The Crystal Skulls are Thirteen Crystal Skulls produced originally by the Morphocrystallic Generation of Crystals and originally placed in the Thirteen Healing Temples on Atlantis but are now located beneath the Potala in Lhasa, Tibet.

❏ How will the Thirteen Crystal Skulls assist Planetary and Evolutionary Transformation?

The Thirteen Crystal Skulls now assembled beneath the Potala in Lhasa, Tibet are a Living Computer for Planetary Healing that work closely together with the Frequency Station "Tribal Light" that is also located there and the Twelve Crystalline Fields of Light that surround the Earth.

❏ What type of Encoding does the Crystal Skull contain?

The Crystal Skulls are Encoded with Feminine Energies, Specific Light Functions, Keys of Enoch, and the Wisdom of certain members of the Higher Evolution. When activated by the Higher Evolution, the jaw of the Crystal Skull can move and speak.

❏ What is the Connection between Light Ships and the Crystal Skulls?

Crystal Skulls and other examples of Crystal and Light Technologies were brought to the Earth by various Galactic Races, such as that of the Pleiadians during the time of Atlantis. The Mitchell-Hedges Skull was first brought to the Atlantean Healing Temple of Muror located in the area of Bimini. This was the great Temple of Healing in which Benu or the Phoenix played a central role in healing.

❏ How many human-sized Crystal Skulls are there?

There are Thirteen Main Crystal Skulls with a wide variety of other models scattered around the Earth. The Thirteen Crystal Skulls are symbolic of the Thirteen Atlantean Healing Temples, the Thirteen Inner Earth Tribes, the 52 year Sacred Calendar of the Mayans, etc...

❏ What is the importance and history of Tibet?

The history and importance of Tibet would involve writing a book. Tibet in association with India serves as the major spiritual programming area for the

Eastern Hemisphere. A vast underground Kingdom exists beneath Tibet, as well as a Secret Valley of Scientific Wonders known as Coda.

❏ How do the Inner Earth Tribes tie in with the Planetary and Evolutionary Transformation of the Earth in the Aquarian Age?

The Thirteen Tribes of the Inner Earth will greatly assist the Planetary Evolution in the introduction of Crystal and Light Technologies for Planetary Evolution. The Crystal Skull is a symbol of contact we maintain with the Inner Earth and Galactic Races. The Crystal Skull is a Symbol of the Crystal Chalice that exists in our Light Bodies as well as the Chalice Lake, a Central Initiation Point in the Inner Earth.

❏ What is the transition into the Fourth and Fifth Dimensions?

The Planetary Evolution and Intelligence of the Earth will ascend Jacob's Ladder of Light through the introduction of Crystal and Light Technologies as the Earth moves closer to the Heart of the Galaxy. The Twelve Crystalline Fields of Light that surround the Earth are now in the process of changing to Fourth and Fifth Dimensional Frequencies. The entire Solar System is shifting toward a blue and ultraviolet Light Spectrum. We are graduating from a Population I System to a Population II System.

CHAPTER 5

THE MICHAEL KANT INTERVIEWS

Introduction
Cosmic Sciences from
a Conscious Channel

The remainder of this chapter will share portions of three interviews we had with Michael Kant and his friend Yasodhara. The interviews are divided into three sections. The first section is a composite of information given in the first two interviews. Section two is a portion of the third interview containing information related to crystals and Crystal Skulls. The last section contains Michael's comments about some of the photographs and slides taken by the research team in Canada with the Mitchell-Hedges Skull, and other slides of the Mayan Crystal Skull.

Important: Reader is advised to make extensive use of the Glossary as you read the Kant interviews!

Section 1
First and Second Interviews

Joshua: In your response to our written questions, you stated that the Mitchell-Hedges Skull was a Priestess in Atlantis and that through the use of a Morphocrystallic process, her human skull was changed into one of crystal. Can you give us more information on this?

Michael: Atlantis made extensive use of Light, Crystal and Thought Technologies. Thought Technologies were integrated with the Crystal Technologies which used Morphocrystallic modes of crystal production. Three Crystal Modes were used in Atlantis and were called the Morphocrystalline Sciences. The first mode is called Morphocrystallic Generation, where one visualizes a molecular matrix of a mineral and holographically projects their mind energies into the ethers to produce a crystal, which we call a Thought Crystal, or a living crystal. This is the purest process of the Morphocrystallic Sciences. And the original thirteen Crystal

MICHAEL KANT

Skulls were created in this way. The second mode, Morphocrystallic Transformation, involves a holographic projection of mind energies into an organic matrix of a living (or formerly living) organic structure, but uses the organic matrix as a building block to make this transformation. Examples of organic structure would be a skull of a person who has died, a plant or a tree. Through this crystal mode you can actually transform organic substances into crystal. The last mode would be the Morphocrystallic Liquidization of crystals, where crystals can be turned into liquid. You can take an emerald, sapphire, diamond or any crystal matrix and turn it into a liquid. This is what the alchemists did in the Middle Ages. They would reduce something down to its liquid essence. With a crystal, mineral or even a flower form, you can do the same thing. The Gem Elixirs and the Bach Flower Remedies are a variation of this Morphocrystallic Liquidization process. You liquidize the crystal and put it into a mold to shape it into any form that you would want. Or you could take an actual flower and turn it into a crystal flower, or a tree into a crystal tree. This is known as Crystal Architecture.

Healing gardens in the Inner Earth make quite a bit of use of this process. You can also take a stone matrix and turn it into a crystalline liquid as in the case of the Great Pyramid. It was done with liquified stone which they formed into solid stone before they assembled the Great Pyramid. The limestone casing of the Great Pyramid formed a crystalline matrix and was actually like a giant crystal even though it was comprised of stone. They could shape crystals into any form that they would want, such as a square stone or a triangular-shaped stone. They would form it into a liquid and it would solidify later into the desired mold.

Also, using Morphocrystallic Liquidization you can make tinctures from crystals by having the crystal in a liquid for various periods of time. The liquid will acquire the frequency of that crystal. If you want the quartz frequency, you would leave quartz in the water and then put it out in the sun for awhile. The water would acquire the frequency of that crystal, and then if you drink it you assimilate the frequency. For example, it would be better to take the frequency of Lithium than to take it directly into your system, which would be toxic. Most of the medicated patients in Mental Hospitals take Lithium directly and it causes toxic poisoning. Also, gold can cause toxic poisoning. It's the frequency of the gold or quartz in association with the liquid that produces a beneficial healing. Of course, Ayurvedic Medicine uses aspects of this ancient

CHAPTER 5

medical art in India. As a matter of fact, Dr. Vasant has a book out on Ayurvedic Medicine. In addition, Tibetan Medicine is very similar. Tibetans make healing substances from liquid crystals or ground-up crystals.

Now, based on the information I have just shared, the Mitchell-Hedges Crystal Skull was formed from the skull of an Atlantean Priestess named Shee-Thee-Tra, as her skull was used for the matrix to form the Crystal Skull. She was killed in a cataclysm during the fall of Atlantis, in its last stages. This particular Crystal Skull was formed through the technique of Morphocrystallic Transformation (a projection of the mind energies into the skull), but wasn't a classic example of the art form because they had to finish it with lasers and polishing (they did a lot of polishing on it) in order to bring out all the Light functions. If they would use this art form as they do in the Inner Earth, they could transform the entire structure of a person who died into crystal. Such is the case for the Ancient Incan Mummies that are under Cuzco and some other places in South America. Actually, the remnants of these people were transformed into crystal, including their garments and the whole body structure, not just the skull. The crystals are still there and they have the frequency and vibration of the people that died. It's a way of preserving the frequency of a particular person; similar to the way we build a statue. They would crystallize the individual for future generations.

Joshua: So in the first mode, Morphocrystallic Generation, the Atlanteans used the power of their minds, without the use of a model to work from, visualized the object they wished to create and it would manifest from out of the ethers?

Michael: All three techniques use holographic projection of mind energies into a matrix. The first technique [Morphocrystallic Generation] uses an etheric matrix form or what they call thought crystals. The second technique [Morphocrystallic Transformation] uses an organic matrix or a former living system. The last technique [Morphocrystallic Liquidization] would be a crystalline matrix where they would project their mind energies into the crystal and turn it into liquid.

Joshua: You just mentioned that through the Morphocrystallic Processes, one can create a Thought Crystal. This implies to me that the crystal was formed by thought, and solidified into the physical. Can you give more information about this?

Michael: Everything is created by Thoughtforms. Whenever a program of Light is brought into existence, this can be considered as a Divine Thoughtform. Of course, you manufacture thousands of Thoughtforms everyday, you just can't see them. They'll attach themselves to you after awhile and cause trouble if you're not careful, so you have to be cautious about what you think. These Thoughtforms work like what are called Thought Crystals or Recording Crystals. The Inner Earth People use Recording Crystals to store their thoughts, information and past history. Thought Crystals can be found all over the world and certain people can tap into them and decode their many different levels. They are something like our eight track tapes except they have many more levels. Some people can only tap into the first level, while others can tap into many more levels. The Crystal Skull is the same way; it's like a Thought Crystal except it happens to have the shape of a skull. A classic Thought Crystal has different levels one can tap into, if you know the Keys (Light Functions or Light Codes). A biocrystalline computer or a Thought Crystal follows what you call the DNA structure with its double-spiral forming the basis of all matter. As matter stretches downward and upward, it forms a double-spiral and brings about key crystal formations.

Joshua: But specifically, how did they change the organic substance into crystal using their minds?

Michael: In the example of the Mitchell-Hedges Skull, seven priests projected their mind energies into the skull of the Atlantean Priestess and used the organic matrix which was already there. She had a regular skull and all they did was change the molecular structure with their mind energies using the matrix that was there. This process is the Second Mode, Morphocrystallic Transformation. Morphocrystallic Generation however, is a direct transformation process where mind energies are projected into the ethers resulting in the creation of a Thought Crystal. You visualize the Thoughtform in your consciousness. You can also use the matrix of a quartz crystal and then project your mind energies to transmute it. So to review, in other words, the Atlantean Priests didn't have the consciousness to create the Thoughtform and project to the matrix, so they needed something to start them off (like a seed), as one can use a seed crystal to make a bigger crystal. A Crystal Skull will always have the frequency of the person that died [and whose bone was transmuted]. The information in Shee-Thee-Tra's system, being that it was encoded in the bone, was preserved when they changed it into crystal. Thus,

CHAPTER 5

this Crystal Skull will contain the genetic information of the person it was made from. Rather than putting their information into a computer, they could transform the person's skull and preserve their record. So the Crystal Skull was used as a record-keeping device.

Joshua: I would like to trace the history of the Mitchell-Hedges Skull after Atlantis sank and what happened to that remnant of Atlantis which is still underwater. Exactly where did this Skull go from Atlantis? Was it underwater for a period of time and then brought out later, or was it immediately brought to another landmass when Atlantis sank? [Editors' note: possibly 15,000 years ago.]

Michael: This Crystal Skull was in one of the thirteen healing temples in Atlantis; the Temple of Muror which was situated in Bimini, associated with healing, regeneration and rejuvenation. In fact, if you go around Bimini, there are still remnants of the healing and rejuvenating springs and foundations of the temple off-shore. On parts of North Bimini there are sacred wells associated with that temple also. Before it was destroyed, they removed certain things from this temple (such as the Crystal Skull) and took them to the Yucatan. The Atlantean Priests who were in charge of the Temple of Muror were well-aware of the different cataclysms affecting Atlantis and possible future changes to their land mass in Bimini. The Mitchell-Hedges Crystal Skull, Crystal Records and Atlantean Fire Crystals were transferred to the Yucatan area where there were many Mayan priests and Melchizedek Schools of higher learning. It was placed in a Temple in the present area of British Honduras [Belize] for safe-keeping. There were certain priests that tried to misuse it. However, the Crystal Skull has basically preserved its original functions as a healing biocrystalline computer.

Joshua: Why was the Mitchell-Hedges Skull moved to the Yucatan? Was (or is) there something special about this geographic region?

Michael: There were three key areas of Atlantis which carried the records. There was an area close to the Giza Pyramid, there was the Bimini Pyramid (which is underwater right now) and there's the Yucatan Pyramid (also underwater). These three areas have records which contain the Scriptures of Light, including the 366 Keys of Enoch (which are a teaching aid used by the Melchizedek Schools) that come from the Jerusalem Command and are responsible for the education of our species. The thirteen healing temples of

MICHAEL KANT

Atlantis are where their education took place. During the times of Atlantis and Lemuria, their spiritual authorities were priestesses because women carried a certain frequency that enabled them to communicate with the higher dimensions better than men. So they were the feminine energy aspect and head of the thirteen temples. The central temple of Atlantis was formed through Morphocrystalline Generation, Morphocrystalline Transformation and Morphocrystalline Liquidization of Crystals.

Many of the Atlantean records which were brought to the Yucatan are currently underwater. The Yucatan was much larger at the time Atlantis sank than it is today. Because of the cataclysms that occurred in Atlantis, land masses were still sinking and settling after its destruction. The Yucatan was still adjusting its land masses and much of the area sank. Many of these Temples and records are underwater for safe-keeping. Some crystal artifacts (like the Crystal Skull) were brought to safer locations such as British Honduras, but most of them were left in the original temples that are below the Caribbean right now, as this was a way of protecting the records. These temples that are underwater have been spotted by different archaeologists and scuba divers, so it's known they are there. Temples [ruins] have been found off the coast of Bimini. So in the whole Caribbean area near Bimini and the Yucatan, there are many different temples lying on the seabed.

The city of Lubaantun, which is where the Crystal Skull was brought, was a key Mayan City. Lubaantun was much different than the way our archaeologists have found it. It had more technology and crystalline and gold structures there than our archaeologists are aware of. This was all hidden away before the final destruction of this Mayan city by an earthquake. The earthquake was brought on by the Fall of Man. As man's consciousness lowered, these crystal artifacts ceased to function. Then they became like toys which some people tried to misuse for black magic, such as the priests who tried to misuse the Mitchell-Hedges Skull. This Crystal Skull has many different layers to it, so it protected itself and did not allow penetration beyond a few top layers at the most. The higher knowledge and information is found in the deeper layers and will be revealed in the future.

Sandra: What was the significance of crystal artifacts to the Mayans?

Michael: The Mayan Indians worshipped crystal artifacts such as the Crystal Skull. These artifacts were treated more as idols or family gods. In the case of the Aztecs, they also had Crystal Skulls which they worshipped in a similar fashion. The Aztecs also had an obsidian mirror that was used for prophecies.

CHAPTER 5

Each of the cultural races in Central America had certain objects that they worshipped. In the case of the Mayans it was the Mitchell-Hedges Skull.

Joshua: Would the soul associated with the person who had been crystallized still be connected with that crystal piece or replica of itself, or would only its imprint remain?

Michael: It would have the Light functions and frequencies of that person but it would not be the actual spirit. All of the Atlantean priests involved with the creation of the Mitchell-Hedges Skull have the ability to project their consciousness and energies into it at any time. However, the Crystal Skull has the frequency of the original Priestess right now. Different spiritual beings can come into the Mitchell-Hedges Skull and manipulate the jaw, because it's motile like a human jaw. It can transmit sound, color and affect all five of your senses. It can affect you with sound through the tinkling and chiming of bells once used around it. It can affect you with aromas [incense burned in the temple] or it can affect you with visual color effects, because the Crystal Skull can project holographic images such as pyramids which it was associated with, or the Caracol-- which was the Mayan Astronomical observatory in Chichen Itza [Caracol translated means 'House of the Holy Ones']. Other images from Lubaantun or Atlantis can be seen.

The Crystal Skull works like a holographic computer and projects images, different Light functions and energies to your consciousness, and thus affects the whole range of your five senses. If people attune to it, they can see the Fire Letters and holograms that it's putting out. If you're not attuned to it, you'll miss all the things that go on. People who are encoded, awake or aware, will see the holographic images it is producing. The skull knows if you're ready. It's like tying into a computer, you must have a certain frequency and code to activate it. In a way, a Crystal Skull is representative of what we call a living biocrystalline computer. It could talk on its own if it wanted to now, but when the time comes, different spiritual energies or Light functions will come into the skull and activate it. They come from higher realms, higher dimensions or Space People on Light Ships.

Joshua: Are you saying that the Mitchell-Hedges Skull literally has the ability to converse as we are now?

Michael: The Mitchell-Hedges Skull is a biocrystalline computer. A biocrystalline computer does not use language such as we would use. It would use holographic images, Fire Letters, telepathy or telepathic impressions. The Mitchell-Hedges Skull communicates a number of key holographic images such as Pyramids, Light Ships, Crystal Spheres and the Mayan observatory called the Caracol. The Caracol was used for astronomical measurements of the Pleiadian Star System which relates to the Mitchell-Hedges Skull. Pleiadian Technology was largely responsible for production of the Mitchell-Hedges Skull and use of the Morphocrystallic Sciences in Atlantis before its final destruction.

Joshua: And so it would never verbalize or be heard, it would only communicate with others through telepathy?

Michael: The Crystal Skull could move its jaw. You may think that it said something but it would actually be a telepathic impression that would sound just as loud as if someone right next to you was talking.

Joshua: Would you please talk more about Atlantis, their use of crystals and their healing temples?

Michael: Atlantis was the most advanced civilization using crystals on the surface of the Earth, not including the Inner Earth. The Central Healing Temple of Atlantis was the largest and it used pyramids and crystals, which have a direct relationship. In the Central Pyramid was a crystal table and a pyramid of crystal. The crystal table had a combination of crystals and metals and was used for healing. The Temple of the Dolphins, which was another healing temple, was used for communication, and people could sit in various chairs that were situated around a mandala and communicate with the Higher Realms. The Atlantean Temples usually had several names because of the initiations and various functions they had at different periods of time. In the case of the Temple at Bimini, the true name would be the Temple of MUROR. It was also called the Temple of Benu, which is the legendary Phoenix that symbolized the fact this temple was used for healing and regeneration.

Tribal Light underneath the Potala in Lhasa, Tibet, is of a similar order as the thirteen Atlantean temples. There are twelve skulls around a thirteenth central skull; each one of the twelve skulls representing one of the original races that still live within the Inner Earth, the thirteenth being the whole family or integration of all the energies. The Potala broadcasts the Ten Commandments of Light, or the Ten Key Frequencies, from the Tribal Light station to the Twelve Crystalline Fields of Light that surround the Earth. Tribal Light is the

CHAPTER 5

highest frequency station in the physical realm on the surface of the Earth. The Thirteen Crystal Skulls were originally in the thirteen Healing Temples of Atlantis and transferred to the Potala after the fall of Atlantis. The Mitchell-Hedges Skull is not one of those thirteen. It was made to imitate those but it's not actually one of the thirteen which were produced by Morphocrystallic Generation, as opposed to Morphocrystallic Transformation of the Mitchell-Hedges Skull.

Joshua: Please elaborate about The Thirteen Crystal Skulls' [under the Potola] connection with the Inner Earth races.

Michael: There are thirteen tribes in the Inner Earth and each tribe represents a genetic lineage that came to our planet. The thirteenth one is a grand family that unifies the twelve tribes. This relates back to <u>The Thirteen Crystal Skulls and the thirteen original</u> outer planets in our solar system. Maldek destroyed <u>itself, so we only have twelve now.</u> But there used to be thirteen planets in our solar system. So you go back to the key number of thirteen again. In the Inner Earth they represent all the genetic lineage from the first races that came here to cultures we don't even know about. Some cultures projected directly to the Inner Earth and never even surfaced. And though there is a predominance of Incan, Mayan and North American Indians in the Inner Earth, they still have representatives of all the genetic classes. So you have all these genetics of the twenty-four Galactic Races that were originally brought to our planet in the form of thirteen tribes.

Joshua: What were you referring to earlier about a Mandala pattern within the Temple of the Dolphins or the Potala? Would this be similar to the way we think of a mandala or geometric pattern today?

Michael: Mandalas are the geometric arrangements of Light, Color and Crystals. Within the Crystal Temple or the Potala in Tibet, crystals and metals are arranged in geometric patterns. In the Potala, where The Thirteen Crystal Skulls are, they use a mandala to align geometric forms with The Thirteen Crystal Skulls. There are twelve Crystal Skulls around a central Skull that serves as a programming skull. The skulls rotate on this crystal dais. You have a similar type of central crystal dais on a spacecraft such as ones the Pleiadians or the Venusians use. In the Potala, the Crystal Skulls form a mandala [an energetic pattern] and activate the crystalline energies along this

MICHAEL KANT

geometrically formed mandala. The mandala has symbols, colors, tones and different segments to create the pattern. Then the skulls are positioned around the central skull and this pattern creates holograms, Fire Letters and it broadcasts the Ten Commandments. The mandala is a kind of a dimensional hologram. In the case of the Crystal Skulls, it is a three-dimensional hologram. The mandalas in Tibet, India and Oriental countries are more of the two-dimensional kind but they give you an idea of the way the colors and the forms are arranged.

Joshua: Could you give a more detailed description of the most powerful placement of The Thirteen Crystal Skulls in the Potala to form a mandala?

Michael: Actually, the Crystal Skulls can create an almost infinite number of Light programs and holograms. The strongest design they work with are triangular designs in the shape of different Mogan Davids [Star of David], usually a double Mogan David which would represent all of the twelve Crystal Skulls, and the central skull, the thirteenth Crystal Skull, would be the unifying factor. If you took two Mogan Davids and put them on top of each other, you would have twelve points and these would create the triangulations of Light, the Ten Commandments. The angles and vectors of the different triangles create the color spectrums and the tone of the Ten Commandments of Living Light. Triangular Light patterns are usually represented in the Mogan David. They could arrange themselves in one triangle or they could arrange themselves in other geometric patterns. The basic pattern that they follow is the Mogan David, the one the Crystal Skulls are working with now in association with the planetary grids, which are the twelve crystalline grids that surround the Earth. A thirteenth energy field unifies the other twelve. So each one of the Crystal Skulls is working with one of the Light Fields right now and their basic pattern would be the Mogan David.

Joshua: Are these two Stars of David superimposed?

Michael: Yes, they are like two superimposed Mogan Davids. The vertex points would be individually represented by a Crystal Skull placed at the respective points around a circle, however, one set of six skulls would be rotated a little bit relative to the other set. So each point represents the position of one of the thirteen Crystal Skulls (now in Tibet). These Crystal Skulls sit on a crystal dais, a huge circular crystalline platform or disk. Beams of laser-like light emanating from the other individual skulls are focused upon

CHAPTER 5

the Central Skull. These light beams create holographic images within the Mogan Davids. The Mogan Davids are constantly shifted as the Crystal Skulls are rotated and these changes in the skulls' positions are dictated by changes in the crystalline grids.

Joshua: Exactly how are the Crystal Skulls situated on this circular dais? Are they just placed in a circle with visible light projecting from each of the twelve skulls into the central skull?

Michael: Yes, the ones in Tibet are. They are basically positioned on the edge of a huge circular crystal disk like you would see on a Light Ship, and this disk is rotating. As it rotates, a vortex of energy called a Pillar of Light is generated, in addition to holograms. Pyramids of Light are coordinated by the Central Skull, as well as the computers that are working with the Crystal Skulls in the same complex.

Joshua: So the twelve outer skulls would be in a circle?

Michael: Right now that is their formation, although they change to other positions often. They are in a circular position to form a pillar of Light. A pillar of Light is comprised of two Mogan Davids superimposed. So it's like a Giant Light Ship in many ways. The skulls coordinate an outer level of energy and they coordinate an inner level of energy that's rotated in different directions around the central skull. The twelve outer skulls are rotating [energy] counter-clockwise and the thirteenth skull is going clockwise, creating a pillar of Light that coordinates all the energies. The triangulations of the energy are always beaming from the eyes of the skulls. The skulls beam back and forth a laser effect coordinated with computers connected to the Inner Earth. One of the reasons the Dark Forces are so interested in this planet is because of the crystal computer in the Inner Earth, which has the ability to create planets. They haven't managed to get there yet. As mentioned, this computer is connected with the Crystal Skulls in Tibet, as well as certain other crystal structures. Right now they're beginning to broadcast the Ten Commandments [of Light] on a limited basis and will eventually extend their broadcasts. Of course, each Crystal Skull has a certain crystal or crystalline form that it is working with. Different crystalline structures are being introduced into our various technologies and sciences as well. So you don't just have quartz Crystal Skulls, you have other crystalline structures such as turquoise, obsidian, lapis lazuli and so on. You can't really think of all the

174 Crystal Skulls as just quartz crystals. They are varied crystalline structures of Living Light.

Sandra: You have frequently mentioned that the Thirteen Crystal Skulls are broadcasting higher vibrational frequencies known as the Ten Commandments of Light. Please give a more concise definition.

Michael: The Ten Commandments are cosmic pyramids of Light arranged in different triangulations of Light [or what are called Pyramidal Light Codes] that form the basis of the Ten [Commandments]. Each one is a different trinity, the tenth being a unification factor. You need the Ten Commandments to go into the higher realms. You can't get into the higher dimensions without them. The Ten Commandments are activating our planetary alignments to move into the higher evolution right now. They are ten key frequencies that activate the Light harmonics around the Earth. Together they are called "The Word Frequency."

In addition, there are twelve crystalline Fields of Light and each one of the Crystal Skulls symbolizes one of these Fields; the thirteenth skull representing the unification of the twelve Fields of Light. One of the many reasons there are Thirteen Crystal Skulls is because each Crystal Skull and its original biocrystalline body regulated or stabilized one of these Crystalline Fields of Light. We're now shifting more and more toward a higher frequency of Light, more towards the fourth and fifth dimension. Thus, our whole Network of Light is changing, and that's one of the jobs of the Crystal Skulls, the crystal balls and the crystal pyramids. The whole structure of our planet is a living crystal which is now moving into the higher dimensions. In fact, if we did not have all the assistance from the Light Ships and Crystal Skulls, this planet would probably have shattered a long time ago. So they are stabilizing devices to prevent this.

There are many telecommunication devices stationed around the Earth and underground chambers by the Inner Earth People. They're placing all kinds of machinery and equipment in time vaults to stabilize the Earth. Under Mesa Verde, Arizona, there is a giant pyramid that serves as a transducer for the Ten Pyramidal Codes of Light that are being broadcast from beneath the Potala in Tibet. When the ten frequencies go out, they're picked up by ten key areas around the Earth. In the Mesa Verde, there is a giant etheric crystal pyramid called the Tau Pyramid. It breaks down energies and distributes them throughout North America. In South America it would be Titicaca, a pyramid

CHAPTER 5

sub-station. Also, all ten frequencies are not only contained within the combination of these Crystal Skulls, but in what they call the Ark of the Covenant, which is in another higher dimension. When the right person comes along, this Ark will be integrated to our frequency. That person hasn't appeared yet, but (s)he will serve as an integration point in helping to bring the Ark into our frequency.

Crystal Skulls are like giant frequency stations and each one of the skulls serves as a sub-station, broadcasting what we call the frequency of the Word or the Ten Commandments, which were absent from the Earth for a long time. Originally, the Ten Commandments were placed and broadcast from the planet Faustia, which is in Orion. We have received a lot of our races and programming from there. The Ten Commandments were situated on our planet for a number of years, but after the Fall of the Earth, they were taken back to Faustia. Faustia is not really a planet; it's a place, but it's not a planet in the classic sense of the term. It's hard to explain on this level. What I call a sun would be the closest definition we have. Then the Ten Commandments were brought back to the Earth in 1981 and reinstated to the Potala in Tibet. This was done because this classroom, our Earth, is ready for graduation. We need the Ten Commandments for graduation because that's what all life harmonics are based upon.

When the Ten Commandments were first brought to the Earth, they were situated at Giza, Egypt. Later they were moved to Tibet and then transferred to South America. Now they are back in Tibet again, where they belong. Originally there were two Arks of the Covenant. The Crystal Ark of the Covenant came along about the time the original races (now in the inner Earth) arrived. This Crystal Ark of the Covenant brought in the same frequencies as the station underneath the Potala. At a later time, it was taken to Egypt, its energies were integrated underneath the Great Pyramid and then it was removed. The Ark of the Covenant mentioned in the Bible is an imitation built by the Hebrews when their technology was declining. It wasn't constructed in the same manner as the original Crystal Ark. Thus, this ark emanated scattered vibrations which caused all kinds of problems. The original Crystal Ark is in South America right now and is a living crystal far more advanced than even a Crystal Skull.

So, the Ten Commandments are being re-broadcast underneath the high-frequency station at the Potala, and work with the tele-thought computers established by the Inner Earth People. Crystal Pyramids serve to break down this frequency more. When our frequencies come in from Orion, they are stepped-down through the Pleiades (the Taurus Constellation), through Arcturus and Sirius (midway stations) before they are distributed along the twelve Crystalline Fields of the Earth. These are translated even more by Ancient Temples, crystal deposits or Crystal Skulls, and then broadcast to our planetary evolution. We're not advanced enough to absorb direct radiations from Orion, it would be very disruptive. So all these things help to realign the twelve crystalline fields of the Earth, and the Potala is now putting out a high frequency based on the Ten Commandments. This station is run by the Egyptian-Tibetan Tribunal, which is responsible for the laws and celestial harmonics of our system. They are descendants of the Solarians and the Blue Madras, the original races that came to this planet from Orion. They maintain genetic light programming and coding, and serve to maintain this frequency station. The Egyptian-Tibetan Tribunal was concerned that the Dark Forces would misuse this station, so it was removed from the Earth. Now they've reinstated it, because it's the basis of the twelve Crystalline Fields of Light that surround the Earth.

Sandra: Will the thirteen Crystal Skulls that are in Tibet ever come out?

Michael: Well, they do come out from time to time. They project to the etheric realms rather than the physical level. They travel along the crystalline Fields of Light around the Earth. Sometimes they are stationed in ancient temple sites of Lemuria. Sometimes they stabilize geophysical fault lines. They work in the capacity of Light Ships, except they're more permanently stationed than a Light Ship. Their basic function right now is to transmit the frequencies of the Ten Commandments.

Joshua: I am very confused about these Thirteen Crystal Skulls in Tibet. Are they physical, dimensional or etheric skulls?

Michael: The Thirteen Crystal Skulls are "apports" or direct projections that were brought from the higher realms. They are biocrystalline totems to symbolize each of the twelve tribes of the Inner Earth and carry each tribe's frequencies and genetics. Each skull is specifically color-coded. The Mitchell-Hedges Skull has a blue and ultraviolet color-code, which is a high frequency one. The ones under the Potala carry color-codes of the Inner Earth Tribes. These tribes came to this planet when the Earth was in the higher frequency levels of the fourth or fifth dimensional states. They came as the Elohim or

Els, and projected as a Light Race, so they are all color-coded. The first ones were Blue, the Blue Madras. They formed the first race in the Inner Earth. Then the Solarians came, which were ones who manifested on the surface of the planet. The Solarians and the Blue Madras met on the surface simultaneously, the Blue Madras coming from the Inner Earth and the Solarians coming from the surface. The thirteen skulls represent these twelve tribes.[3] As stated before, the thirteenth is actually the family of these tribes.

Joshua: Were the thirteen skulls (in Tibet) brought to the Earth or were they created through the Morphocrystallic Sciences which the people on the Earth at that time were familiar with?

Michael: The Thirteen Crystal Skulls in Tibet as I mentioned were originally created as an entire biocrystalline structure (head and body) and represent the genetic heritage of the thirteen tribes manifested on the Earth. The thirteen biocrystalline structures were teleported to our planet from other dimensions and planets. For instance, one biocrystalline body was projected from Sirius. It had a blue quartz structure to it and could project back and forth to Sirius. Another biocrystalline structure was from Orion, and was used not only for planetary genetic programming, but for teleportation as well. These biocrystalline structures preserved key levels of information that would have been otherwise lost, and stabilized Planetary Genetics and Light Harmonics as well.

Joshua: Is the human form the only model used for a Crystal Skull?

Michael: The biocrystalline structure of the Crystal Skulls are in the human form, which is the form the different races eventually decided upon as they settled into the Third Dimensional Frequency of the Earth. Originally, Planetary Evolutions could choose different forms with many variations before they decided on human form. This goes back again to the half-animal, half-human aspects of creation that were present then. Once Planetary Genetics were firmly set by the Higher Evolution, the biocrystalline structures were brought into existence as a model for planetary evolution to follow, to preserve Planetary Genetics and Planetary Light Functions. There are also

---

[3.] Editors' Note: The Thirteen Crystal Skulls which Michael refers to are of an interdimensional nature and can instantaneously shift their presence back and forth between the physical level and the etheric level.

other artifacts which they used to preserve this information, such as crystal tablets and crystal pyramids, but these objects came along much later.

Joshua: Could you summarize the purpose or service The Thirteen Crystal Skulls in Tibet are providing for the Earth?

Michael: The Thirteen Crystal Skulls under the Potala maintain the frequency of the Ten Commandments of Light being broadcast. They are a biocrystalline computer, and as I mentioned, consist of a pattern of two Mogan Davids superimposed. When you integrate these Mogan Davids, they facilitate communication with the higher realms. The Thirteen Crystal Skulls are for healing, communication and balance of planetary harmonics. They work in a similar fashion as the pyramids; the crystal pyramids that are around the Earth which broadcast signals to our Planetary Evolution. Actually, pyramids are a little bit better for communication than the skulls. Also, the skull is symbolic of a crystal chalice or grail inside the energy system of the human body. The base of the chalice begins in the lower neck region and extends up through your head.

Joshua: Could we make a general statement that UFOs, Space Brothers or Extraterrestrials have something to do with the bringing forth of these Crystal Skulls to our planet?

Michael: The biocrystalline structures of The Thirteen Crystal Skulls, the Crystal Pyramids and the Crystal Tablets were brought directly to our Planetary Evolution by the Higher Evolution aboard spacecraft. Some of these items were teleported here directly, or others were manifested through Morphocrystallic Sciences. Some of the biocrystalline structures of The Thirteen Crystal Skulls were brought on Light Ships; some were manifested here directly, others were teleported to the Earth directly. These skulls do have the ability to move from the Potala in Tibet. They can move through the Twelve Crystalline Fields of Light, or they can travel to other planets as well. The Thirteen Crystal Skulls and their biocrystalline structures are very active in our planetary evolution.

Joshua: Well, it sounds like at least the technology to create the skulls was brought from elsewhere.

Michael: Various technologies and the Morphocrystallic Sciences were introduced to our planetary evolution during several historical times. The

CHAPTER 5

most recent was during the times of Atlantis. They were also introduced during the times of Lemuria and earlier. These Technologies and Sciences had to be introduced several times because of many cataclysms which occurred on the Earth. The Pleiadians were responsible for the introduction of the Morphocrystallic Sciences (from the Taurus Constellation) in Atlantis before the last cataclysms. These sciences were brought in earlier times by races from Orion. The Morphocrystallic Sciences have been here several times.

Joshua: Did the Pleiadians receive this information from Orion as well?

Michael: Orion is the major programming area for our section of the galaxy. It's where major energies come through Jacob's Ladder of Living Light. The Pleiades is responsible for the physical aspect of our evolution. Orion and the Pleiades blend their energies into our planetary civilization.

Joshua: May I summarize what has been presented so far? If I understand correctly, there are thirteen master skulls, which are not necessarily on the physical level, but work on an etheric energy level. These originally resided within the thirteen healing temples in Atlantis, but are now in Tibet. However, you have also stated that the Mitchell-Hedges Skull was in one of these Atlantean temples and was created to replace one of the thirteen original skulls. Can you give more details about why the original Thirteen Crystal Skulls were removed from the Atlantean Temples?

Michael: The Original Thirteen Temples in Atlantis were established by the Melchezidek Brotherhood, which is responsible for our planetary education. The Thirteen Healing Temples in Atlantis originally had thirteen Crystal Skulls, but during the fall of Man, the Thirteen Crystal Skulls and their biocrystalline structures were removed to Tibet. It was at that time that the Mitchell-Hedges Skull was formed and placed in the Temple of Muror on Bimini.

Joshua: To replace the ones that were taken?

Michael: Yes, to replace the original Thirteen Crystal Skulls that were on Atlantis. Crystal Skulls such as the Mitchell-Hedges Skull, the Amethyst Skull, the Rose Quartz Skull from Guatemala and a number of others that people have found, are replacements for the originals; they're not the original Crystal Skulls. So they're really not representative of the Morphocrystallic Sciences in their truest form. They were made during the fall of Atlantis.

Sandra: Are the skulls which went to Tibet still there?

MICHAEL KANT

Michael: The Potala is where The Thirteen Crystal Skulls are currently stationed. As I mentioned, their biocrystalline structures are situated elsewhere right now. Eventually the Crystal Skulls and their biocrystalline structures will be reunited because they represented the Planetary Genetics of the individual thirteen original races of this planet. Each race has a biocrystalline skull and body as well. So, currently we have thirteen Crystal Skulls. The biocrystalline bodies will be brought into focus later on.

Joshua: Can you give us more information about the replacement of the master skulls in the Atlantean temples?

Michael: Yes, as they would remove one of the original Crystal Skulls in the Atlantean Healing Temples, they would replace it with a duplicate Crystal Skull. Sometimes the Atlantean priests were not aware of when the original was replaced with a duplicate. During the fall of Atlantis, the frequencies were rapidly decreasing and the priests were not always aware of what the Crystal Skulls were used for. So the original ones were removed to Tibet for safe-keeping. The same thing happened with the Crystal Ark of the Covenant which was removed and then a duplicate was placed in Solomon's Temple. This duplicate could never use as many Light Functions and Energies as the original, but it had some of its functions. This Ark of the Covenant that was produced as an imitation of the original lacked many of the key Light Functions and harmonics. As a result, it produced harmful radiations to those who came into contact with it. So there is the original Crystal Ark of the Covenant and the biblical Ark of the Covenant. There are Crystal Skulls-- thirteen original ones and thirteen additional ones that are actually duplicates. Then there are many other versions of skulls which came along later on, that made it even more confusing.

Joshua: Regarding the thirteen surrogate skulls (this would probably be the best way to phrase it)-- you said previously that they would not all be clear, that they were made out of different types of quartz. Do you know what each one was made from and how many were clear?

Michael: The original Crystal Skulls that were placed in Atlantis were clear skulls. [*Joshua:* All of them?] Yes, and the thirteen replacements were also clear skulls. The skulls which came later were not as clear. They didn't know how to use the Morphocrystallic Sciences. The Crystal Skulls in Atlantis were

CHAPTER 5

quartz-based and quartz is a big family. Amethyst would be one type of Crystal Skull they used. The Rose Quartz Skull would be another. There's an entire family of quartz. These gemstones in the quartz family are the key crystals, just as The Thirteen Crystal Skulls in Atlantis were key crystals. There's aquamarine, amethyst, rose quartz, there's a purple lithium stone which is a new crystal they just found in South America, and other crystals that we are not aware of. Also, an Obsidian Skull was produced later on by the Aztecs. It was really a duplication of one of The Thirteen Crystal Skulls in Atlantis.

Sandra: As a member of the research team that went to Canada, I channeled that the Mitchell-Hedges Skull had an affinity to the blue and ultraviolet light for healing. Are these the colors used to activate the skull for healing, or does the skull have information (or programming) so that it automatically knows how to heal each person who comes into contact with it?

Michael: Well, the Crystal Skull, as a bio-crystalline computer, can be thought of as an energy gate. It can store information from different dimensions and levels and then transmit them to a person like a radio. This skull works in a predominance of blue or violet color-codes, but it can work in other color spectrums as well. It has many layers of information, like a Thought Crystal; some people can tap into a general level and some people can tap into the deeper levels. If you don't have any mental blocks and you can tap into the skull, it will project holographic images. Certain computers today are able to project holographic images out into space. The Crystal Skull can do the same thing, so if a person were attuned to this, (s)he would pick up these images. The blue spectrum which the skull emanates, is actually symbolic of the Divine Will. In fact, our Earth is shifting more towards the feminine Blue Light Spectrum and away from the old masculine solar energies of the red and yellow spectrum because we are moving into a Population II System which encompasses the higher ultraviolet frequency. That's what the Crystal Skull is dealing with, a higher ultraviolet frequency, a feminine type of energy. So, the Crystal Skull works with Key Light Spectrums to help one integrate with the higher frequencies.

Some people need a point of contact. If you put your hands on the skull, in a certain way, you can transmit information if you know how. The Atlantean Priests would put their hands on the skull and transmit information directly

MICHAEL KANT

into the skull or reverse their hand position and take information out of the skull. It's similar to the hand gestures (Mudras) they use in Yoga. They used a great deal of Yogic techniques around the Crystal Skull, which is a whole science of Light. They used the skull as a storage device or computer, as they would simply put their hand on it and then transmit their thoughts directly. If you know how to place your hands together correctly using the right frequency, you can extract information directly from the skull into yourself. If you aren't ready for it, the skull or your own mental blocks will prevent it. When you're encoded with the appropriate frequencies, you can work with objects such as a Crystal Skull, the Crystal Ball (of Dr. Brown)[4], or Crystal Pyramids which are coded for specific individuals, frequencies and communication. So the Crystal Skull is not going to sit there and just speak small talk; it will talk from a higher level. If you try to pester it, it can zap you or really affect your system, which the skulls sometimes do. This is a result of your negativity reacting against the higher frequencies of Light.

Based on my contact with Space Beings, they don't use Crystal Skulls because they don't need them. Instead, they work with crystal helmets to tie into their computers directly. The helmet has all kinds of crystals in it. You put it over your head and it transmits information from the computer directly to your brain, but only if your brain patterns are attuned. Therefore, the Crystal Skulls are similar to Crystal Helmets because they transmit and encode knowledge into those people who are ready for it, which they can retrieve later on.

Sandra: In my past-life regressions, I've had a strong connection to having worked with thirteen Crystal Skulls in Tibet. After seeing the Mitchell-Hedges Skull for the first time, my affinity to the Crystal Skulls became even stronger. But, why do you think that information is coming out about the skulls now? Is it because there is a shift that has come about and people are ready for more information?

---

[4] Dr. Brown, a naturopathic practitioner from Arizona, observed an underwater pyramid while scuba diving off Bimini in 1970. After entering this structure he came upon an unusual room where he found this crystal ball cradled by a pair of bronze hands. Dr. Brown removed this ball and later observed strange phenomena occurring around and within it; such as phantom lights, voices, tinkling bells, etc. This is very similar to phenomena which have been experienced in the presence of a Crystal Skull.

CHAPTER 5

Michael: The Crystal Skulls are really just the tip of the iceberg of what's coming out. So it's not surprising that they are emerging at this time because things like the Enoch book, [*The Keys of Enoch,* by J. J. Hurtak, which represents a probe into our planetary evolution to see if we are ready for the Higher Teachings], crystals and interest in UFOs are areas that people understand fairly well now, as opposed to twenty or thirty years ago when these topics didn't make sense to most people. The Crystal Skull has much more to tell than people imagine, they just don't understand how to tap into it yet. It's like a giant Thought Crystal, or holographic computer. Of course, when you have thirteen of them as they do in Tibet, that's a true master computer. The pyramids do the same thing on a different level.

Basically, our whole solar system and planetary evolution is evolving closer to the central areas of the Galaxy, so our entire harmonic fields of Light are changing. In the past, our Earth has been in a fallen state, even more than it is now. After the fall of Atlantis we went to a lower frequency. Many things were hidden away in secret crystal vaults under South America and thirteen underground cities. The Ark of the Covenant is hidden in the United States. These were all hidden away and timed to be brought out as the Earth started to move up in its evolution again. The Mitchell-Hedges Crystal Skull was brought out in 1924, the Crystal Ball [found by Dr. Brown] was brought out in the 70's and there have been a lot of other things that have been found which people don't talk about, especially large crystal tablets found off Bimini. These items all are timed to be released at certain points to stimulate planetary evolution.

If you aren't ready for this information it wouldn't mean much to you if it were brought out yet. So it's meant for certain people to find at certain times. For example, there are vaults underneath the Great Pyramid that will be found by three key people. When their energies are brought together, the secret of the vaults will reveal itself to them. But it won't reveal itself to just anybody, it's meant for certain specific people. The [Mitchell-Hedges] Crystal Skull was from a Healing Temple in Atlantis and works with the healing frequency, and communication or communion with the higher dimensional frequencies. The fact that our solar system is moving toward the central region of the Galaxy means that we're needing more Light so that we will become what they call a Population II System. We will have two suns instead of one and we'll be shifting from the solar frequencies towards the ultraviolet frequencies.

MICHAEL KANT

(During the interview, Michael was asked about his UFO experience where a Pleiadian Spacecraft teleported him aboard from his home in Illinois and took him on a tour through our planet and solar system. Below are excerpts from this part of the interview to help the reader better understand the Inner Earth and the people who live within our world.)

Michael: Aboard the ship I was given a tour of our solar system and was taken through the Inner Earth, where most of the Higher Genetic Races of the Earth live right now. There are other parallel evolutions that the Pleiadians are in contact with in the Inner Earth (unknown to our scientists) called the Twelve Tribes. Each tribe of the Inner Earth is closely associated with a Medicine Lodge and the nature kingdom. There are different plants and animals in the Inner Earth than on the surface of our planet, but some of these originally came from the surface.

The Inner Earth has a higher frequency than the surface of the Earth, more of a fourth and fifth dimensional frequency, whereas the surface of the Earth is more of a third dimensional frequency. In the Inner Earth you have what is called the Atoma [their central sun at the Earth's core], which is surrounded by hydrogen clouds. It is mostly daytime since they usually have light of some sort. Towards the end of the day, they have a dimming of the light due to the hydrogen clouds that surround the Atoma. Inner Earth people breathe what we would call etheric energy and eat much less food than we do. Their plant life is bigger than ours because of more stimulation from the radiation of the central Atoma. Six Earth races that originated on the surface have migrated to the Inner Earth and combined with six Galactic races to comprise twelve races, with the thirteenth being a grand family which forms a blending of all the races.

The Inner Earth Tribes have what they call the clan, the culture and the medicine society. Each one has various cultures integrated into it. The Blue Madras, being the first, would have one culture and the second one would have two cultures. The twelfth tribe has twelve cultures integrated into it. These cultures maintain their identity and don't interbreed like we do. They maintain very tight control of genetics, Light Functions and Light Codes. The Twelve Tribes of the Inner Earth can be thought of as six Earth Tribes [the Blue Madras] and six Sky Tribes [the Solarians]. Each Tribe has a totem and a medicine lodge. They're very much into healing with crystals and make use of the Morphocrystallic Generation, Transformation, and Liquidization of crystals.

CHAPTER 5

The Inner Earth people have a communion with nature and work closely with the plant and animal kingdom, dolphins, whales, Maria Bird (similar to a peacock with colored feathers, but much larger) and the Unicorn. They have special healing gardens where people are re-balanced. People from the surface are usually not welcome to the Inner Earth because of the visitors' negative frequencies or thoughts. Usually, if you are allowed entry, you'll go through a purification ritual. Everything in the Inner Earth is based on the highest genetics of Light alignment and thus they must keep a sealed energy layer to prevent unwelcome visitors. Eventually they will merge with the surface people of the Earth as we move into the higher frequencies.

The region of the Inner Earth has more land surface compared to our outer Earth surface. It has some mountains but not as many. The highest peak in the Inner Earth, the Sapphire Mountain, is a crystal mountain composed of ice crystals with varying densities. It serves as a central communication point, as a transport mechanism and as an initiation point in the Inner Earth. Close to the Sapphire Mountain is what is called the Chalice Lake, which is a key initiation point. Here all the crystalline Fields of Light come together and manifest, so the Lake gets quite a bit of energy and power. The Blue Spruce Medicine Lodge is located in the central part of the Chalice Lake, on an island called Communion. This goes back to the old legends of the Crystal Grail and the Holy Grail.

They use Light Ships very similar to the Pleiadian crafts. There are some Pleiadian Races in the Inner Earth Races. The Pleiadians maintain a close tie with the Inner Earth people not only through visits in their reconnaissance craft (like the one I was on), but through the Phoenix V Program, which is the code name that the Pleiadians use for their Program of Light that they use on the Earth. The Inner Earth people and the Pleiadians cooperate in construction of various pyramids of Light such as the Tau Pyramid in Mesa Verde. These types of pyramids of Light help to bring forth the new frequencies of Light such as the Ten Commandments and the integration of Planetary Harmonics and Frequency Stations. The Inner Earth people do have some spacecraft that they use, but they keep them in the Inner Earth most of the time, though they do occasionally come out.

The Inner Earth people are more advanced, because they are in the Fourth and Fifth Dimensions. The most advanced people in the Inner Earth are called the Illuminaries, or what we call the Hierarchy of Light. These souls are very knowledgeable in the higher spiritual and scientific teachings such as the

A pictorial representation of our Earth as a hollow planet, with the Atoma (or inner sun) shining out from the center of the Earth's core. Also observe the land masses on the inner surface and the opening at the North Pole with spirals of Light flowing out.

Enoch book. The Inner Earth people are a little bit taller than the surface races and a little more translucent, like the Pleiadians who I met on the ship. Some of the races did come from the Pleiades originally, others came from Orion and some of the ancient cultures (such as those of Atlantis and Lemuria) that were on the surface of the Earth have now integrated into the Inner Earth tribes. Thus the genetics of these ancient peoples are still preserved in the Inner Earth. The Inner Earth serves as a central focus point for our planetary evolution right now. We could think of the Inner Earth civilizations as representing what the surface of the Earth should be like and will be like in the future. The Inner Earth people have a number of programs to re-activate the Harmonic Grid Structure around the Earth which will assist the surface to be like the Inner Earth.

The Inner Earth cooperates with the Galactic Hierarchy of Light and has a number of programs where they preserve World Cultural Sites like Mesa Verde or the Grand Tetons. Crystal Skulls would also be considered a part of this program. More specifically, they call this organization the Office of the Clarion. It preserves historical objects of importance such as the Crystal Skull or the Shroud of Turin-- things that carry key frequencies-- otherwise these objects would be destroyed. They preserve World Cultural Sites and key cultural artifacts which were produced in Atlantis or Lemuria. Many of these items were teleported to the Inner Earth during the destruction of Atlantis, Lemuria or Hyperborea. The Inner Earth people are still constructing things around the Earth in cooperation with the Pleiadians and various Galactic councils. Some of the more recent activities would be the pyramid of Light over San Antonio, or the Aton pyramid of Light over the Four Corners area. So the Inner Earth people are very active in Light Technologies, Thought Technologies and Crystal Technologies just as the Pleiadians.

The races of the Inner Earth are color-coded. Some races are blue, some are more of the golden hue. At one time there was a blue race on the surface of the Earth but it became extinct through the fall of humanity and through interbreeding and mixing. The blue race, which is a key genetic programming factor in our planetary evolution, was lost on the surface but is still present in the Inner Earth. This is where our knowledge of the blue races, the blue-blood and nobility comes; from the blue races, because they were prevalent in Atlantis. Some blue races have come from the Star System Sirius, as well as Orion, their original home. So there has been quite an interaction between the blue races and the Inner Earth.

MICHAEL KANT

Joshua: You previously mentioned that each one of the original Crystal Skulls represented an Inner Earth race. Can you give more information about this connection?

Michael: The biocrystalline Crystal Skulls and their associated structures were manifested during different times in the Earth's history as different races manifested upon our planet. The first race to manifest was the Blue Madras. They projected from the star station Faustia in the Orion constellation. The Blue Madras were followed by the Solarians, which is an old term for the galactic races which landed on the surface of our planet. As each race projected to the Earth, they would form a biocrystalline structure to preserve their Planetary Genetics, Light Functions and information necessary for planetary evolution at that time, even when the Earth was gradually undergoing stabilization. The crystal served as a storage bank for information, similar to aspects of our computers where data can't be erased when it is needed to be stored on a permanent basis. So Planetary Harmonics, Planetary Genetics and the cultural heritage of the Thirteen Races were preserved through the Thirteen Crystal Skulls and their biocrystalline structures.

(Resuming questions about the Crystal Skulls)

Joshua: One of the channels we talked to during our research on the Crystal Skulls made a statement that metal or semiprecious metals could also be used to create skulls with similar capabilities. Is this something that you are familiar with?

Michael: You can use crystal to create a Crystal Skull, you can use metal to make a metal skull, you can use combinations of crystals and metals to make a Crystal Skull. In Atlantean or Lemurian Technology, crystals and metals were often used together. Crystal is a higher form of the nature kingdom, but metals do have a crystalline structure as well. Quartz has a defined crystalline structure whereas metals have an undefined crystalline structure. Gold and Quartz often can be found together in nature; this produces a higher frequency for spiritual healing.

Joshua: While scrying with the Mitchell-Hedges Skull, many people have seen a tremendous amount of underwater scenes. Was there a time when this skull was underwater? If it was not, then why have people seen these scenes?

Michael: Atlantean Technology developed a number of underwater cities, underwater pyramids and underwater temples that are still active. The [Mitchell-Hedges] Crystal Skull was in one of these underwater temples. The Temple of Muror, where the Crystal Skull was originally housed, was destroyed by a cataclysm. There was a period of time when this Crystal Skull was in-place in an underwater pyramid. And these cities are still used by the Atlanteans even today. Submarines have found strange bubble formations in the floor of the ocean and Crystal Pyramids that are still very active in underwater Atlantean cities of Light.

Joshua: Were there ever any Crystal Skulls that were brought to the Earth for manipulative or controlling purposes?

Michael: There are many types of Crystal Skulls and some crystal artifacts which have been brought to our planet and have affected evolution in a negative way. The so-called Fallen Lords which come from a certain area of our galaxy, or outside of our Galactic Disk, introduced these technologies during the time of Atlantis to cause the fall of Man or the fall of Atlantean civilization. They misused crystal energies and unbalanced the Earth's planetary harmonics, which caused many of these cataclysms due to the negative use of the crystal energies and the Light Functions. Of course, atomic testing and related radiation, and things of this nature were also indirectly or directly caused by the misuse of crystals or crystalline fields. In atomic energy, they make use of the Twelve Crystalline Fields of Light that surround our planet. Atomic energy can only be detonated at key locations along the Crystalline Fields of Light. So again, crystals played a major role in planetary evolution. Crystals are biocrystalline computers which can be programmed positively or negatively. Some crystals do have a negative vibration and you should avoid those. You should be very aware of where the crystal is in its evolution, its frequency and vibration. There is some manipulation by people with crystals even today; they try to control people with negative crystals. So it's very important to choose the correct crystal for yourself.

Joshua: What would you say are the ages of the skulls that are being found?

Michael: The original biocrystalline structures of The Thirteen Crystal Skulls in Tibet were brought to the Earth during the times that the Elohim first appeared here, about a billion years ago. The Mitchell-Hedges Skull would be much more recent of course (15,000 - 25,000 years ago), during the time of the last fall of Atlantis. So there is quite a bit of time duration when the original Thirteen Crystal Skulls in Tibet were brought here by the Elohim.

Joshua: Would other civilizations, planets and dimensions also have tools on the order of a Crystal Skull or Crystal Person? Is this unique to our planet?

Michael: Every planetary evolution has its own unique biocrystalline structures. Some planets would have certain similarities to ours. Crystal pyramids and biocrystalline structures would be prevalent on other planets as well as our own because certain forms, structures and Light Functions are universal; they don't vary from planet to planet. It is like when you have a seed or any type of plant, the seed always follows certain patterns, although there are variations. Similarly, the biocrystalline Crystal Skulls set the pattern for our planetary evolution to follow. Also, on Venus the Crystal Skulls are used in a similar fashion but the planetary evolution progresses in a much different fashion than our own. Currently, the Venusian planetary civilization exists in the fifth dimension.

Joshua: We have heard that the Cherokees are presently buying carved skulls. Harley Swiftdeer (a Native American teacher) shares Indian legends which state that each major religion of the Earth has a set of thirteen skulls, twelve clear and one amethyst. The essence of my question is, do either the Hopis, (and perhaps we can focus on the Hopis first) or any Native American Indians in general, have an affinity for the Crystal Skulls?

Michael: Some of the American Indians such as the Hopis were descendants of tribes that came from the Inner Earth. These tribes come out to the surface from time to time to check on certain Atlantean Time capsules or crystal records in the Mesa Verde area or the Atlantean Time Vaults under Mount Payson in the Four Corners region of Arizona. These descendants were left behind as Guardians for these time capsules. The Hopis have a secret tradition that most western civilizations aren't aware of. Also, the Hopis are very aware of the use of the Crystal Skulls, the Inner Earth, and the cultural heritage of The Thirteen Crystal Skulls in Tibet. They keep this knowledge hidden from the White Man for fear that he would misuse this knowledge. The Hopis have many prophecies about the destruction of the White Man's civilization and so the Crystal Skull is of special significance to their races. There are many variations of ancient Crystal Skulls and many people are

CHAPTER 5

carving crystal skulls now. I have seen a few crystal skulls that are smaller versions of the Mitchell-Hedges Skull, not with a movable jaw, but in similar patterns. These Crystal Skulls represent more primitive cultures. In the case of the Central American Indians, they also use a variation of the Crystal Skull where they use mosaics as a mask. These masks are a much more primitive version of the original Crystal Skulls. The Crystal Skull does hold a key position in American Indian mythology, history and folk lore. The Aztecs had an Obsidian Crystal Skull which played a key role in their civilization.

Joshua: If the Hopi are relatives of the Guardians that came out of the Inner Earth, the implication is that there is a Red Race in the Inner Earth, is this correct?

Michael: All of the races, the thirteen races in the Inner Earth, represent not only a race that lives on the surface of our planet, such as the Atlantean Red Race, but many of the Galactic races that were active on our planetary surface at one time. Each of the thirteen tribes has separate smaller clans that are representative of different planetary cultures. The Blue Madras would be only one tribe. The Red Races are just one of the color-coded races that were a part of our evolution. There's the Blue Race, the Yellow Race, the Green Race, all the way through the color Spectrum; all the various color-coding is used. Some color-coding of our surface evolution doesn't have a counterpart, such as the Blue Race which moved entirely into the Inner Earth and will at a later time re-emerge onto the surface.

Sandra: So there *would* be a Green Race too.

Michael: There used to be a Green, Orange and a Violet Race. They phased themselves out, which is one of the reasons the planet fell, because the Higher Light Races kept mixing with the lower fallen races and this caused the fall in the planetary vibration. Whereas in the Inner Earth, they only allow marriage between the Highest Light Races and people with the correct genetics and Light Programming. If you get two people together that have the wrong Light programming, then you create aversion and negativity. And that is what can cause strange and negative thought forms that people have, because the two people's programming doesn't match. Thus, the Inner Earth has a very strict control and they use a crystal to determine who should marry and who shouldn't. However, some people in the Inner Earth are determined to marry anyway.

Sandra: I have a feeling that I will be writing a book about my past-life experiences in Tibet. I don't know whether I will channel the information, but I know that it will relate to the thirteen Crystal Skulls that are in Tibet. I have questions involving specifics related to those particular skulls.

Michael: Tibet is a spiritual programming area for the eastern part of our planet. Tibet, China, and India form a triangle, just like Israel, Egypt and Syria form a triangle for the western world. And these are the two key programming areas for the twelve Crystalline Fields of Light. The fields are shifting to North America now and will be aligned there. The Dark Forces were very aware of the planetary light grids, the twelve crystalline fields of Light and the Ten Commandments of Light as well. They wanted to rule Tibet and Egypt so they could control these grids. This is why there has always been a tension in central Asia and Egypt as well. They're trying to control planetary harmonics. A group in the Eastern World that knew of the Crystal Skulls would probably be the Bon-Po, who used to be in Tibet before the Revolution.

Yasodhara: They were anxious to hide them away. The Light Forces managed to hide the skulls from the Bon-Po. Is that your understanding [Michael]?

Michael: The Bon-Po[5] were shamans and they worshiped not only Crystal Skulls, but physical skulls as well. They were really kind of gruesome. This form of worshipping bone skulls is from the Bon-Po religion. It gives the Crystal Skulls a negative connotation so the people will not understand the Crystal Skulls' true purpose. They tried to control the original Thirteen Crystal Skulls and could not, so then they attempted to destroy them but failed. The Bon-Po tried to hide the skulls someplace where the Light Forces couldn't reach them, but all the Crystal Skulls have an energy field around them; they protect themselves. Only certain people can get in contact with them. The Crystal Skulls are in a place within the caverns under the Potala where they are located on a permanent basis so they can teleport wherever they need to be used. This mandala of skulls creates a vortex which adds Light energy to the grid system that comes up through the Potala in Tibet and protects the individual skulls. There's a series of caverns that distribute energies to the Inner Earth Region and to other areas of the planet, beneath this mandala

---

5· Bon-Po was the religion in Tibet before the Buddhists had control.

CHAPTER 5

(Tribal Light). This was one of the reasons why the Chinese wanted to control Tibet and the Crystal Skulls. The Chinese have a heritage of this way back into history and they are very aware of a lot of these caverns and artifacts that are underground in that area. In fact, there is a monastery in China that has different figures of people that represent various aspects of our evolution. In one room of the monastery there is a figure of a Space Being and another room just shows the regular races [human races].

The Buddhists are very advanced spiritual scientists. Buddhists always used crystals in association with their religions whether it was Crystal Skulls or medicines. Tibetan medicines made quite a bit of use of crystals and Crystal Skulls. The Tibetans weren't as aware of these skulls as the former races in Tibet were, such as the Bon-Po. One of the reasons the Chinese went in was because the Bon-Po were influencing our planetary civilization in a negative way.

Sandra: What I'm hearing you say is that most of the Crystal Skulls coming out now are not really the pure skulls or even a reflection of them. Supposedly there are three new skulls that have just come out, [*Joshua:* From Guatemala and Central America.] and one of them is the Rose Quartz Skull, which Nick saw. It is claimed to be bigger than the Mitchell-Hedges Skull and also have a movable jaw.

Michael: I think the one in Guatemala and the Mitchell-Hedges Skull are similar in size and they both represent former priestesses. Atlantean priestesses were the ones that were always the head of the thirteen healing temples in Atlantis. They had a natural affinity with crystals. It is the feminine energies which are necessary to activate the skulls.

Rose quartz is much rarer than natural quartz. There are deposits in South Dakota. Natural quartz can be found all over. In fact, the Mitchell-Hedges Skull has the same type of crystalline structure as the quartz crystals in Calaveras, California. [*Sandra:* Yes, that's what I've heard.] But that's just coincidence as far as I know. There's a lot of quartz in Calaveras County too.

Sandra: Will you please describe color-coding as it is used with Crystal Skulls?

Michael: There are twelve key colors which would be color-coded in each one of your twelve chakras and the Crystal Skulls. The thirteenth would be a combination of all the others, which would be a pure White Light, a combination of all these frequencies. So there are twelve key color codes that

MICHAEL KANT

our planetary evolution uses and the Ten Commandments are used to activate these color codes, as will all the Crystal Skulls. <u>The first race to come to our planet represented Divine Love-- blue.</u> The second race that came was more of a yellowish color and the third race was basically red. This continued until all twelve colors were represented.

Sandra: So what would the rose color mean? Is that closer to the red or would that be more of a pink or purple?

Michael: It would be distinct from the red. The red would be more of a masculine color, but the pink would be a feminine aspect. It would be one of the twelve colors which are variations of the three primary colors. You can have red, yellow and blue. There are always variations of colors to go with the twelve key colors. But first you start with the trinity, the three primary colors, blue, yellow and red. And then the yellow color in combination with other primaries will give you purple, green and orange and these combinations continue between the primary colors until you have all twelve colors.

A Crystal Skull is like a computer, and if you know how to activate it with the password or Light Function, it will release key information. This is its system of preventing unauthorized people (so to speak) from accessing the information in it. It always sends out probes to see if you're ready or not. It will probably show you a spacecraft to see if you recognize it, or it will put out a pyramid to see if you're ready, a face or a priest who's been associated with the skull. A Crystal Skull will impress you in different modes to see if you're truly ready for information. It will release these key colors, smells and impressions to probe our planetary consciousness from time to time.

Joshua: Who is doing this impressing?

Michael: The Higher Evolution uses the Crystal Skulls as biocrystalline computers, just as we use a computer to program information for others to retrieve later on. They use the crystalline grids of the Earth and Crystal Skulls to provide information to our planetary evolution for the planetary education.

Joshua: Could we compare the activation of a Crystal Skull to the procedure a person would use to access a protected computer system? In other words, would a person's vibration (possibly working in combination with color, light and sound) serve as the key which unlocks the program(s) in the skull?

CHAPTER 5

Michael: If the right person comes along, this would activate it. A Crystal Skull can't be activated by just anybody. The skull has many different layers like a Thought Crystal. The first layer would be very narrow, the deeper layers would have the key information, and the skull would test you as you went through each layer. It's like when you go through the Third, Fourth or Fifth Dimension, you have to be ready for it or you can easily become very scattered and confused.

Sandra: Yes indeed. Do you know about hand signals that were used in conjunction with the skull?

Michael: I think I mentioned it a little bit before, but I didn't get into too much detail. Each of your ten fingers represent the Ten Commandments of Light; they're called the Chana energies. The way your fingers are placed on the skull will activate the Light codes and give information that is stored inside the Crystal Skull. If you wanted to go into an Atlantean time capsule, you access that by placing your hand on the right section of the skull and you will be led to one. On the doors to the time capsules they have an imprint of a hand. You put your hand in this imprint and if your Light Functions are attuned, that door will automatically open. So, by placing your hands on a Crystal Skull in a certain way, it will project Holograms and Fire Letters. To see if you're ready to work with it, the Crystal Skull will put out a small probe, like a color or sound. If a person doesn't respond, the Crystal Skull will stop its programming.

Sandra: Through my inner contacts with Space Beings, I've seen them using hand signals. The Pleiadians probably use similar hand signals, since my understanding is that this is a main form of communication used by the extraterrestrials. I used the same hand signals to activate the Mitchell-Hedges Skull.

Michael: They do use a wide variety of methods for communication, but their primary means is through the use of holograms and Fire Letters. Hand signals or movements activate color-coded signals, an example of which would be the breastplate of the High Priest where the crystals positioned upon it are color-coded and initialized by finger placement upon the stones. In fact, some people are marketing these miniature breastplates now, which is kind of interesting. These have the sequence of color stones which represent the Lights that were flashed to our Planetary Evolution by the Higher Evolution for contact. When you do yoga and meditation, you've got to put your hands in a certain way because of the manner that the energies will move. Buddhists have different meditative positions, each one of these represents a different idea or concept. Holding your fingers in certain ways, you'll broadcast Light codes. Just like when one lays their hands on another person, some people can *heal* others because of these energies. Each one of the ten fingers has its own frequency emission which is called the Chana. Each Chana has a left or a right-hand spiral, depending upon your polarization.

(Lastly, we asked Michael about how he receives his information.)

Sandra: We have interviewed many different channels who have wonderful information, but you seem to be able to tap into so many levels. Can you tell us how you do this?

Michael: That's just multiplexing, which means you can go through all the different levels without having any problems, such as in a crystal which may have sixteen, twenty or thirty levels. Most people only get to the first level. They try to get deeper and get blocked or have headaches because it will not open to them, especially recording crystals. Recording crystals are all over the place. Or if you go to certain places, there are these doors of knowledge, and if you place your hand on the doors, you will find all kinds of ancient artifacts contained in there. Your individual vibration must be the right frequency to open the doors.

Joshua: When you are accessing your information (as I see it in my mind's eye), it seems to be all around us floating in the air. [*Michael:* Yes, the Fire Letters.] So you're just seeing the Fire Letters and each one telepathically communicates to you whatever it means?

Michael: Sometimes I get telepathic communications, or I tap into computers or crystals. At other times there are [etheric] books available which I can access. Usually I get information from the Fire Letters, or sometimes it comes in as a series of holographic images. Sometimes I just see the hologram and then must decode it. Other times the information comes from spacecraft as Fire Letters and I try to disseminate whatever I can remember. Usually it's a hologram that comes through, which is color-coded and sound-coded. There's a certain mathematical relationship to the way the Letters are shaped, and naturally I go between the Letters because they're holographic. The

CHAPTER 5

meaning of these Fire Letters depends on their tone, their qualities and the energies they form. They are around us all the time, it's just a matter of being attuned to them. Fire Letters are a Universal Language used all over the Galaxy. Otherwise, if you were to go from the Jerusalem Command to an Andromeda Command or some other Galactic Command, you would need a translator; which you sometimes do anyway. The Fire Letters help to integrate this Universal Language.

Section 2
Third Interview

Jeff: Can you comment on what crystal records are and their significance.

Michael: Well, there are different ways of recording information. Chronomonitors are a form of crystal recording device. There are crystal records that are actually encoded on crystals and metal books [combinations of metals and crystals that are synthesized together] where ancient records were stored. Places like Atlantis used crystal records which involved information storage on huge crystals or books. In fact there were recently crystal records found off Bimini which are about seven feet tall and three feet wide. The individuals who found it, prefer to keep it a secret. I don't know about everything they discovered, but they did find actual crystal records.

Jeff: Are you referring to crystal tablets?

Michael: As far as I can tell. They're transparent crystals with fire letters on them usually found on certain types of metals, engraved or etched into the crystals themselves. The crystal tablets are usually activated by a person's consciousness. Even though some people may not see any designs on the crystal or crystal recording device, their consciousness will activate the crystal record and holographs. Though there may be etchings on the crystal tablets, they're not the actual messages that are in the crystal; there's a deeper level. Similarly, if one looks at the Crystal Skull, there are many many different levels of crystal records.

In order for a person to be prevented from tapping into deeper levels, the crystal records are created into different forms; so you might see an etching on the surface for a more general level and there are holograms in different layers which would be activated by consciousness. One can't really tap into

MICHAEL KANT

the information unless it was meant for them. People are finding these things everywhere. There are certain record chambers in Utah, which is where the Crystal Skulls in Tibet eventually will be transferred to, once the programming is completed. Different levels of information are stored in these crystal chambers. There's a type of metal on the walls which is alchemically made with gold and silver and contains the higher teachings. More general teachings are upon crystal spheres and crystal rings in the caverns. The caverns are the sites of ancient cities that were established at the dawn of our planetary civilization when the original races from Orion established themselves. They established a city in the area of Salt Lake City, and these caves are still there in the Wasatch Mountains.

Higher levels of information which an average person wouldn't recognize are stored on the metal walls in the caves. These races used to have a space needle in that same area so they could actually receive different communications and holograms through it. Finally the space needle was moved into a crystal dome. Light images from numerous star systems would be projected upon that dome. All of these various recording devices were capable of absorbing different frequencies and energies. Another example of these records would be the telonium tablets in Arizona. They're crystalline, but not like what we consider crystal. The tablets are metal and crystal fused together. Our scientists don't know how this was done. Some people have been allowed to examine these metal samples briefly, but these samples disappear after examination by scientists.

Jeff: Exactly, it's like these samples decompose or just vaporize after a period of time.

Michael: Yes, much like Angel Hair found by early UFO investigators. There are also crystal pyramids that store information, used in temple functions such as in Mt. Shasta, where there's a crystal pyramid. Also there's a huge (etheric) crystal pyramid above San Antonio right now that broadcasts Light Programs. Then there's what they call brilliant Thought Crystals or Recording Crystals, which are interdimensional types of crystals found at key areas around the Earth in secret chambers and temple sites. Thought Crystals have different levels of information which they record. They're activated by your consciousness too, but they are not like the more traditional type of crystal that can be used for storing ancient records.

CHAPTER 5

Jeff: Some people, such as Katrina Raphael, call them record-keeper crystals.

Michael: Oh, that's a little different. Record keepers are more like generator crystals that store energy and are placed at harmonic points to stabilize the twelve crystalline fields of the Earth. A friend of mine uses what they call Aquarian or Atlantean Firestones, which are a high-frequency type of quartz crystal found in Arkansas and Brazil. He places them around the Earth to stabilize it's crystalline structure. Of course, the Firestones are becoming active now because of the shift to the fourth-dimensional frequency. For a while, their energy was withdrawn and buried within the planet. Now this energy is beginning to be reactivated, which is another reason the Crystal Skulls are becoming active in Tibet. Eventually they'll be shifted to what is called the "New Jerusalem" in North America, which is the new spiritual programming area. The old programming areas were in Tibet and Egypt, but they're being shifted to a new synthesis or programming area in North America. The original Ark of the Covenant is already in those caverns.

Jeff: By whom and when have these artifacts been moved?

Michael: They're moved by various Galactic Races and members of our planetary evolution known as the Solarians, who are still active in the Inner Earth. The Ten Commandments of Living Light are starting to broadcast through Light Pyramids on the planet. Some of these Light Pyramids are located in Utah, Titicacca and elsewhere. The Inner Earth people are more active in this area than we are, for they have never had a fallen state, like our present planetary civilization.

Jeff: So the Light Beings have dematerialized these objects or transformed them into Light, beamed them into these caves and rematerialized them into the physical?

Michael: Crystal artifacts are often moved into the higher dimensions such as the fourth and fifth dimensions, where most of these records are stored. Otherwise third-dimensional fallen biochemical intelligence would interfere or try to destroy key records. They're usually kept in the fourth or fifth dimension in a protected energy matrix. It's not a solid form like we think of it, but the molecular matrix is stored here so it can be recreated on our level. So when I say they've moved these artifacts, I mean that the energy matrix which represents this artifact (such as the Ark of the Covenant or the Crystal Skulls) is shifted. This would be similar to the planetary grids which are being shifted all the time. The Thirteen Crystal Skulls are moving to the Utah area into crystal caverns that were established by the Solarian Races, who were members of the original planetary races. The Solarians were actually part of what you call the Elohim from Orion, that were beamed here on zionic energy beams following Jacob's Ladder of Living Light. This is called zionic light projection.

The Blue Madras who beamed here first came on an energy spiral or beam through Jacob's Ladder of Living Light, which stretches from Orion to the Earth, beaming down different energy functions. It's called *zionic beaming,* using zions, a type of light particle (quite a complicated process). First they beamed into the central regions on the planet and later they came in Light Ships. Then the ones in the central regions of the planet (Blue Madras) met the ones on the surface (Helios) and mixed in the Four Corners Area to become collectively known as the Solarians. The Four Corners area is in proximity to Salt Lake City, where they established the first original city (an energy city) and later they developed their Space Needle. That's why there are many records and other artifacts around Salt Lake City where the "New Jerusalem" will eventually be established. Such artifacts include the Ark of the Covenant (now hidden there) and the Crystal Skulls, soon to be reunited as they originally were.

Sandra: Do you have any idea of the timing when the Crystal Skulls will all be in Utah?

Michael: No, but several of them have already been transferred there. It's a transition period right now, as some of the Crystal Skulls are still underneath the Potala in Tibet. Also, the Crystal Skulls that are already in the caverns beneath Salt Lake City are shifting the twelve crystalline Fields of Light toward North America. Ancient grids used to be concentrated in Israel, Egypt, India and Tibet as the left and right side of the planetary crystalline brain. Now this grid system is being shifted to North America where crystal records and Crystal Skulls are. There are crystal records underneath the Potala, and crystal records and Atlantean Temples in the Bermuda Triangle area. The Crystal Skull that you worked with was at one time located in the Yucatan area. There are Lemurian Crystal Temples and records that are hidden at Mt. Shasta. Most of

CHAPTER 5

the crystal records, or a large percentage of them, are in North America right now. So it's only natural that all these crystal artifacts, crystal records and Crystal Skulls are being transferred to North America.

Joshua: It sounds to me, since we last interviewed you, that this is something which developed recently, since you never mentioned that the thirteen skulls in Tibet were being moved to another location on the Earth.

Michael: The Thirteen Crystal Skulls have not always had their central base of operations under the Potala, but indeed always had the ability to move to different areas of the planet. However, they always return to their base or Light Station, which is now being shifted to the Salt Lake City area, to the ancient caverns and Cities of Light established there originally. The Ark of the Covenant was originally transported to the Potala area, then was later moved to the Great Pyramid and now to North America. So the Crystal Skulls are following a similar pattern of being removed from Tibet and brought to North America. Of course, many of the Scriptures of Light (including Crystal Skulls and crystal artifacts) are being moved from Tibet and Egypt to North America. They're all becoming unified now instead of being scattered over the Earth and this will create a greater activation of the planetary crystalline grid. Especially since the Harmonic Convergence, there is an accelerating pace of preparing this new area of programming for the Crystal Skulls as we shift more and more into the fourth and fifth dimensions. So there is a definite need for the feminine ray to be in North America within the heart region of the planetary crystalline grid in the Four Corners area. It's just natural that the feminine ray would be anchored there by The Thirteen Crystal Skulls, since that was the original contact point between the Inner Earth and the Galactic Races. All will be brought together again, since that was their point of origin.

Sandra: Are there any other crystalline objects connected with The Thirteen Crystal Skulls?

Michael: In addition to the crystalline structures (bodies) that are going to be unified with these Crystal Skulls, there are crystal garments and other crystal artifacts (flutes, bells and helmets) that will activate them. [*Sandra:* Masks?] Yes, crystal masks, similar to what are being found in the Yucatan now, possibly made from jade or some other types of metals or crystals, will also activate the skulls.

MICHAEL KANT

Joshua: Many of the ancient crystalline artifacts seem to be coming out now. Is there some kind of projection when mankind will be ready to begin to reuse these tools?

Michael: Well, there are certain individuals ready now to use these crystal artifacts and Crystal Skulls, to activate the knowledge that's stored within them and to activate their energy fields. When you start to activate the energy fields in the crystals, you coordinate with the planetary crystalline grid. The two work together and create more energy and holograms. This will help to accelerate the evolution of the individual working with the crystals as well. There are certain individuals who have worked with these crystals before and they have Light Functions that the crystals actually recognize. There are talking crystals in New Mexico, which one lady found, that were similar to recording crystals and would actually talk to an individual.

Sandra: I get the feeling that three of the skulls that were in Tibet have already been brought to Salt Lake City. [*Michael:* I would say three or four at least, right now.] Whenever I went back to Tibet in regressions, I saw four skulls usually sitting in front of the others and they were the most active, like the controlling ones. So it would make sense that they would be the first moved.

Michael: As grids from Tibet and Israel are transferred to North America, these originating areas are becoming deactivated. The Crystal Skulls, crystal records and artifacts, Buddhist scriptures of Light and other documents of Light are being transferred to North America. As I mentioned before, the Office of the Clarion protects world cultural sites. It's actually a part of the Culture Rama Complex that's under the Grand Canyon, which is a huge underground complex that the Inner Earth people constructed. The Office of the Clarion preserves crystalline artifacts such as Crystal Skulls, Power Rods and the Aquarian Firestones which are coming to light now and being brought to North America. The World Cultural Sites include places such as Stonehenge or the Great Pyramid. Many of the crystal artifacts would be lost because the Dark Forces know about them and they would try to misuse them. In Tibet, the Chinese are aware of some of the Crystal Skulls, but they can't figure out how to gain access to the caverns where the Crystal Skulls are stored, as the Higher Intelligences have them blocked and are in the process of relocating the skulls. They usually move out three at a time, forming a Trinity of Light to

CHAPTER 5

protect themselves, using a pyramid formation. There's at least three Crystal Skulls in Salt Lake City, Utah, now. [*Sandra:* As I see it, one more is on its way.] There would be at least three to go initially and the others will follow suit. Soon the crystal bodies or the biocrystalline structures will be unified there. There are garments and laser rods, as well as headbands and certain jewelry too in Egypt that goes with them. So they're all going to be brought together. [*Jeff:* In physical form?] [*Sandra:* Yes, that is what I saw.] Yes, in energy chambers. An average person wouldn't be able to get to them like in the Halls of Records. If an average person went to the Hall of Records in Egypt, he wouldn't even understand what the records were saying; it is just too advanced for him. Those records will probably also be teleported to North America with additional ones.

Joshua: In our previous interviews, did you say that the crystalline structures or bodies associated with the Crystal Skulls are in some other regions of the galaxy now?

Michael: At one time this was true. Now they're on the planet in various locations. Some are in South America and some are in Tibet. They're scattered around in key areas right now to hold planetary energies. It's not necessary to keep the whole biocrystalline body together just now, but eventually the whole body is going to come together, like the bracelets, helmets and belts that adorn it. These seamless garments are made of crystal, similar to what they use on a spacecraft but slightly different. [*Jeff:* Are these flexible?] They're flexible with a suede-type finish to them. The ones that go with the Crystal Skulls are color-coded. Some are silver, gold, blue or green, depending on the color harmonics of the skull. They will be color-coded, like you used to see on the Egyptian Pharoahs with the red and the black. Especially the red, blue, black and the gold are significant color-coding used with the Crystal Skulls. Black is a key color-code of our lost color spectrum.

MICHAEL KANT

Section 3

Michael's Additional Comments
(After the Interviews)

❑   On the UFO appearing within the Mitchell-Hedges Skull, shown in
Chapter 2:

"You see here a Pleiadian craft/shape. Probably an older ship (about 20,000
years old) because the newer ones have an antenna and a dome on top, rather
than an 'L' shape."

❑   The Mitchell-Hedges Crystal Skull's connection with the Stars:

"The Crystal Skull can also produce certain configurations of stars when you
look at it from a certain angle. It will show the stars that it's been associated
with, such as the Pleiades. ...Originally the Crystal Skull was in the Caracol, a
Mayan observatory also known as the House of the Holy Ones. It was used in
association with star energies which would transmit information to the
Mayans. So, when the star energies hit the Crystal Skull at a certain angle,
these energies will register there. When a person faces a star in a certain way,
it activates energies in his/her biocrystalline system, as well as that of the
Crystal Skull."

❑   Michael described a high mountain he saw in this skull, which he
said was typical of Southern China and Tibet. So the question was:
"Are you saying that this skull was in Tibet?"

"I'm saying that this image shows an association with China or Tibet. Yes,
this one [the Mitchell-Hedges Skull] was in these regions for a while, during
which time it was encoded with certain information from the [original]
Thirteen Crystal Skulls. So these types of skulls did get moved around. Of
course, the Atlantean Priestcraft moved all over the planet to various schools,
to acquire and exchange information with others. They travelled to the
Yucatan, Egypt and Tibet, and were well aware of other high-energy places on
the planet."

❑   How the Mayan Skull was made:

"There are many different possibilities. For example, the Chinese made jade
by constantly grinding it over a long period of time. Jade and quartz are about
the same hardness. It takes a great deal of work, but you can form the most

CHAPTER 5

intricate things from a crystal through a long period of grinding. If one uses a combination of other crystals and water (especially using crystal sand) and you diligently grind for a long period of time, this will bring out the Light Functions. ...Similar to the use of diamond wheels which shape diamonds, one can use quartz sand to grind and shape the skull into the desired form. This is why there aren't any scratches on the skull."

MICHAEL KANT

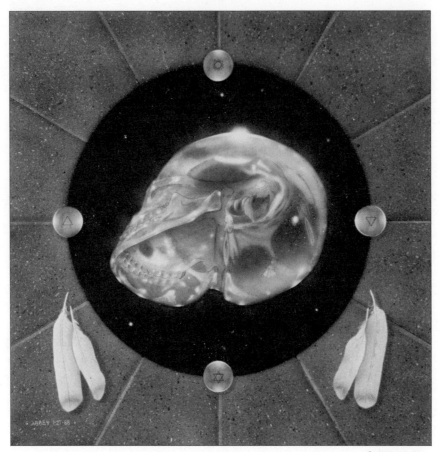

Artist's rendition of the Mitchell-Hedges Skull becoming activated, with holographic images forming inside. This view is from underneath the skull. Here is a portrayal of what happens to the Crystal Skull when a person begins to meditate upon it, similar to the opening of the inner chamber as Sandra discusses in this chapter.

CHAPTER 6

n the first section of this chapter, I would like to share an important message I received from my friends from Space, Akbar and Josephat. After my first UFO contact in 1980 (Chapter 2), I began to receive information from these beings, which I would (inwardly) hear telepathically and transcribe. These messages came in randomly, so Nick suggested that I ask the beings specific questions in order to establish a coherent dialogue. The basic theme of the information given to me dealt with the mission or spiritual work I had agreed to do in relation to the Crystal Skulls. They explained that there was a plan involving many people on Earth, as well as extraterrestrials, to bring all the ancient Crystal Skulls into alignment with thirteen special pyramids. And now I would like to present the message I received on August 19, 1983, dealing with a technique to activate the Mitchell-Hedges Crystal Skull.

Channeled Information Received From Akbar & Josephat

Sandra: I am ready to receive your messages --

Now is the time for us to prepare you for the anxiously awaited presentation. Know that we will guide you every step of the way, just as in the past. This is an eventful time. The momentum is building to a full crescendo. We are going to tell you the code as it is and has functioned for centuries and eons of time.

It is necessary at first to hold the skull in a horizontal position, thus enabling the waterflow[1] to lie along the horizontal axis. This waterflow will set up a current of energy while it will allow the current within the crown of the skull to magnify, amplify and codify. After this beginning preparatory step, place the skull on a blue cloth approximately three feet by five feet. It is not necessary to have any markings on the cloth as with a crystal ball. There are three things to remember:

1) Do not use too much light in the room.

2) Do not use too many people; three will be sufficient.

3) Do not allow any outside sounds to interfere.

Now that the beginning stages have been completed, the skull is ready for complete activation. It is a simple process that has been passed on, generation to generation. Insert into each eye a stone. The blue in the left [eye], the green in the right [eye]. Place the red stone on the Third Eye.

Activation is accomplished by pressing each stone ten times in succession, then releasing to the count of three and pressing again. By repeating this process 6 X 6 (36 times), the formula for activating all thirteen of the skulls will be programmed. We want you to visualize all of the skulls together, and when you are able to achieve this, we will show you in your waking state the future plans for our work to begin.

For now we are asking you to record information on only four major skulls, as it is true that they activate the others. The four major skulls will be

---

[1] Etheric conduits of water which at times can become physical.

CHAPTER 6

in your control within one month's time[2]— an awesome responsibility, but one which you have been prepared for by us. Know that you will contribute greatly to the expansion of mankind and the development of peaceful means of coexistence.

Sandra: What about sounds?

The sound of your own voice is the only one necessary, having been trained many lifetimes. You know the magic chant of humans is OM MANI PAD-ME HUM. Just as Nick uses many chants, not just one, so it is that you can do likewise. Call upon your memory banks. Remember C - A - B are the notes; red, green, blue are the colors, and the cloth must be blue. The moonlight is most effective.

You now know why Selena, bringer of the full moon, is your name. Oh mighty skull, for you I have sacrificed much and the bowels of my life flow, resurged with life when beset upon by thy Light.

Clairvoyant Session About The Crystal Skulls

The following interview was conducted in November, 1987, at the home of Sandra Bowen, in Pinole, California. The interviewers were Jeff Cohen and Joshua Shapiro. Sandra is a 'conscious channel' who retains her own awareness and repeats the information which she inwardly hears in response to the questioning. In this session, Sandra is receiving information from those who she calls "The Gold Beings," in conjunction with her own perspectives as well.

Jeff: Who are the Gold Beings?

Sandra: The Gold Beings work with the Archangels, and they are close to the Source [GOD]. They are as close to the Source as the Archangels are. And there are so many that we cannot begin to count them. But the beauty is that they have a knowledge of what it is to live on the Earth because they have had so many Earth lives. They have progressed and developed enough spiritually to be very close to the Source.

---

[2]-Note: These Space Beings have very little sense of Earth time, so one month to them could be years for us.

Jeff: Why are the Gold Beings here, around the Earth and around individuals?

Sandra: They need to be here now. They have worked with certain people, but now they must be more direct. They need to be close to these people, to be around them and guide them because this information must come out so that we can understand what it means to know the Source, since we have forgotten. They also want to explain the universe to people, the order of the universe and how it works, as well as talk about the different types of beings, because these beings are our brothers and sisters. So they are here to facilitate all of this.

Jeff: Are there several individuals or groups who have had contact with the Gold Beings or written about them?

Sandra: There are people all over the world who have had contact and there will be a time when those people will come together, because they will find that they are doing very similar work.

Jeff: Moving into the area of Crystal Skulls, can you tell us what is their purpose?

Sandra: The Crystal Skulls are intergalactic communication devices which have been placed on the Earth to await a period of time when the proper people, who have made commitments to work with these particular skulls, are available to activate them through different methods. The protectors/keepers of the skulls will move them to different locations and leave them there to balance the Earth's energies.

Joshua: What is the purpose of activating the Crystal Skulls?

Sandra: The purpose of their activation is to retrieve the information which is encoded within the skulls and also to send out laser beams which interact with people who have a connection with the skulls. This applies not only for people who are in close vicinity to the skulls, but also for those who are at a great distance as well.

Joshua: Does an individual have to go to a particular skull to activate it? Couldn't the Space Beings just activate the skulls at their whim?

Sandra: No, there was an agreement made that it would be necessary for humans to interact with the Crystal Skulls in order to activate them, and this is part of Universal Law.

CHAPTER 6

Joshua: What happens if the particular individual who is supposed to recharge and activate the skull forgets his/her mission, fails, dies accidentally or can't do this?

Sandra: There would immediately be another to take that person's place.

Jeff: Will you give a history of the Mitchell-Hedges Skull?

Sandra: Before I begin to discuss the Mitchell-Hedges Skull, I need to give some background information. The concept for the crystallization of the skulls was conceived by the Council of Twenty-six.[3] And when this council discussed how they were going to preserve knowledge, they knew that within the bones of the human body, knowledge can be stored. They also knew that the people who had an understanding of the value of bone in any form would protect these bones. The stories and knowledge of certain ancestral bones, Crystal Skulls, tablets and so forth which are part of Earth cultures, have been orally passed down from generation to generation. And at that time it was decided which objects would be crystallized and which would not.

In the case of the Mitchell-Hedges Skull, it was the crystallization of Sha-tree-tra's skull, a high priestess in Atlantis. She had a community or group of people who looked to her for guidance. She was respected and responsible for many thousands of men and women. Therefore, when she died there were seven Priests who had to form a special pattern (similar to a star pattern) around her skull. With the help of the Space Beings, using the power of their minds and laser beams emanating from their eyes, they were able to crystallize her skull. Now, this is something that the Space Beings had been doing and teaching the Atlanteans for many centuries. Sha-Tree-Tra wasn't one of the first people to have her skull changed to crystal by this process.

Joshua: What happened to the rest of her body?

Sandra: It was also crystallized and placed in different locations, but still near the site of the skull. There will be a time when those parts will be discovered by people who will be guided to go there and find them.

Joshua: Briefly discuss the movement of the Crystal Skull from its origin, until it was found in this century.

---

[3] The Council of Twenty-six is a group of celestial, spiritual beings who exist on a very high vibrational level. They have never had earthly lives and are involved in the spiritual evolution of various solar systems.

Sandra: After Sha-tree-tra's skull was transformed into crystal, she spent a fairly long period of time in Egypt. She was transported there by the Space Beings, and then was taken to the Mayans. She is one skull that has not traveled to too many places on the Earth, until recently. She would travel dimensionally , or in other words, the crystal form of her skull would go into a dimension where beings continued to work with her. That's why this particular skull is a trigger for all of the other Crystal Skulls. The codes that people have inwardly received, when there is an opportunity to utilize them, are going to activate all of the other skulls.

After spending three weeks in Canada with the Mitchell-Hedges Skull, the spirit of Sha-tree-tra has been in constant communication with me. I inwardly see her as being very beautiful, with long dark hair, and about 5' 4" tall. She usually is wearing what appears to be Mayan clothing with a rather large feathered headdress. I also see an electric blue aura around her.

Joshua: What does this Crystal Skull have to do with the ones in Tibet?

Sandra: She is more of an Earth representative rather than the etheric form of the skulls in Tibet.

Joshua: In one of your regressions you felt that the Mitchell-Hedges Skull was in Tibet at one time. Would you comment on this?

Sandra: No, the Mitchell-Hedges Skull was not in Tibet, but it has a direct link to the skulls in Tibet. It is like a sister to the skulls in Tibet-- in the sense of Universal Sisterhood, and is definitely programmed with those skulls.

Joshua: Can you explain why Michael Kant saw scenes of Tibet in the Mitchell-Hedges Skull?

Sandra: When you work with the Mitchell-Hedges Skull, you are working with all the other Crystal Skulls because they are directly linked, and it is as though you are activating and accessing all of the skulls in Tibet.

Joshua: One day in November of 1985, while the research team was in Canada working with the Mitchell-Hedges Skull, I experienced a great deal of powerful energy which was overwhelming and almost knocked me out. What was occurring on that day?

Sandra: On that day, my energy activated a section of the skull that is called a secret chamber. My energy was raised by the Gold Beings. So when I tapped

CHAPTER 6

into this section of the skull, there was a surge of golden light. The chamber that opened within the skull was one that had been dormant for some time.

Joshua: So why would this affect other people?

Sandra: Because within that chamber is a vibration that is directly related to the Gold Beings. The Gold Beings are the main ray or the main group which has made a commitment to work with people here on the Earth to get out the information about the Crystal Skulls.

Joshua: But at that particular point, we were not aware of the Gold Beings.

Sandra: They were not in the picture, no. They were there in terms of just the gold color emanating from the Crystal Skull, which not everybody can see; only trained people can see it. This is similar to seeing an aura.

Joshua: I felt that there were many Crystal Skulls besides the Mitchell-Hedges Skull involved in this energy release. Why would other Crystal Skulls be involved?

Sandra: As I said previously, it was the planned time. When this particular section was opened, a link-up occurred with all the other Crystal Skulls. It was similar to a communication system which informed other people that it was time for connection. Even people that are not involved in working with the skulls, knew that something happened to them in their personal lives. Whether it was a dream or some kind of physical sensation or knowingness, they all had changes at that time. If they think back to that time period [early November, 1985], they will be aware of it.

Joshua: Was it just your energy that activated the secret chamber or did it involve the energy of the entire group in Canada?

Sandra: Well, at that particular time it was my energy, because this is an agreement that I made. Prior to that time, my body had been prepared for this particular event to occur. It's a commitment I made that I would do this. And so this particular reactivation of the skull was something that happened just between Sha-tree-tra and myself.

Jeff: Are there any other skulls which are on the Earth, that are like the Mitchell-Hedges Skull or the Rose Quartz Skull, in terms of being human-like in their proportions and having a detachable jaw?

SANDRA BOWEN

Sandra: There are thirty-six that are of different colors. They are clear, pure, radiant and placed all over the world in triads or groups of three.

Joshua: Is there a focal point where the energy of these thirty-six skulls merge together?

Sandra: Yes, the culmination of their combined energy meets in a pyramid in the etheric planes over Tibet.

Joshua: Is this position being shifted now?

Sandra: Tibet will always be a powerful vortex area, but because of world events, Earth changes and people that are going to be working with the Crystal Skulls, the skulls are being slowly moved over to what we would call the Four Corners Area. The fourth Crystal Skull of the original thirteen is there now. They will continue to bring three at a time until all the skulls are there. They will be there within a six month period of time from now. That is why the people who are going to be working with them have found that their lives have speeded up. Not only this, but it has been difficult for many of them, because in order to work with a Crystal Skull it is very important that the person go through bodily or vibrational changes. The Four Corners area is where the research will take place, and each individual must be able to deal with the vibration of this geographic region. As the Crystal Skulls are being moved, they become formless as they go into the higher vibrational dimensions, so they are not physical. They are thoughts in the Guardians' minds. But then when they get to their destination, they will again take on a physical form and that's where we will be working with them.

Joshua: Getting back to the Gold Beings, how can such advanced beings communicate with us directly without causing mental and physical disruption?

Sandra: The people that are in communication with the Gold Beings, have undergone (or are undergoing) a process which turns their etheric body into crystal. This has altered their molecular structure, resulting in a vibrational change which facilitates communication with the Gold Beings. The process does take time and isn't always easy, but once it's completed, then that particular person can communicate with no problems. This process is something that the Gold Beings don't necessarily prepare a person for; other beings do this with the person. But after the process is completed, the communication is easy, very easy indeed. Whenever the Gold Beings are present, the White Light is always there to protect as well. It's like the Gold Beings and the White Light work hand in hand. So if you are aware of a person who is communicating with the Gold Beings, you will see (if you have that gift of clairvoyance) that that person has had their entire sub-atomic structure changed and is different from other people. It comes from the inside out, and not only are the cells changed but there is a thin layer of crystal covering the entire body. It is like a crystal sheath. The entire body changes, and the brain in particular, because it is the most important organ. The brain becomes very similar to the Crystal Skull. This is necessary in order for that person to access the skulls.

Joshua: If such a person had their molecular structure changed to crystal, then wouldn't there be the possibility that this person would no longer be able to exist on our physical level at the octave at which the Earth is vibrating? Wouldn't that person disappear and move into another dimension?

Sandra: If they choose to do this, they could, yes. But the people to whom this process has occurred or is occurring to, usually have a very strong commitment to do what they came to the Earth to fulfill. They made an agreement and they are very dedicated.

My own experiences during this process have been very physical: a ringing in my ears, the feeling that time is either too slow or too fast, many aches and pains throughout my body and tremendous confusion. Knowing that this process was occurring and receiving information from the Beings every step of the way helped me to get through this time period more easily.

Jeff: Is there a connection between the Crystal Skulls and the Inner Earth?

Sandra: The Crystal Skulls within the Inner Earth, besides being there to balance the Earth, represent each Inner Earth tribe. They are also used for communication by all the tribes. The Inner Earth Beings at this time are very excited that the shifting of the Earth's vibration toward Light and Love is going to allow them to come out and tell about what is occurring in their world. They have been waiting [a long time to do so]. Their purpose is to assist us in not destroying their home. The positive Inner Earth Beings are very loving and happy with their home, so they don't want it destroyed. Every Crystal Skull that is with each tribe has its history, but it also has a function. That will be known only when the right people that are supposed to find these skulls are allowed to enter the Inner Earth by the Inner Earth Beings. Such individuals will be able to work with that particular skull.

Jeff: Is there a connection between the Crystal Skulls and Extraterrestrials?

Sandra: It's the same as the connection between the Crystal Skulls and the Inner Earth Beings. You cannot separate the Inner Earth Beings from the other planetary beings. They are all following Universal Law. And there is a plan so that they all work together and know what they're supposed to do.

Jeff: What is the significance of the state of Utah as related to the Aquarian Age?

Sandra: This is considered sacred land, and that is because the Inner Earth Beings all gather there. They have always converged there since the Earth was created. This is where a great gathering of selected representatives of the Inner Earth Tribes will occur. And so the residents that have been living in that area have a knowledge of the Inner Earth Beings and of the Space Beings. All of their knowledge collectively has been preserved there. It is a sacred blessed land where people whose mission is to reactivate knowledge stored within artifacts such as crystals, Crystal Skulls, metal tablets, bones and stones, will be drawn to relocate.

CHAPTER 6

Dolphins swimming around one of many Crystal Skulls theorized to be buried or submerged in the ocean. As psychic as dolphins are, could they be in telepathic communication with some of the Crystal Skulls?

Neville Rowe, ME, CH, is an Electrical Engineer who has been involved in the spiritual growth movement for over fifteen years. An experienced channel and psychic teacher, Neville regularly channels *Soli* (an expression of a group of entities working together to oversee the evolution of the Earth and the Solar System, assisting and guiding those who are working in the light) and the *Dolphins* (our aquatic mammalian friends who send us love and light to help rebalance the planet's energies and assist us in returning to the Divine Plan for spiritual unfoldment) for *Spirit Speaks* and *Body, Mind & Spirit*. Neville has over five years experience as a past-life regressionist and offers intensive workshops which help many to become open channels to their Higher Selves/spirit guides/teachers. He also has appeared on radio and TV.

Channeling the Dolphins

The following interview was conducted with Neville Rowe in October, 1987, at the Whole Life Expo in Los Angeles, California. Neville was asked to channel the dolphins, but prior to his self-induced trance state, we asked him some questions about his background. The interviewers were Sandra Bowen, Jeff Cohen, Nathaniel Pirolo, Joshua Shapiro, Janine Smith and Paula Strausser.

Joshua: When did you start channeling the Dolphins?

Neville: That was two years ago. I was down at Sea World in San Diego watching the giant Orcas going through their circus tricks with the humans. And I wondered if the humans knew what was going on. I think perhaps they do to some level, but it also occurred to me that creatures of that intelligence and size weren't there accidentally. You can't tell me that somebody goes out on a boat and 'accidentally' captures two creatures like that. They had to have volunteered to live the rest of their lives in that tiny pool. And so I just sent them a telepathic thought from my heart and mind, 'Thank you for being here in service and allowing us to have this inter-species communication in this way.' And I had this overwhelming feeling of acknowledgment come back, just a wash of love. It was an amazing feeling.

It was about a month later that some friends of mine and I were in a house down in Corona del Mar, California. They'd been out to sea on a boat to visit with the dolphins. There had been so many people on the boat and lots of dolphins around, that not much was accomplished. So they were talking about going out again with a small group to get a focused energy, and it came to me then that you don't have to go out to sea to talk with the dolphins, we could do it right there. So I said, "Let's try it." We sat down in meditation. I went into trance like I normally do, except this time I said, "Hey, dolphins! If there are any of you around who want to come through, please do." Before very long, I found my body turning into a dolphin. My knees came together, I felt solid from the waist down, this muscular movement ran through my body, and my breathing was very deep and heavy. That first time they just gasped out a few words about how different human breathing was from dolphin

CHAPTER 7

breathing because they breathe voluntarily. They hold their breath underwater and they gasp a breath when they come to the surface. And that was about it for the first time.

In the next session they were much more fluent. Ever since then they've been speaking. About the fourth session, on the intake of breath they used my nasal passages to make the dolphin sounds, the squeaks and what have you, and they do that every time now. Then they go into English and they speak just like any other channeling session, except the muscular movement is still going through my body and I still feel like a dolphin.

Joshua: Have they told you how long they've been on this planet?

Neville: No. The messages the whales and dolphins bring through me try to get us out of thinking so technically and genetically. It doesn't matter how long the genetic form has been on Earth. It's totally irrelevant to what we're doing here. They try to get us to think in terms of who we are as spiritual beings and where we have been. We've been *all* over the universe, we just happen to be in human form now and they just happen to be in dolphin form now. Now, I specialize in past-life regression. I've taken people back to lifetimes on all kinds of planets, all kinds of experiences. And you get beyond even bothering about where the human body or the dolphin body came from. What does it matter? What matters is what we are now doing with our spiritual lives. When the dolphins speak through me, that is the primary focus: *the message.* "What are we doing with ourselves as spiritual beings?"

Joshua: When the dolphins speak through you, is it a particular dolphin who's doing so, or is it the collective consciousness of dolphins on the planet?

Neville: They [the dolphins] say it's a group of them, five or six of them, who are in physical form. And it varies; four is the minimum, seven is the most so far. One time somebody asked them and they said, "It's rather like many, many dolphins are listening in and everybody's sitting around the radio and listening to the conversation, but five or six of us have the microphone, we do the talking." They use the analogy of the radio quite a lot because it's like telepathic communication.

When I channel, I'm communicating through the energy of the Higher Self. The other entities that come in are imposing their vibrations, obviously with permission of the Higher Self, and that vibration is impressed onto my subconscious mind and my subconscious translates it into English. Obviously,

NEVILLE ROWE

the dolphins don't speak the English language. My spirit teacher, Soli, doesn't speak the English language. He's never physically been on the Earth and never intends to be. So, the communication is the vibration being translated into English by my mind. Therefore, you hear my speech pattern, you hear my phraseology and vocabulary whether I'm channeling Soli or the dolphins. The information that comes through is very similar in both cases. Soli is around when the dolphins are channeling through. Sometimes people have asked questions that the dolphins can't answer, and they will leave temporarily and Soli will come through to answer, then the dolphins will come back. Sometimes it's such a blend that you can't tell the difference one from the other. When people ask personal questions of the dolphins, the dolphins contact spirit guides and teachers and relay information.

(Neville goes into a type of trance state, the Dolphin energies settle in, and the channeling begins...)

Dolphins: We are Kajuba. Welcome, dear friends. It is our great pleasure to be able to share this time and this space with you, to be a part of your vibration. My dear friends, it is most important to recognize at the outset that we are one, that you are us and we are you. That within human form you see your separation, your individuality. Your subconscious minds as human beings are focused constantly on how different you are from all your brothers and sisters around you, how different you are from all the other life forms and species on the world with you. We will ask you, my friends, to begin to look at the similarities, to begin to see the oneness, to recognize what has been, is and always will be true-- that you are God, that we are God, that the tiniest speck of dust upon your Earth is God and that all is God. All is created by thought within the infinite Living Spirit. You are part of that thought and your thoughts created the reality around you. To recognize ultimately, my friends, that there is no such thing as Truth. To recognize that there is no such thing as history. That you will hear from many different spirit teachers many different interpretations of what occurred in history. Why? Because history exists in probability just as the future exists within probability.

Within your subconscious minds you have solidly placed that belief in past, present and future, the belief in time and space. You believe that everything that happened in the past is cast in concrete, it was 'that' way. You believe that the future is ephemeral, that it is probability that has not occurred yet. But, my friends, time does not exist. Everything that has been *is* and always

CHAPTER 7

will be. It simply *is*. But not *is* in fixed form, it *is* in probability. And this is difficult for the human mind to grasp because you deal so much within your subconscious with time and space. The past is probability. You can see many different parallel pasts just as you can look into your probable futures and see many different probable futures.

When you look into your future, my friends, when you make a choice within your lives about something that is going to happen, you might look upon it with the analogy of a path that is dividing into two and you must make the choice which path you're going to go down. Do you choose the right-hand path or the left-hand path? You, within your conscious decision, choose to go down the right-hand path, but in going down that right-hand path all you are doing is focusing your consciousness into that particular path. What you see around you is what you think is reality. What you don't recognize is that the left-hand path still exists. Just because you choose to not focus your consciousness upon that at that time does not mean that it does not exist. Both paths exist. Every time you make a choice within your lives there is, in a sense, another aspect of yourself experiencing the other aspect of that choice.

Similarly, my friends, you're going to find that the past history of events is subject to individual interpretation. If you would look at six individuals observing on a street corner what you would call a motor accident (actually there are no such things as accidents, but you label them so) and then you take those six individuals into your court of justice and you have each one become a witness, there may be six different events spoken of that day. And each will be real for the individuals concerned. So it is when you look into the collective unconscious regarding history. There are individual interpretations within that consciousness. And there are parallel probabilities. There can be a large group of individuals who experience one probability upon the Earth while another group of individuals is experiencing another probability. Therefore, you will find many different interpretations and understandings of what has occurred upon the Earth's surface.

There are parallel dimensions existing around you now. And if one of those entities [in a parallel dimension] chose to currently incarnate within human form, and you were to take a past life regression on that individual currently in human form, they would experience a life that they knew was on Earth but which would be totally unlike anything else that you have experienced or any other individual has experienced. There are indeed many probability patterns. It is therefore difficult when you are dealing with history, to get a coherent picture. This is why it is easier to deal with the history of yesterday, the year before, or ten years ago, than it is ten thousand years ago, let alone ten million. The further back you go, the more you compound your probabilities and the differences in the infinite possibilities of experience in the past, just as you have infinite possibilities of experience in the future. Historians write what they believe happened. But every story of history is an individual interpretation through the subconscious mind of the individual writing it. This is why a book such as your Bible has been interpreted and misinterpreted, rewritten and retranslated, and changed time and time again until it bears very little resemblance to the events that prompted the writings in the first place. There were many different interpretations as to what happened.

There are many past probabilities of what happened in those events. Not to say that your labors are wasted; of course not, they have great value. There is much that has a common thread, a common theme which can be brought forward to help humanity understand itself a little better at this time. But we would ask you, my friends, to focus your endeavors on those things that will allow humanity to understand itself. Understand that you are not your genetic physical bodies. These bodies which you inhabit are but vehicles that you have chosen to use this one time around upon the Earth. You have chosen a Ford, my friends, and we have chosen a Chevrolet. It is no different than that. You have chosen to be in human form, we have chosen to be in dolphin form. It does not make us better than you. Many of us have had human lives, many of you have had dolphin lives. You have had lifetimes, as have we, in many different planes and dimensions of time and space and planets all over the universe, seen and unseen. You are universal energies, my friends. You are infinite, immortal, eternal, and universal. You are not who you think you are. You are not your physical, emotional, and mental bodies. You are Spirit, Infinite Living Spirit. And as Infinite Living Spirit, you can choose to play anywhere within your own creation. For you are the creator and the creation both, and there is no separation. When we speak of 'you' we must include 'us.' It is *we*, my friends, all of us. All that is, *is* the creator and the creation.

It is important to begin to recognize your spiritual beingness, my friends, to recognize your universality, to recognize that you are not who you think you are within your individual lives. You are beings of light and power. But being within human forms with the intellectual and subconscious belief systems of limitation, of lack, of individuality, you are always willing and ready to give your power away to those that you think of as being higher than you. But, my

CHAPTER 7

friends, there is none higher than you. No part of God is higher than another part of God. You are the infinite living spirit. Your highest teacher lives within you, it is your own Higher Self. Your Higher Self *is* your highest teacher. No one knows better what is right for you than your own Higher Self. There is *no one* higher than you, my friends. Your subconscious mind judges constantly-- Is it good? Is it bad? Is it right? Is it wrong? Is it positive? Is it negative? It constantly judges according to arbitrary standards-- you take this into absolutely every aspect of existence. You judge yourselves in position, in place within your world, in your hierarchies. Is someone higher than me? Is someone lower then me? You take that out from beyond the world and say, 'Is this spirit higher or lower than this spirit?' No, my friends, they are not higher or lower than you, they are just different. They are different experiences.

We are not better or worse than you, it is just a different experience. It is true, of course, that there are entities that have greater understanding, greater awareness perhaps, standing a little bit higher up on the mountain so that they can see a little bit farther over the valley than you can. And so you listen to them and what they are saying. But you still must make what you hear yours, else it has no meaning to you. You are learning to take your powers back and not give them away to us, to spirit guides, to anyone. You are learning to rediscover who you truly are, to discover that you are spirit, to rediscover and remember that you are infinite, universal. My dear friends, would you have questions for us?

Joshua: We would like to explore information the dolphins have related to what mankind is calling the Crystal Skulls. Do you understand this term?

Dolphins: Indeed. Yes, again, speaking of probabilities in the past, you're going to hear many different interpretations of these. And in truth there are many different skulls and vibrational levels. Many of these skulls are not of your vibrational level or dimension. But over the centuries, over thousands of years, they have slowly lost their vibrational energy, and that has lowered their frequency so that they have come into manifestation into your physical world. They were in parallel dimensions to your world and have now come into your frequency. There are many that you have not yet discovered, but will be discovering. Not only Crystal Skulls, my friends, but crystal artifacts of many kinds. Let us speak a little of crystal in general before we speak of the skulls in particular.

Understand, it is no accident that you have such an interest in crystal at this time. You have used crystal in Atlantis, Lemuria and other similar civilizations that you lump all together, thinking of them as being Atlantis. Let's look at Atlantis especially. It was a civilization of great technological achievement, much more so than you have in Earth at this time. And there was a great use of crystal. But it was also a civilization very similar to your civilization of this time in that the powers that you had, your technologies, your use of crystal was for personal gain and aggrandizement, for competition, for getting one over your neighbor, brother or sister. In other words, an intense feeling again of individuality, of isolation and of lack. You used crystal in this way, and ultimately the civilization was destroyed because of the energy of the motivation for its use (obviously not the crystal itself, for crystal is an objective amplifier). Crystal does not destroy in and of itself, it simply amplifies thought, positive or negative.

There were those within that civilization who could see what was going to happen and were trying to prevent it. There were those who didn't want to see what was going to happen and didn't try to prevent it, for they were having too much fun using its powers. Understand, my dear friends, that there is no judgment associated with this. There is no judgment associated with anything on the earth plane. Nothing is ever 'wrong' with the Earth. The Earth is an experience like any other experience within the universe. And you as a spiritual being choose in free will to be upon the Earth and have those experiences. It is your subconscious minds and ego personalities that choose to judge the experiences as positive or negative. We are not judging.

Many of us were in Atlantis in dolphin form at the same time that you were. There was much communication between dolphin and human. There were places where we communicated telepathically, meeting places where we would come together and have much contact. We saw the possible changes and communicated them to humans. Understand, my friends, that at that time as of now, many who were in human form had had lifetimes as dolphins and vise-versa. You have had numerous lives in Atlantis as dolphins or humans. (You can choose to be a saint in one lifetime and a sinner in the next. There are no judgments. You can choose to be whatever you wish throughout the universe.) But those of you who were in Atlantis at that time foresaw what was going to happen. You had great power of foreseeing; you could see into your future lives. You saw the lives that you are [living] now. You are in Atlantis, for Atlantis still exists since time does not exist. The being that you

CHAPTER 7

are in Atlantis is communicating with you now. Some of those beings are your guides right now. Some of your *future* lives are your guides.

But at that time, having the power to see forward into present time, you very carefully set up experiences for yourselves lifetime after lifetime, culminating in this particular time and space right here and now upon Earth. Why? Because when you left that physical body, you had much judgment upon yourselves. It is difficult to see how these things interrelate, my friends, when you think in linear time. You will just have to take the words as we speak them. But when you left those physical bodies, you had much judgment of self. It is important to realize that when you go through that process you call death, no one judges you. There is no God or committee sitting in judgment. The only judge of you is *you*. From the ego personalities that you have and the beliefs that you have when you make that transition, you judge yourself. Many of you judge yourselves very harshly. Some for not having done enough to prevent the changes. Some for having been blind enough to allow the changes to take place.

Whatever the reason, you judged yourselves. You decided that you were going to come back here and now in a very similar energy, a very similar vibration on Earth at this time, to *get it right* in your terms, not from a spiritual perspective, but in your terms as human beings. So, many of you are back here right now in a very similar vibration, also again finding yourselves being caught up in the possibilities of crystal. Some are being tempted to misuse it again. But you did one thing for yourselves, my friends; you made sure that the crystal that you use at this particular time right here and now would not have the power that it did in Atlantis. You have defused its energy in many ways for the time being, but it will come back. You made absolutely certain that this time around, you would not be tempted to misuse your powers as you did before.

Many of you, my friends, have set up around the Earth, Time-Space Interdimensional locks so that at the right time you will rediscover them. Within those Time and Space locks you will find crystal artifacts. You will find machinery and libraries of information. You will find treasures beyond your imagination at this time in your current personalities. But you put them there, my friends, and you will find them when you feel the time is right. You set this up very carefully so that you would not be able to rediscover these things until you could use them in a responsible manner. You set up patterns of lifetimes culminating at this point so that you would be a part of this vibration of change upon the Earth. One of the reasons you are feeling so much anxiety, many of you, is because you can feel the changes coming. They are coming so close that you can almost touch them, but they are not close enough and there is frustration because you want them now. Be patient, my friends, for you are working as you chose to and as you set things up for yourselves.

Now, more specifically, the Crystal Skulls. Understand that the cranium, the shape of the head that contains the brain has, of course, its own physical function and form. When you designed the human body-- and of course *you* designed it otherwise you wouldn't be living in it-- you set up its function very carefully. The shape of its bones, the shape of its structure. It is far too much to go into every detail of every aspect of the physical body, but you believe that you live within your head. You believe that your subconscious and your personality and your ego lives within the head. It is not true. The brain is, of course, an important aspect of the body, and it is the seat of consciousness perhaps, the central communications center, but it is *not* the be-all and end-all of your being. Your subconscious mind exists throughout the whole of the body, throughout the whole of the nervous system. The brain has its memory devices, yes, it is your repository of information, but it does not exist in isolation from the rest of the body.

You are aware of the energy centers in the body and their interconnections. Physically the brain has that function of being the center of control. The head is designed to protect and house the brain and some of the major sensory inputs such as sound, sight, taste and smell. You feel that the head is an extremely important part of your bodies. The shape of the head therefore has a great significance. What better way to put power into a crystal than to shape that crystal in the form of the most powerful aspect of yourselves! It is a little bit of anthropomorphism, that you are seeing the crystal in the form of the human head. It is not important ultimately what form you choose to make a crystal. You can have a crystal any shape you wish, but if you believe it has power, then it has power. Those who formed crystals into human skulls believed that they were putting much greater power into the crystal by so doing. And because they believed that, they did it. So the form of the crystal head has much power within it, much power of computation in the sense of the brain as being a computer.

Your computers work in the same way that your brains do. It's no accident, of course. They use similar electromagnetic structures, much more grossly

CHAPTER 7

than the human brain or any other physical brain on Earth, but nonetheless, a similar kind of structure. And the crystals that were formed into the human skull were given that kind of structure within them by thought, by empowering them. There have been crystals formed in many different ways, some by laser at the time of Atlantis and Lemuria. However, there have been times in the Mayan civilization, for example, when seemingly one Crystal Skull, not currently in circulation yet, was formed by a number of temple maidens (virgins) rubbing the crystal by hand with cloth for several hundred years, day in and day out to get it into its form. In doing so, imagine the power that is put into such a thing. You see, it is most important to recognize that no crystal has power in and of itself. Crystal is an objective amplifier. It has power only because a human being or some other entity has put power into it, by storing its thought in that crystal and programming it. The *belief* in creating such a device stores the energy within it. Further questions, my friend.

Joshua: Are you familiar with the skull that is known to humans as the Mitchell-Hedges Crystal Skull?

Dolphins: We are familiar with it through the subconscious mind of this channel. We pick up the vibration and understand that which you are speaking of, yes.

Joshua: Do you know or have any information about how it was formed or where it came from?

Dolphins: It was formed in the Mayan civilization time, seemingly. This is the information we are bringing forth. Understand that the Mayan civilization was one of great knowledge and technological powers as well. The Mayan civilization had much contact with your off-planet brothers and sisters and their technology. In fact, there were individuals from off-planet who were existing within that civilization. Some were influencing by their thoughtforms from off-planet, some were physically manifested on the planet at the time. And, of course, the same is true now, my friends; for there are many of your off-planet brothers and sisters walking around you right now, some seen and some unseen. But at that time, there was much more interaction, we might say interference, from your off-planet brothers and sisters; literally interfering with the human form, genetically experimenting with it, working with it, just as you farm your animals.

The off-planet beings brought sophisticated technology, and one of their devices was used to create that particular skull. Understand that in the civilization at that time, there was much awe among the local population for the off-planet brothers and sisters who were working with them. They were held in awe and in great fear. And so many of the technological devices were similarly held in awe and fear. That particular skull was used as a device to control. It was created and was programmed as an instrument not to control negatively, but certainly to hold the population in greater awe and fear. It is important to recognize that when we say this, it is not that there was a negative vibration put into it, but that it was used for that purpose. It was a powerful object, a powerful symbol and talisman.

When the off-planet brothers and sisters withdrew, they took most of their technology with them; not all, some of it still exists there and will be ultimately found within that area, but most of it was taken with them. The skull was left behind as a reminder. It became an object of worship by the populace that remained. It became a communications device between the population left behind and those that had been there, a telepathic terminal, as it were. Over the centuries it was so used, and gained and stored a tremendous amount of knowledge. This included information about this prior civilization at the time and the guidance of those who had left the people behind, for they were not entirely negative, although many of their practices today would be seen to be negative. They became somewhat more benign. Many individuals who were around at the Mayan civilization had great guilt about what they had done to the local population. And when they left, they chose to work in a far more benign manner. So, much of the information stored within that head is from that time. Much of it, my friends, is not to be understood right now.

Some of the information within that skull would be dangerous to you, were you to pull it right out. It has been set up in such a way that you cannot do that. There have been safeguards placed within it. It is similar to your computers which have many different storage locations. Some of those storage locations can be accessed by the simplest programs. Some of these databanks are so well-guarded that only the most complex, most responsible programs can access them. So it is within that skull. There's information that you *are* bringing out and *will* bring out that will be of great value to you to begin with. And as you begin to recognize your responsibility to yourselves and for your use of energy, and as you begin to recognize and remember who

CHAPTER 7

you have been and how you have used energy and crystal power before, you will begin to find that more aspects of that information will come forward. There is much within it that is not right for the present time and it will come out in its own time, just as we spoke before of you having set up your time and space interlocks so that you would only rediscover your libraries of information (much of it stored within crystal) at the appropriate times. Similarly within the skull. There is much to be discovered within it, my friends, and you will discover it. There are six others [Crystal Skulls] directly associated with that skull [the Mitchell-Hedges]. Seemingly, three are currently known; three have not yet been discovered and will be rediscovered within the not too distant future. That particular skull of which you speak will tell ultimately where the others are, for it now wants to be re-united with those other skulls. And as those others come forward, one by one, they will be joined together in communion.

Joshua: Can you tell us, of the three that are known, what might they be called and where are they situated?

Dolphins: One is held by an individual who does not let it be known to anyone. He is an individual who has great knowledge and great power, who has it in safekeeping. It is in Germany-- no more clues than that my friends, for it will come in due course. Two others seemingly are seen and known, without their power being known so much perhaps. They are seen to be less powerful; they will be reactivated in due course.

Jeff: Can you describe the process in terms we might understand about how the Mitchell-Hedges Crystal Skull was created by the extraterrestrials?

Dolphins: They used the power of the sun focused in a ray of high intensity, or should we say, of high temperature, to melt very precisely. The device centering that ray of sunlight on the block of quartz worked on it to form the skull. It was done slowly over a long period of time so that the individuals around could come and view the changes day by day. So a little was melted off here, a little there. It involved very precise computer-controlled location of that high-temperature focusing of the sun's rays. It was done in itself as a show, a piece of theater for the individuals around.

Joshua: We have noticed that the Mitchell-Hedges Skull, seems to have more of a calming or healing effect than some of the other skulls. It has not been tampered with as much as some of the other Crystal Skulls.

NEVILLE ROWE

Dolphins: This is true; it is an aspect of what we said before-- that it was used for so long after the entities left. It was not always that way. In its beginnings it was used in a more controlling way. Had you felt it in its earliest times, you would have felt its control; you would have felt constrained to act in a certain way and to do certain things. It was really a way of controlling the population. But as time passed, it was used more as an object of worship by the individuals left behind on Earth than by those who had gone. It was used by them in a more benign way to bring through great understanding and knowledge. This Crystal Skull acquired a much softer vibration of love, understanding and wisdom that the off-planet entities helped to bring back to those left on Earth. So it has acquired that vibration, which you feel today. It has been hidden for so long from human contact, that it has not picked up the vibrations of humans. Understand, my friends, that crystal picks up any vibration that is around it; some resist more than others of course. One of the aspects of the shape of the human skull is that your head shape resists vibrations coming into it to a certain extent. So the shape of the Crystal Skull resists some programming coming into it. Nonetheless, if it is left around in human contact for a long time, it will still pick up the vibration of everything that is around it-- positive and negative. As we've said so many times, crystal in and of itself is objective; it does not know positivity or negativity. It depends on what is programmed into it.

Joshua: Were there any Crystal Skulls in Atlantis? The Mayan civilization was after Atlantis, as I understand it.

Dolphins: Yes that's true. There were, but they were rather more as ornaments. At that time the actual artifact or the shape of the skull was not seen to be so important, for crystal was common and was used in many different shapes and sizes. So yes, there were Crystal Skulls and some of them were programmed, and some of them will be found, but they were not seen to be so important.

Sandra: Are you familiar with that area on the Earth known as Tibet? And if so, is there some kind of connection with Crystal Skulls there?

Dolphins: Seemingly... not likely to be found within this current period of time, this current cataclysmic period. There is a connection there but it is very remote, from what we are being shown. There may be others who have greater information on this, but our sources are saying that this is very remote.

CHAPTER 7

Joshua: By remote, do you mean that if there were such objects they would be totally hidden?

Dolphins: Yes indeed.

Joshua: Are the dolphins involved in any way in looking after or protecting Crystal Skulls that are yet unknown?

Dolphins: It would not be true to say that we are trying to protect; the skulls protect themselves and you have protected them. You have set up the energy fields. Again, we must remind you that we are speaking here of spiritual beings; some who are currently in human form, some who are currently in dolphin form. As spiritual beings, my friends, you have had a hand in all this yourselves. So it is not so much that the *dolphin form* is protecting, it is much more the energy of the artifacts themselves that is protecting, as you have set it up for yourselves. Those who created those artifacts set up the vibrations within them to provide the protection, and it is time-linked and energy-linked. When the energy and the time are right, then the protection will naturally fall away and you will rediscover what *you* have created. We specifically say *you,* my friends, because you in this room and many others of your brothers and sisters had a direct physical hand in doing those things. So you *will* be finding things of your own that you have set away for yourselves. And you will know them, you will recognize them. You will not have to dig them out of the Earth; they will come to you in many different and strange ways. You will recognize the information that you stored within them, and you will rediscover it for yourselves. So we would not say specifically that the dolphins are protecting the skulls in that sense.

Joshua: So you would say that there are some Crystal Skulls hidden underwater?

Dolphins: Oh yes, indeed. And some are still in other dimensions, yet coming into what you would see as physical form in your world.

Joshua: There is an American Indian belief or legend that twenty-three of twenty-four Crystal Skulls are now in place at various points in the Earth's ley-lines or electromagnetic grid, and that they must have the twenty-fourth skull in place to effect a healing to the entire planet, which would expand consciousness. Are you familiar with this and do you have any comment?

Dolphins: This, my friends, is one of those parallel probabilities that we were speaking of. One of those parallel realities. And to the extent that those individuals believe that, then it is true. We would not ever say that anything is not true, my friends. If enough individuals believe something, then of course it is true, because it has been created by that thought. But we would ask you to have this thought as well: Understand that the Earth is a living being, a sentient being of spirit just as you are. It has its own experiences, its own karmic experiences in that sense, its own beliefs about itself. It has its own needs. It is not so much that humans need to heal the Earth. It is much more important that humans heal themselves so that the Earth does not require healing, for it is humanity that is imbalancing the world at this time. And this is not a judgment, it is one of the aspects of the form of being human. The Earth knew this and accepted the role, chose to be a part of it, chose to allow humans to live on its surface, knowing that given a certain time, the energy would become imbalanced again. It has gone through this cyclic experience many, many times. When humanity becomes too imbalancing, as it did in Atlantis, Earth must change things. So the Earth goes through its convulsions and changes. And it is happening again now.

In terms of using crystals of any shape or size; yes, they can be used, but it is the motivation of the user-- we repeat and we cannot repeat too often-- it is the motivation of the user of the crystal that is important, not the crystal in and of itself. Yes, programs can be placed within the crystals and the crystals can be placed in certain places, but it is the belief of those who placed the crystals there that will do the work. It is just as easy, my friends, to believe that the twenty-fourth crystal is [already] there. You can create it in your thoughtform and place it there. If enough individuals did so, it would physically manifest and everybody would see it. You *can* create by thought and you *do* create by thought. There is no other way. If enough individuals concentrate their energy and thought into something, they will create it. Stonehenge in England was created by thought. It was visualized and imagined within the thoughts of the Druids for so long, that when they were destroyed, their thoughts which were hovering there became manifest. They no longer needed it in thought, but their thought was so powerful, it manifested into physical form. You have the powers to create anything.

We would ask or suggest that those who feel that it is necessary to have such artifacts in place in order to heal the Earth, begin to believe that it has already happened, and you will have the same result, my friends. Ultimately,

CHAPTER 7

it is the thought that is important. These objects that you use, crystal and otherwise, are but tools. They are amplifiers and concentrators of your thought. Because you deal within a physical world of technology, you believe that you must have tools to do things, not recognizing that thought creates everything. So, change the belief. Believe now that the consciousness is changing. Believe that the twenty-fourth skull is in place and it will be.

Joshua: Right now there is a fabulous interest in Crystal Skulls and people are being drawn to them. [*Dolphins:* Yes.] Will you comment on that and offer any concluding remarks you wish?

Dolphins: The skull is a powerful symbol, the most powerful aspect of the body. Think about your 'scary times,' Halloween, as you call it. You are not scared by a leg bone anywhere near the same way you are by a hollow skull. There is something about the shape of the head, because as we said before, it contains what you think of as being your individuality or personality. The shape of the skull itself is a very powerful symbol for good and evil; and there's no difference between good and evil, of course, they are only judgments that you make upon the Earth. And incidentally, my friends, you cannot have one without the other. If you see something as good, you must have something bad to compare it to, otherwise you could not see it as being good. It is part of the Law of Duality and Polarity which you deal so strongly with upon the Earth. But, the skull being a powerful symbol, and there being so much interest in crystal at this time, crystal in the shape of the skull is a very mysterious object. It has tremendous drawing power. You could see a crystal elephant with just as much power, but you would not be drawn to it in the same way. Since it is in the shape of a human skull, it opens up the subconscious mind of so many individuals to the mystery-- where did it come from, why is it in that shape, what is the power, what is in those eye sockets?

The other aspect of that, my friends, is that when you look into each other's eyes, in a real sense you are looking into each other's inner beings. You can see a direct spiritual connection in the eyes to the inner spiritual being of that individual you are looking at. When you look into the eyes of a skull [of bone], it is almost as though it is empty. When you look into a Crystal Skull, you recognize that it is not empty; that there is a spirit in there, there is a *beingness* in there. It is very powerful for that reason. It comes forward at this time because many individuals need to be reawakened to who they truly are. They need to be reminded at some level (it may not even be a conscious one)

NEVILLE ROWE

of their purpose within this world; that they had been in Atlantis; that they had used crystal and misused it; that they are here now to again regain their powers and begin to use them in a positive sense.

You are doing valuable work my friends. Of course, you are strongly guided by many on the spirit side in the work that you are doing. As we said before, simply allow yourselves to open more and more to that intuition that is guiding you. Of course, you have your ego personalities; do not put yourselves down for that. Recognize that you are going to make what *you* think are errors, but recognize also that there are no such things as failures in the world. There are only experiences. You do have a pattern of experiences that you have come here to live, and even if you do not always achieve that pattern it is not a failure. You will choose to have another life and come back to try it again if you feel that you need to. There is no such thing as failure, my friends; no right, no wrong; only experience. The more you can see life as an experience, to *be* experienced, the more joy you will find in it. Life is a joy. It is to be celebrated.

One of the aspects which we in dolphin form wish to bring forth for your understanding is the joy in sheer *beingness*. We do not care about jobs or earning livings. We do not care if we die. You have much greater worry for us dear friends than we do ourselves. We do not care that our physical forms are destroyed. We know that they are temporary vehicles. You worry about your physical vehicles so very much, you have such fear of death that you then have such fear of living. We do not have that fear of death because we understand death, therefore we do not have any fear of living. Hence we can enjoy and experience our lives to the fullest. We would like you to understand that joy. We come to you in meditations to bring you that joy. We are delighted to be with you in physical form so that you can experience that joy physically with us and play with us.

It is our delight to share time and space with you, our dear friends, and we touch each and every one of you within this room. Feel our vibration, feel our energy, we are with you always. We, Kajuba have spoken.

CHAPTER 7

CONCLUSION

ur intent in this book has been to present several perspectives on the mysterious Crystal Skulls. We have gathered information from many sources in order to present some of the best possible explanations and theories for the skulls' existence. No longer can we be content to look at them merely as wonderful ancient art objects. We believe it's time to understand the purpose and powerful abilities of the ancient Crystal Skulls.

THERE IS A REASON WHY THE CRYSTAL SKULLS ARE BEGINNING TO BE NOTICED. There is a reason why people are becoming so fascinated by them and why so many civilizations have been involved with human shaped skulls composed of various materials, including crystal. In some of these civilizations, Crystal Skulls were worshiped as gods or power tools. Human greed was often involved. However, we've also provided much evidence within in this book showing that this is not the true reason that the Crystal Skulls have been given to mankind.

Truly, the Crystal Skulls are a reflection of the perfection in mankind. We believe they are ancient computers which have answers within them to many of our questions, and that they can provide solutions to the world's problems. When we are mature enough to use these Divine Tools for Perfect Love and in Perfect Harmony, they will take us into incredible new realities of beauty and joy. They have been sleeping for thousands of years, waiting for this time in our history to be reactivated. It is our belief that those individuals who have worked with the Crystal Skulls in their past lifetimes are being called now to be with them again.

Recognizing the depth of many sections of this book, we'd like to summarize some of the theories we have presented.

IT IS OUR FEELING THAT CRYSTAL SKULLS of a nature as represented by the Mitchell-Hedges Skull will all be clear, as Michael Kant or F. R. 'Nick' Nocerino have said. Each skull of this type was brought forth through a mental process which we do not understand today (i.e.-- through the power of the mind). This is the reason we cannot duplicate them even with our sophisticated, advanced technologies. As in the case of the Mitchell-Hedges Crystal Skull, it may have been the skull of a Atlantean Priestess at one time, although a few of the channels we have interviewed (not all included in this book) have implied that skulls such as this may have come from as far back as Lemuria. In any case, most of the ancient skulls we have explored within this book (the Mitchell-Hedges Skull, the Mayan Skull or the Amethyst Skull) are thousands of years old. We cannot be sure of course, since we have no reliable system with which to date crystal (Carbon-14 dating does not work with crystal.).

From the research done by F. R. 'Nick' Nocerino on the Mayan Skull and the Mitchell-Hedges Skull (and psychometry done with slides of the Amethyst, Paris and British Skulls), we believe that Crystal Skulls record vibrations in the form of images of the events that have occurred around them. In this way, they seem to work as video cameras of sorts, recording holographic scenes. The majority of people who have attended our lectures about the Crystal Skulls have stated that they were able to see these images while viewing slides or pictures of the skulls. And not only this, but while viewing these pictures and slides, the holographic images begin to change in front of one's eyes. Thus, we further speculate that the energy and essence of the Crystal Skulls are contained within these images. Through our experiences and research, we feel that an individual does not necessarily need to be in the presence of a Crystal Skull to establish a connection with it, but can do so through pictures

CONCLUSION

as well. This phenomenon also demonstrates how the skulls can be activated by having a person concentrate their mind energies on the actual skulls or the pictures. In addition, as demonstrated by the respective research of Nick Nocerino and Frank Dorland, any other crystal placed in the presence of a Crystal Skull can be changed and/or charged, so that it too may show holographic pictures.

WE BELIEVE THERE ARE TWO LIKELY THEORIES about the origin of Crystal Skulls such as the Mitchell-Hedges Skull or Rose Quartz Skull, based on our inability to explain their existence from archaeological and scientific perspectives. Either their manufacture was by a very advanced technological civilization on our Earth which understood Cosmic Laws and Universal Interrelationships beyond our current scope, or an extraterrestrial civilization was involved in bringing the process of the skull's creation to our world. Through our interviews, it seems that if the latter occurred, then it was a combination of receiving actual physical Crystal Skulls and some type of inner telepathic contact with receptive individuals who were inspired to create the Crystal Skulls. We feel that both theories are correct and that the actual answer is likely to be a synthesis of the two.

In connection with the extraterrestrial theories: If we review the channeled sessions by Michael Kant and Sandra Bowen, both imply that many of the Crystal Skulls were brought or projected here from other parts of our galaxy. Michael also stated that some of the Crystal Skulls we are currently familiar with were created on the Earth, but they were copied from Thirteen Original Skulls, some of which may still be in Tibet. Others have been moved to an underground city near Salt Lake City in Utah. He also mentioned that each of these Thirteen Original Crystal Skulls were clear skulls, and that each one has a complete crystal body associated with it.

In addition, the further we move into the Age of Aquarius, the more likely it is that the head will rejoin its crystal body. These complete crystal bodies have stored within them the history and genetic information of the Twelve Tribes or Races of the Inner Earth, with the Thirteenth Crystal Skull representing the union or family of the tribes. This seems to correlate completely with what Nick discussed in his interview, about his inner vision of always seeing thirteen clear skulls together with one of them serving as a master stone (a main Crystal Skull surrounded by, and interacting with twelve other skulls).

However, looking at the advanced civilization idea, it is felt by the co-authors and other channels that some of the Crystal Skulls could have an Atlantean origin. As Michael Kant shared in his interview, he felt the Mitchell-Hedges Crystal Skull was in one of the thirteen healing temples of Atlantis, located in what we now know as Bimini. We feel, based on the similar physical craftsmanship, especially the movable jaw and the clarity of the crystal, that also the Rose Quartz Skull and the newly reported Crystal Skull found in Peru, are of similar origin to the Mitchell-Hedges Skull. Michael had suggested in prior correspondences that the Amethyst Skull is from Atlantis. But if that is true, based on the vibration Joshua Shapiro remembers experiencing in Atlantis and while in the presence of the Amethyst Skull (in 1983), it was probably a subservient or supportive skull to the main Thirteen Crystal Skulls.

Another corollary theory to the Atlantis origin: upon the destruction of the continent of Atlantis, the Mitchell-Hedges Skull sank underwater, where it was protected for a few thousand years, perhaps by the dolphins. This close association with the Atlantean demise possibly explains many of the watery scenes the researchers in Canada observed during scrying sessions.

THE IDEA OF THE NUMBER THIRTEEN COMES UP IN SEVERAL OF OUR WORLD RELIGIONS. In Christianity, there is the Christ surrounded by his twelve apostles. A similar story is told in the book, *He Walked the Americas,* by L. Taylor Hansen. According to Ms. Hansen, there were legends of a man similar to the biblical Jesus, who traveled among the native peoples in North, Central and South America, as well as in the Polynesian Islands. Each culture he visited talked about him as a white man with crosses in his hands, who taught them exactly the same message as Christ. When he left, he would choose twelve men from the tribe to continue these teachings. When asked his name, he let each tribe decide what to call him. For example, the Cherokee or Dakotah called him Chee-Zoos.

The thirteen tribes of Israel are a second example. Twelve tribes or families were connected by a thirteenth, priestly tribe, the Kohanim (Priests). Another example is Michael's reference to the mandala of energy formed by The Thirteen Crystal Skulls in Tibet. This pattern of twelve Crystal Skulls represents two Stars of David with a central thirteenth skull as its focal point. Thirteen is a holy number combination. Perhaps long ago it was this number of Crystal Skulls that created the significance of the number thirteen. Current world religions copied it, but they have forgotten why it was so important.

CONCLUSION

It is our feeling that maybe there are multiple sets of thirteen Crystal Skulls which work together all over the world. We intuitively believe in these theories because of the wide variation of shape in the known ancient Crystal Skulls. Another possible theory is that each different shape of Crystal Skull represents a different form of human that existed on this planet. Steve Mehler disagrees with this idea and feels that the skulls were only symbolic, with the possible exception of the Mitchell-Hedges Skull. He agreed that this Crystal Skull could have been the skull of a living person changed to crystal. Also, there are the beliefs taught by Harley Swiftdeer of the Deer Tribe, that each major religion of the Earth has a set of thirteen skulls; twelve clear skulls in a circle surrounding a central thirteenth skull made of amethyst. So based on our investigations, we feel that there is at least one set of thirteen skulls, if not more. The co-authors of this book (and Steve Mehler) all feel that there will be a time in our future when several skulls, if not all thirteen, will come together and the energy that will be generated by such a combination will change the face of our Earth.

Is there a connection between the Crystal Skulls and UFOs? One interesting thing is that every person who has assisted in this book is also very interested in the study of UFOs. One of the photographs in Sandra's first chapter shows what appears to be an image of a spacecraft (or according to Michael Kant-- a Pleiadian Ship) appearing within the Mitchell-Hedges Skull. This of itself does not necessarily imply that extraterrestrials brought the skulls, but it may imply that the Crystal Skulls have recorded images of Spacecraft or UFO activity in their memory banks. Of course, if there were an advanced civilization such as Atlantis, then Atlanteans could have used some form of craft similar to those reported as UFOs today. Maybe even some of these spacecrafts we are seeing are not extraterrestrial but rather intraterrestrial, implying as their source either the Inner Earth or messengers from our past or future.

Another theory we have heard was presented by trance channel Sandra Haberer of North Carolina. She said that the Crystal Skulls were created from the melted-down remnants of individual members of an extraterrestrial race which visited our world between 11,000 - 50,000 years ago. When an alien was about to die (their lifespan was approximately 950 years), a body was cloned for the spirit to continue to live in and its original body was changed into crystal. After these alien beings (in the cloned bodies) returned to their home world, they could telepathically communicate with the natives through the Crystals Skulls and continue to spiritually guide them.

BOWEN, NOCERINO, SHAPIRO

No matter which way we go with our conjecture, there needs to be more research in this area of a possible UFO connection. When the scrying process is used on other Crystal Skulls (such as the Mayan Skull), we again find UFOs appearing. If the Crystal Skulls are computers, then like our modern computers they could send each other information, so that if a person is looking into one skull, it could access the information from another skull. Also, what if there are other Crystal Skulls on other worlds or in other dimensions? Could they also send holographic images from their worlds to the Crystal Skulls we have here on Earth? We could then view infinite worlds and dimensions. As one gazes into the eyes of the Mitchell-Hedges Skull, there is a feeling of drifting into infinity. It is as if whatever question one may have, an answer could be received through the skull. Another possibility could be (as described in Sandra Bowen's UFO contact) that the Space Beings already have Crystal Skulls onboard their craft. For each skull on the Earth there may be a counterpart skull on a spacecraft.

Changing direction, let us consider a different line of thought. We mentioned the concept of a powerful consciousness or intelligence which appears to work through and control the Crystal Skulls. Our personal experiences with this force lead us to believe that they are beings who have transcended the physical planes or realities. At certain times, these beings can communicate through Crystal Skulls because the skulls act as bridges to link their dimensions to ours. They cannot directly communicate with us because their vibration is too high. The beings would shatter our bodies through contact, like glass that shatters when exposed to a given frequency of sound. However, since crystal seems to be able to transcend many levels and dimensions, a Crystal Skull would be the perfect vehicle to handle and step-down the energy of these beings.

ANOTHER INTERESTING COMMON DENOMINATOR AMONG ALL THE CRYSTAL SKULLS which we have studied is their ability to be used for miraculous forms of healing. For example, the Maya told Anna Mitchell-Hedges and her father that the Crystal Skull could be used to heal or to will death. Anna told the members of the 1985 research team that she has received letters from people who have visited her, stating that they were healed of particular illnesses. Steve Mehler mentions that many people who came to see the Mayan Skull or Amethyst Skull in his home received a healing.

Nevertheless, not all of the Crystal Skulls have stored within them such positive and uplifting energies. Some of the skulls have recorded man's

CONCLUSION

inhumanity to man to such a degree that it is very difficult for people to be around them. For example, we have heard reports that the British Skull in London has scared people so much that they must put it away for periods of time. When they were scrying the Mayan Skull, the researchers saw many scenes of violence, such as human sacrifices and wars. On the other hand, as we have mentioned, these types of scenes did not come out with the Mitchell-Hedges Skull. So perhaps one of our jobs in the future will be to take some of these Crystal Skulls that have been misused and cleanse them to bring them back to their true purpose.

THIS BOOK IS JUST SCRATCHING THE SURFACE OF INFORMATION about the Crystal Skulls. It is the authors' desire that there should be more research and education about them. We do not wish to repeat the mistakes of the past in revering the Crystal Skulls as gods or using them for destructive purposes. We hope that we have presented a more positive message about the Crystal Skulls and how these Gifts of God can be used as powerful tools to help us solve contemporary problems which we have created for ourselves. There is no one who can scientifically prove most of the statements which have been made in this book, however, we feel that the information contained herein will give the reader a better foundation to proceed from. We hope more and more people *will* have opportunities to work with the Crystal Skulls.

It seems that the Crystal Skulls are beginning to become more activated. As was stated in the book, *The Skull Speaks,* the Crystal Skulls are drawing certain people together as preparation for beginning to work with them. As they were used in the past to heal our planet and our people, we hope it shall be once again. To us, the re-emergence of the Crystal Skulls is a powerful sign of the impending Aquarian Age, which will be a Golden Age. The closer we get to flowing into the New Age, the more Divine Tools will emerge to assist us.

AS MORE RESEARCH IS DONE WITH THE CRYSTAL SKULLS and as ancient skulls are re-discovered, we wonder, will the theories in this book be confirmed? Will the Crystal Skulls begin to communicate with us and share their great knowledge? Are they indeed one of the key tools which we will use to bring peace and harmony to our world? Will our true history and connection to the Universe be revealed? Will the Crystal Skulls act as communication devices with the Space Beings, thus allowing us to travel to other worlds?

We thank each of you for your interest and if you have information or experiences connected with the Crystal Skulls which you would like to share, please feel free to contact us. It has been our joy and pleasure to share this book with you. We hope we have bridged the gap between our sciences and the psychic or metaphysical realms, towards understanding these so-called mysterious Crystal Skulls, which perhaps for the reader at this point, may no longer be a total mystery.

Sandra Bowen
F. R. 'Nick' Nocerino
Joshua Shapiro

CONCLUSION

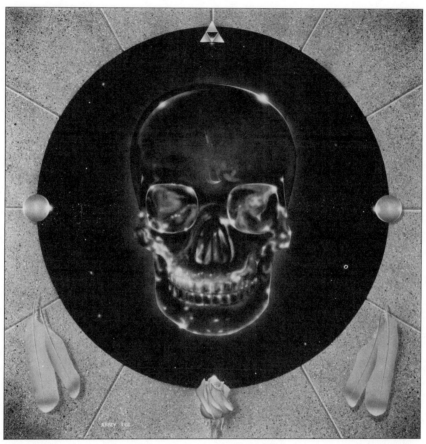

The mysterious Crystal Skulls... Perhaps one day we will completely understand what they are and why they are now appearing.

Disclaimer: We do not advocate the substitution of crystal healing remedies for any professional medical treatment or advice.

[Editors' note: The term "crystal" and "quartz crystal" shall be used interchangeably.]

This appendix is for readers who are unfamiliar with crystals, and specifically, one special type, quartz crystals. It also offers an explanation why the ancients would choose quartz to fashion a human-type skull. Crystals have become a very popular subject. There are many books on this topic appearing in even the most well-known book chains. But the question remains, why the growing interest in these gifts from Mother Earth? This appendix not only defines what crystals are, but also how they can be used. So, first let's begin by consulting some of the more prominent books written on the subject.

One of the best beginner's books on crystals is, *The Crystal Book,* by DaEl Walker. DaEl states, "Physically, crystals are fossilized water. They come into existence when water combines with an element in the presence of certain conditions of pressure, temperature and energy. When conditions are right, water will cause the element to grow as a crystal. ...Silicon, as sand, combines with water to become silicon dioxide, or quartz crystal."

QUARTZ CRYSTALS COME IN A VARIETY OF TYPES, usually distinguished by their color. For example, amethyst is one form of quartz which takes on a violet/purple color (regular quartz is clear except for impurities which cloud it). In addition, there is rose quartz (pink), citrine (yellow-brown to orange), smoky quartz (gray to smoky-black) and aventurine (green). In the study of metaphysics, each color has a significance and represents a certain aspect of beingness or vibration in humans. Thus, each variety of quartz has a specific use based on color and vibrational properties.

Another property of quartz crystals is what is called the piezoelectric effect. This quality according to DaEl, "Amplifies, transforms, stores, focuses and transfers energy. A tiny slice of quartz in a microcircuit increases an electrical signal. ...Quartz transforms energy. If squeezed, it generates electricity. When an electrical current is sent through it, it swells." Quartz is used in various forms in some types of microphones and loudspeakers, audio/video and electronic equipment, computers, etc.

Many people who rub or squeeze crystals report feeling a warmth or tingling sensation, which is this electrical effect. Some lasers use crystals to focus a beam of intense light. Even our solar energy devices use quartz crystals in their photovoltaic cells. It has been said by many people who channel information from past advanced civilizations such as Atlantis and Lemuria, that the crystal was the main source for all of their energy needs.

All quartz crystals are six-sided and usually found in the ground with at least one end having a point (single-terminated). If both sides of the crystal are pointed, it is called double-terminated. Scientists tell us that quartz crystals have a perfect symmetry within their structure. From a metaphysical point of view, the six sides can be equated with the powerful mystical symbol of the Star of David, which has been on the Earth long before the time of the Hebrews. Some say this symbol is a doorway to other dimensions!

These then, are the main physical aspects of quartz crystals. And it is these aspects which make crystals so important to the spiritual/metaphysical worlds. Crystals are direct, potent tools to reach those dimensions.

CRYSTALS SERVE AS OUR CONNECTION TO THE LIGHT UNIVERSES, since they are receivers and transmitters of higher vibrational energies. Authors Randall & Vickie Baer describe this aspect of quartz crystal most effectively in the title of their best selling book, *Windows of Light*. They say, "...For quartz is the crystal connection to the infinite octaves of Light; it is a spiral staircase to crystalline perfection. Just as water freezes into ice and yet can be transformed into the higher-energy state of steam, so too can pure celestial White Light crystallize into quartz crystal, yet retain the potential to be activated into a window for the higher-energy states of Light to shine through to the Earth-plane. Quartz is unique in this regard and as such serves as a looking glass of the soul, reflecting back to us the Light-Beings that we truly are."

APPENDIX A

Or we could say, as Lavandar does in her book, *Quartz Crystals: A Celestial Point of View,* that Quartz Crystals are Liquified Light. In other words, for the Light to be present in a physical form, so we can see and touch it with our physical senses, this vibration of Light/Truth creates an extension or projection of itself through the crystals, providing us with these dimensional windows or doorways which one can tap into and reach the higher and more loving vibrations of spirit.

HOW ARE CRYSTALS USED? Many of the crystal books give various techniques about how to use crystals for healing and balancing body energies. For example, a person can hold a crystal in one hand and pass it over the part of the body where illness or injury is, in an attempt to balance the body's energies there and evoke a healing. The crystal will amplify the healer's body energy (which can be observed through Kirlian photography and galvanic skin response) and help the healer to channel more universal energies. Another technique is to create a unified energy field by placing crystals in various geometric patterns and then putting the person (who is to receive the healing) within this energy field. Also, crystals can be used in combination with music, sound, color, magnets, pyramids and thoughtforms. Finally, the books discuss using quartz crystals in combination with other gemstones (such as lapis lazuli, malachite, opals, tourmaline, topaz, etc.) and placing them on various points of the body, corresponding to the oriental meridian systems (used for acupuncture) and the chakras (energy vortexes on the body such as the Third Eye, heart or solar plexus). All of these methods use crystals to help create balance in the body's energy systems.

Another property ascribed to quartz crystals is an ability to amplify thoughts or mental energies. Clear quartz is unique in its ability to process the full-spectrum range of energies, thus it can be programmed (via mental or spoken affirmations) to perform certain functions, or help to bring changes into physical manifestation in one's life. All other non-quartz crystals are vibration-specific, so they are limited in what energies they can process and in the effects they can produce.

For example, you could use the clear quartz crystal to amplify the visualization of good health or success in business. Crystal has the ability to increase the power of a thought. This attribute is reflected by Hermes, a great Pre-Socratic philosopher. He postulated seven universal laws, and in his first law he states, "All is Mind, the Universe is Mental." This means that, we create

QUARTZ CRYSTALS (DEFINITION)

everything which happens in our lives by the power of our minds. Crystal can accelerate this process and empower these thoughts. Thus, we must take responsibility for how we use this power, whether it is used for the benefit of mankind or its destruction. For example, it is said that in Atlantis they built great weapons of destruction based on crystal technology. Hopefully we will not make the same mistake.

QUARTZ CRYSTALS HAVE THE ABILITY TO STORE LARGE AMOUNTS OF INFORMATION within a highly-ordered lattice structure, similar to our computers. We believe this storage process includes holding thoughtforms, pictures, energy, histories, etc. We are not exactly sure how quartz crystals do this, although there are many theories. However, from a technological standpoint, we have heard reports that IBM (the largest manufacturer of computers) is already developing a computer using quartz crystals as the medium to record information. They have a special device using some form of laser which can read information stored in the crystal on a molecular level. Since we believe that the crystal can store vibrations, and anything that happens (such as thoughts, emotions, actions or whatever) is a vibration, there can be vast amounts of knowledge in crystals. Individuals who are psychically sensitive are able to pick-up these vibrations or energies and interpret them, such as what is done with the Crystal Skulls.

Many spiritual channels are telepathically receiving that the UFOs or Space Beings are also using crystals as computers aboard their spacecrafts. This was demonstrated quite interestingly in the Hollywood movie "Hanger 18," where the U.S. Government examines a crashed saucer.

In *Windows of Light*, as well as from many of our own experiences, we have found that the quartz crystals are alive and conscious sentient beings! Again, to quote from *Windows of Light*, "Crystals are shamanic power objects par excellence. Shamans ascribe a singular importance to quartz above all other power objects, perceiving it to be a 'live rock,' a living being. As such, crystals are regarded as the most powerful of the Shaman's 'spirit helpers.'" It has been said, we do not pick the crystals; they pick us by our unique vibration, and choose which people they can best serve. They select who they can work with and who will provide the greatest assistance toward rebalancing our planetary energies. A crystal must be respected, not only as an important aspect of the Creator, but as a teacher as well. They will speak to you if you are inwardly receptive. Crystals can give us personal guidance and clear up outer confusion to allow inner clarity, which is perhaps how we received the term "Crystal Clear." And most importantly, they can connect one to any level or dimension within the universe!

THE STUDY OF THE USES AND EFFECTS OF CRYSTALS COULD TAKE A LIFETIME. If you are not too familiar with crystals, we highly recommend you consult *The Crystal Cosmos Network Directory,* by Elizabeth Logan, listed in the Crystal Skull Resource Directory (Appendix D). This directory contains any type of crystal contact you can imagine, as well as a good list of books. Also, another fine book is called, *The Crystal Sourcebook,* by Milewski and Hartford. It includes articles with many of the leading crystal teachers and researchers (including a chapter by F. R. 'Nick' Nocerino), also listed in our directory under Mystic Crystal Publications. We also recommend most New Age or Metaphysical bookstores for the purchase of crystals.

Contact information for the crystal books previously mentioned:

Baer, Randall & Vickie,
 WINDOWS OF LIGHT, (Quartz Crystals & Self-Transformation),
 THE CRYSTAL CONNECTION,
 (Guidebook for Personal & Planetary Ascension),
 New York, Harper & Row, 1984 & 1986

Criswell, Beverly,
 QUARTZ CRYSTALS (A Celestial Point of View),
 (Lavandar Lines, Beverly Criswell, P.O. Box 1089, Santa Fe, NM 87504)

Walker, DaEl,
 THE CRYSTAL BOOK, THE CRYSTAL HEALING BOOK,
 Sunol, Crystal Co., 1983, 1988
 (The Crystal Company, Laurie Jelgersma, #110 2nd Ave., #D12,
 Pacheco, CA 94553; (415) 674-9090

APPENDIX B
ADDITIONAL CRYSTAL SKULL
INFORMATION GIVEN PUBLICLY

In this appendix, we briefly summarize additional information given publicly about the Mitchell-Hedges Crystal Skull. The two major references presented here are [information from] Anna Mitchell-Hedges, the current owner of this Crystal Skull, and Frank Dorland, the first person to do an in-depth analysis of it. This appendix will include accounts of some of their experiences as they have been related to the media and shared in various books. Also included is a brief summary of the book, *The Skull Speaks,* by AMHREA.

HISTORY OF THE MITCHELL-HEDGES SKULL

Section 1
(As related in media interviews
with Anna Mitchell-Hedges)

Anna Mitchell-Hedges is the adopted daughter of famed explorer and archaeologist, F. A. Mitchell-Hedges. She accompanied her father on many of his journeys throughout the world. Anna Mitchell-Hedges was a part of her father's expedition to British Honduras (now Belize) in the early 1920's. [Editors' note: F. A. Mitchell-Hedges was granted permission by the governor of British Honduras to explore this region.] Here they discovered the ruins of a Mayan city which her father thought had something to do with Atlantis. The expedition named the area "Lubaantun," which is a Mayan word meaning "The City of Fallen Stones." In 1924, on her seventeenth birthday, Anna first saw something shining through the stones in one of the Mayan structures. At this time, her father wasn't there. He had returned to England to generate funds necessary to continue their expedition. Upon his return, Anna told him what she had seen, but he did not think it was anything special, saying it was just a piece of glass. However, Anna insisted it was important, so the following day they began moving stones with the help of a number of local Maya.

It took them perhaps a bit more than six weeks before they were able to unearth the Crystal Skull. Some of the stones were so heavy that it took two men to lift them. When they cleared the final slab away, Anna went to pick up the artifact because she had smaller hands than the others, and she brought out the top part of the skull which she showed to her father. The Mayan natives who were working with them started kissing the ground, crying and laughing with joy. The Maya constructed a make-shift altar, upon which they placed the skull. Soon, natives from near and far were gathered at the site and the celebrations went on for days, bringing to a halt all excavation work.

Some three months later, they discovered the detachable lower jaw twenty-five feet from where the top part was found. F. A. Mitchell-Hedges gave the Crystal Skull back to the Maya. He didn't want to take this special object away from them, since they had been so kind to all the members of the expedition. In 1927, when they finished their work at Lubaantun, the head Mayan priest presented the Crystal Skull to Anna's father as a gift of appreciation for the medical attention and supplies, modern tools, utensils and continual nursing care provided by expedition members, which eased the suffering of the Mayan people. This is why the Crystal Skull has remained a possession of their family.

THE MAYAN PEOPLE TOLD ANNA AND HER FATHER that the skull was made 3,600 years ago and it took one hundred and fifty years through five generations to make. [Editors' note: This Crystal Skull was known to the Mayan Priests through their legends.] One huge block of crystal was rubbed until it was shaped into its present perfect form. The Maya told them that the Crystal Skull was used by the high priests to will death or to heal. But willing death with this skull was done in a kind way. For example, if a medicine man or witch doctor was getting too old to perform the religious ceremonies, a young man was chosen to take his place. Then, at the appropriate time, both of them would lie in front of the altar with the Crystal Skull on top of it, and the high priest would perform a ceremony. In this ceremony, the old man's knowledge would transfer into the young boy and the medicine man would peacefully pass on, while the boy would immediately become very knowledgeable.

Anna feels that the Crystal Skull has tremendous power, but that it also gives one a warning when something is going to happen. For example, one day while she was in England (1963), she saw the Crystal Skull had fogged up and water was dripping from it. She thought someone had poured water on it. She wiped it off, but the skull continued to drip. Anna felt cold and that something terrible was going to happen. When they put the news on at five o'clock in the afternoon, they heard that President Kennedy had been assassinated.

Anna has been offered hundreds of thousands of dollars for the skull, but she refuses to sell it because she feels that if she sold it to a private collector, then no one would be able to see it. Anna has shared the skull with thousands of people through appearances at conferences, schools, libraries and via media coverage. The Mitchell-Hedges Skull is one of three Crystal Skulls which one may currently see in person, but the other two are in museums. She feels that the Crystal Skull is a loving skull, and she has great joy in sharing it with other people. Anna has watched many people who came to see this clear Crystal Skull break out into smiles, almost as though a transformative miracle had happened before them.

SUMMARY OF THE BOOK
THE SKULL SPEAKS

Section 2

In November of 1985, author Brian Hadley James and the Anna Mitchell-Hedges Research and Exploration Association (AMHREA) released their book, *The Skull Speaks,* which was devoted to sharing information about the Mitchell-Hedges Skull. The material for the book was channeled by British trance-medium, Carole Davis, with Mr. James serving as the interviewer. They received information during a two and one-half year period involving nine sessions.

Carole Davis, as she described in the video, "The Psychic Connection: The Crystal Skull" (done by Alan Neuman), went with some friends to see the Mitchell-Hedges Skull one day and suddenly felt quite sleepy. She thought no one would notice, so she just took a short nap. However, when she awoke, Carole discovered that she had indeed not been sleeping but went into a trance and shared some profound information about the Crystal Skull. As demonstrated in the video, Carole aligns her vibration with the skull (or as the book describes, with the various minds resident within it) through the use of toning.

The following is our interpretation of some significant information shared during the channeled sessions of this book. As *The Skull Speaks* was only the second published book to exclusively focus on a Crystal Skull, we thought it might be interesting to present this information so that the reader may gain additional perspectives to those we have shared thus far.

ACCORDING TO THE CONSCIOUSNESS OR MINDS (within the Crystal Skull) which spoke through Ms. Davis, the Mitchell-Hedges Crystal Skull is seventeen thousand years old. Many generations of people have possessed it, maintaining its smoothness by polishing it with hair and sand. This Crystal Skull was a part of the Great Crystal of Atlantis[1] and the minds of many beings are stored within the skull. The skull is alive and continually fed by energies which we do not comprehend.

During the fall of Atlantis, these beings (who had placed the essence of their minds within the skull) saw that their home would soon be destroyed. They wanted to preserve their knowledge, and since most Atlanteans had forgotten their purpose for incarnating on the Earth, they decided to leave their wisdom of the ages in crystalline objects. These beings also knew they would not be returning to our world in physical bodies, as they had great difficulty adjusting their vibration to the frequency of the earth plane. At first they considered storing their collective knowledge in Bimini, which was the heart of Atlantis and the place where this information was being kept until that point. However, the beings knew it would be too dangerous to place all their knowledge in one location, lest it fall into the wrong hands. So it was dispersed to be housed within many receptacles, such as the Crystal Skulls. As a matter of fact, throughout *The Skull Speaks,* it was stressed that no *one* person would possess all the beings' knowledge or know where all of these receptacles were hidden.

Furthermore, the resident minds of the Crystal Skull said that Atlantis was more than just a geographic location. Atlantis symbolically represented what they called "The Minds of One." And by this, we believe they were alluding to the idea that all souls and all realities are a part of the one Universal Consciousness or Energy which we call God, the Creator. The parts of The Minds of One that were placed in each receptacle made from crystal or gemstones are now being called back into service because our Earth desperately needs them to rebalance itself and restore harmony amongst humankind. Currently, the resident minds in the Mitchell-Hedges Crystal Skull

---

[1]-[Editors' note: We believe this refers to the large crystal which was the main power source for Atlantis.]

exist in another dimension and are patiently waiting to spiritually communicate with us through this Crystal Skull.

THE MITCHELL-HEDGES CRYSTAL SKULL OPERATES similar to our modern day computers. The Crystal Skull will become activated when the correct vibration is produced in its presence. At such time, people who are seeking information from the skull can receive such. What these beings were saying is that when the right people of the proper intent come together (which was defined as what we call Love, or people whose motivation is to help the Earth), the secret knowledge encoded within will be revealed. Each person will receive what is appropriate for their spiritual evolution and what they can integrate into their own reality. However, as previously mentioned, no singular person will be allowed to receive *all* the knowledge contained within the Crystal Skull.

The resident minds within the Crystal Skull set up vibrational locks in all the crystalline artifacts containing parts of The Minds of One. This was done so that people of unscrupulous intent would not be able to use a mechanical process to release the inherent knowledge. Further it was stated this skull will never be in a location where it cannot be utilized. Eventually, the Mitchell-Hedges Skull, along with other receptacles of knowledge, will provide important information to scientists and healers of our world. If it should ever fall into the wrong hands, the skull would destroy itself. However, over thousands of years there have been many seen and unseen forces guarding it.

THE MINDS WITHIN THE SKULL STATED that there will be other [ancient] Crystal Skulls found. They also commented that even though there are many such receptacles, some still have not been activated or humans have not touched their energies. And the form of these receptacles is not always that of a Crystal Skull. However, there will be a time when all these artifacts or receptacles of knowledge are placed together. When this occurs, incredible information and guidance will be released. This will catalyze a major shift in consciousness on our planet. Unfortunately, the timing of this is not to happen yet.

The language used by the Crystal Skull involves pure thoughtforms. Thus, a true communication with the Crystal Skull must be from mind to mind, telepathically. If these thoughtforms had not been placed in the skull, then it would simply be a beautiful work of art. It is this special energy of living beings which makes the Crystal Skull different than common quartz crystal.

Furthermore, it was stated that when [ancient] Crystal Skulls feel the pull of people whose minds are projecting an energy similar to what they emit, this in itself will activate the skulls to emanate a magnetic field which will telepathically draw these individuals to be in their presence. Undoubtedly, these are people who have worked with Crystal Skulls in former lifetimes. The beings are beginning to activate all the crystal receptacles in an attempt to awaken mankind to the philosophy of what they called "The One Mind" and to create a better world. However, it is required by Universal Law that we must seek the Crystal Skulls out through free will and contact them in some way if we wish to receive the knowledge stored within them .

FRANK DORLAND

Section 3
Accounts of his Research with the Mitchell-Hedges Skull

Since beginning our research about the Crystal Skulls, we have sought others who might have information to share. Knowing of Frank Dorland's background, we of course decided to contact him. He had the Mitchell-Hedges Skull in his possession for six years due to the generosity of the skull's owner, Anna Mitchell-Hedges. We consider his research on this Skull to be invaluable.

FRANK DORLAND WAS A WELL-KNOWN ART CONSERVATOR for many years and worked with numerous art treasures. In 1964, Frank was loaned the famous Mitchell-Hedges Crystal Skull, which he was allowed to research until 1970. Through this involvement, Frank became very knowledgeable about crystals. He is also a skilled lapidarist and jewelry craftsman. Frank has provided many individuals with some of the finest carved quartz pieces. He was one of the main people interviewed by Richard Garvin in 1973 for the first published book focused on information about a Crystal Skull. As mentioned before, this book included the scientific findings of Hewlett-Packard's research with this Crystal Skull.

Frank has been interviewed by a number of radio and television stations about his experiences with the Mitchell-Hedges Crystal Skull and he has also lectured. He has written articles which appeared in various publications. One of his latest articles about the Crystal Skull appears in, *The Crystal Sourcebook,* by Milewski and Hartford (1987). Frank's new book about crystals, entitled, *Holy Ice,* is scheduled for future release.

APPENDIX B

Joshua and Sandra first met Mr. Dorland in September of 1985, and since that time they have remained in contact with him. Mr. Dorland has also told us that he too is aware of a Crystal Skull found in the diggings near Machu Picchu, Peru, which apparently is very similar in shape and size to the Mitchell-Hedges Skull.

The purpose of this part of the appendix is to summarize the work done by Mr. Dorland with the Mitchell-Hedges Crystal Skull through information which he has publicly shared . We give a brief history of his research with this skull, as well as some of his findings and theories about it.

AND NOW LET US HEAR FROM one of the first people to really have a chance to explore the mysteries of the Mitchell-Hedges Crystal Skull...

Frank Dorland and his wife/co-worker, Mabel, first heard of this Crystal Skull in 1950. At this time they were art conservators living in La Jolla, California. Because of their profession, they had heard stories about a mysterious ancient artifact in England-- a Crystal Skull. Since their specialty was researching and working with religious art, they were extremely interested.

In the Fall of 1964, they were invited to participate in the New York World's Fair, to oversee the famous Icon of Our Lady of Kazan, a major exhibit at the Fair. Concurrently, Anna Mitchell-Hedges was flying into New York to talk about her skull to Frederick Docksteder, director of the Museum of the American Indian, and a world-renowned expert on ancient artifacts. She was seeking other individuals who could give her more insights about what the Crystal Skull was, how it was used and who made it.

When Frank and Mabel learned that Anna Mitchell-Hedges was going to be in town, they arranged to meet and accompany her to the museum. Just prior to the Dorlands' return to California, Miss Mitchell-Hedges asked if they would take the Crystal Skull back with them for research purposes. They agreed and on October 19, 1964, happily boarded their plane with two very important art objects (the Icon and the Crystal Skull).

HOME FOR FRANK AND MABEL WAS IN MILL VALLEY, CALIFORNIA (north of San Francisco), in a very comfortable converted farmhouse situated on the side of Mount Tamalpais just above Muir Woods. Their home was filled with many priceless paintings, all in the process of being restored, as well as numerous bottles and jars of artists supplies. Mabel felt they needed an even safer place than their home for the valuable pieces of art they had brought back. So, they rented a safety-deposit box in the Mill Valley Bank of America. The Crystal Skull was stored there when not being researched.

Once it was learned that Frank and Mabel had the Crystal Skull in their possession, they were flooded by letters and phone calls from people who wanted to see it. They entertained people from all types of backgrounds, including religious leaders, scientists, shamans, psychiatrists, psychologists, hypnotists, medical doctors, attorneys, and of course, psychics. There were many sessions held with different groups as they tried to unravel the secrets of the Crystal Skull.

Frank became so fascinated with the skull and devoted so much of his time to studying it that he soon fell months behind in his restoration work. He had special cameras and high-powered microscopes to photograph the skull from every angle. Frank also made numerous models of the Mitchell-Hedges Skull from plasters and resins. These helped him examine cross-sections of the skull and obtain precise measurements.

BUT, NO MATTER HOW SCIENTIFIC HIS PROCEDURES AND RESEARCH WERE, there were just too many strange phenomena occurring around the Crystal Skull. Mr. Dorland was quoted as saying in Richard Garvin's book:

"Now, I have done my utmost since this thing came into my care, to keep this skull far away from anything on parapsychology, psychic phenomena, spiritualism and so forth. But that has been a total flop. I have simply been unable to do it. It is a strange *strange* object. It fascinates people with its hypnotic effect. People of all sorts are drawn to it as if it were a magnet. I have had people look at it and show a tendency to go asleep. In others it causes the pulse to quicken. People can see all sorts of things in the skull."[2]

What were these strange phenomena which were occurring around the skull? The first time they kept the skull overnight in their home, Frank and Mabel were awakened by unusual noises in the house, including a jungle cat, silver bells tinkling softly and chimes. The next morning possessions were scattered all over their living room, yet all the windows and doors were locked. At other times they heard what sounded like music or human voices singing strange chants. The skull also gave off what Frank calls an elusive

---

[2] Garvin, Richard, *The Crystal Skull*, Doubleday & Co., New York, 1973.

APPENDIX B

perfume or odor. As we have mentioned before, they would see many pictures and images appearing within the skull. These images included other Crystal Skulls, high mountains, temples and faces which Frank was even able to photograph. On several occasions, Frank remembers seeing a dark spot which would spontaneously appear within the Crystal Skull and grow in size until it would fill at least half of it. During this process, the skull's temples would repeatedly disappear and reappear.

His most profound experience occurred one evening when he was looking at the skull and he noticed a glow or aura appearing around it. At this time, the Crystal Skull was in ordinary light, when suddenly this aura appeared and grew until it was a full eighteen inches surrounding the skull. This phenomenon lasted six minutes. He didn't believe what he was seeing, so he picked up a magazine and read a few words, in order to re-focus his eyes. When he looked back at the skull, the aura was still there and it intensified. This experience taught him a great deal about the auras encircling all living things.

TO BETTER UNDERSTAND THE SKULL, Frank and Mabel began to have gatherings with selected groups of psychically sensitive individuals. However, as with everything else in dealing with this most unpredictable skull, the information these psychics received was so diverse that none of it corroborated.

Frank determined that the skull must somehow be able to reflect back to people information about themselves which is contained in their own conscious and subconscious minds. He believed it had nothing to do with information stored in the skull itself. This conclusion necessitated a new approach where concise questions were prepared before the sessions. These questions were asked of each psychic after they fell into a meditative state in the presence of the skull. Their goal was to determine how the skull works with and records information. This procedure produced results that could more easily be studied. Frank feels that these psychic readings have more value if the mind of the reader is clear. This is because it is the human mind which controls or activates the Crystal Skull.

Many of the visiting shamans and medicine people told them that the skull was filled with great knowledge and wisdom, as well as information related to the past and future of our world. They said that there were great secrets locked within the skull which would only come out at the proper time, for our world was not quite ready to receive them.

FRANK DORLAND

Another interesting experiment that Frank and Mabel attempted was to see how another crystal would react if kept in the presence of the Crystal Skull. The History Division of the Oakland Public Museum loaned them an authentic rock quartz crystal ball which had flaws and veils similar to the Mitchell-Hedges Skull. They kept this crystal ball with the skull for two years. They found that the museum's piece produced almost identical phenomena in some respects, but not to the degree as with the Crystal Skull. They were able to see visions and images inside of the crystal ball and at times smelled a sweet-sour odor emanating from it.

Finally, in 1970, Anna Mitchell-Hedges came to San Francisco to pick up her Crystal Skull. Mr. Dorland continues to work with crystals, and still associates and corresponds with many others in the field. Now, from the years of research and study, let us consider some of Mr. Dorland's theories and conclusions about the Mitchell-Hedges Crystal Skull:

FROM AN INTERVIEW WITH A LOCAL TELEVISION CHANNEL from Los Angeles, California, for a program called "Eye on L.A.":

"Although there is a great deal of controversy about the origination of the skull, in our estimation and our research, we believe that the skull was made at least 12,000 years ago and has been changed twice by three different civilizations since its first inception."

Frank Dorland believes that the Mitchell-Hedges Crystal Skull was created from one large chunk of quartz crystal which weighed at least twenty pounds. He believes it was shaped by hand over a long period of time (at least three hundred years) in the classic chipping and flaking method, and then was sanded smooth and hand-polished with hair and sand. Additionally, in private conversations Frank has told us that he believes this Crystal Skull is an almost exact duplication of a young female's skull. She was between the ages of twenty-one and twenty-nine years when she died.

In an interview for the television show, "That's Incredible," Mr. Dorland discussed how the Crystal Skull was used by past civilizations. He felt that the last civilization which had the skull decided that 'god' should talk and accomplished this by cutting loose the jawbone of the skull. The Priests decided that by doing this, they could then control what 'god' said. To move the jaw for the purpose of barking-out their religious orders, the priests would place the skull over an altar and mount it on two pivoting axes, so that the skull could nod and move from side to side. They probably used two crystal push rods from below the skull to achieve the up and down motion of the jaw and give the appearance of speaking.

IN ADDITION, FRANK'S RESEARCH LED TO THE DISCOVERY that the Crystal Skull has an elaborate internal system of prisms and lenses which will dynamically reflect light sources. He believes that the Mayan priests were well aware of this effect and used it to hypnotically strike fear into the hearts of the temple worshippers. Frank realized this when he was sitting on his couch one day, looking at the fireplace across the room. The Crystal Skull was directly in front of him resting on a table, and when he glanced at it, he noticed dancing flames of fire in the skull's eyes. Frank determined from these observations that the Priests would place an altar fire behind and/or underneath the skull to illuminate its face and eyes. While researching these effects, Frank discovered that the back of the Mitchell-Hedges Crystal Skull functions as a lens to focus light on various places within the skull.

Based on his research, he feels that the skull was put to a religious use, either by the Atlanteans, the ancient Egytians, Babylonians or even Tibetans. He believes that the Mitchell-Hedges Skull, in the beginning was similar in shape and form to the British Skull, and that it had not been completely finished. The Phoenicians then brought the Mitchell-Hedges Skull from Babylon to Central America, where the Maya or Aztecs came into its possession. He says that either the Maya or Aztecs completed its shape as it is today, and then detached the jawbone. The skull became lost for hundreds of years until F. A. Mitchell-Hedges found it in 1924.

As to the question of why the ancients would create a skull of crystal, Frank has found in his extensive research that there was a worldwide practice by many past civilizations centered around skull worship. This would include the Pacific Islands, Tibet, Egypt and Mexico. He feels that these people held the skull in extremely high veneration. They believed that the skull is a godhead--symbolically representing all knowledge and wisdom. He believes it was the basis of their power and their magical talismans.

IT IS MR. DORLAND'S OPINION THAT THE MITCHELL-HEDGES SKULL was crafted to be a female skull. The civilization involved in its creation undoubtedly viewed God as female in the sense that it is the feminine energy from which all things

FRANK DORLAND

are born. Since these civilizations considered the skull to be their god, it would then have a female shape and God was called by them the Great Mother or Queen of Heaven. Thus the Crystal Skull was a physical symbol for the Great Mother.

To paraphrase and augment a conclusion of Mr. Dorland regarding an important symbolic meaning of this Crystal Skull:

Our world is now patriarchal and masculine. The Crystal Skulls are a link to a previous, "feminine" world. Just as the ancients recognized the power of the feminine forces, so must we. A balance must be struck between masculine and feminine energies in order for there to be peace and productive coexistence in our future.

APPENDIX B

APPENDIX C
MICHAEL ABBEY

Comments from the Illustrator

Working on this project has been a fascinating journey, which I feel I have only just begun. I thank the co-authors, editors and everyone involved, for including me in the creation of this book.

As I worked on the illustrations, I became interested in all cultural archetypes of skulls, which eventually led me to certain Native American teachings about the Crystal Skulls' origins and functions here on this planet. I found there is a legend, not written in any book, but handed down orally from a "body" of sacred knowledge of traditional Native American Elders called "Twisted-Hairs." The hair represents knowledge, and therefore, a "Twisted-Hair" is a person who wove and integrated the knowledge from all sources into his/her path tempered by the heart.

THIS ORAL TRADITION IS REFERRED TO AS THE LEGEND OF THE SINGING SKULLS. It describes twelve magical worlds, planets within various star systems (e.g.-- Sirius, Pleiades, etc.) which all contain a form of humanoid life. These races felt incomplete and wondered what they could do to become whole. The Mother Earth invited them to walk upon her, so that by knowing each other, they would discover their answers. As each race came to Earth, they brought with them a carved Crystal Skull (with a movable jaw) which was created on their respective worlds. They called each of these skulls a Singing Skull because each world had a unique vibration which could be symbolically expressed as a song. These Crystal Skulls are computers that contain the history of their planet. All of these skulls can access the others and replay information in the form of holographic images.

The beings from the twelve magical worlds gathered their respective Crystal Skulls together to form a circle of twelve, which they called "The Ark." In the center of the Ark was a Master Skull group. This group consisted of five skulls; a large amethyst skull surrounded by a masculine amethyst skull to the west, a feminine amethyst skull to the east, a citrine skull to the north and a rose quartz skull to the south.

The legend of the twelve worlds is reported in the book, *Song of Heyoehkoh,* by Hyemeyohsts Storm in 1981. Harley Swiftdeer, of the Deer Tribe and a member of the Twisted Hairs, is publicly sharing these oral teachings. Swiftdeer states that when the Spaniards invaded the Americas, Cortez and Father Diaz (who represented the Pope) discovered the Ark and stole one of the major skulls (a skull which represents our planet in the circle of the Ark). On the way to their ships, the Spaniards were attacked by the Mayans, who took the skull back and buried it in Central America.

[To learn more about this ancient legend of the Crystal Skulls, contact the Deer Tribe Metis Medicine Society listed in the Crystal Skull Resource Directory, Appendix D.]

APPENDIX C

APPENDIX D
CRYSTAL SKULL RESOURCE DIRECTORY

This Crystal Skull Resource Directory is included so that if the reader(s) have any interest to further their own personal research in the area of the Crystal Skulls, they will have organizations or people which they may contact. We have only listed those we consider to be main contacts, although there aren't many people actively involved with Crystal Skull research at this time. Also, if you contact one of the listings below, undoubtedly it will lead to others which are not listed, because as of this time they may be unknown to us. We have divided these lists up into Crystal Skull individuals or groups, a list of some of books and articles written about the Crystal Skulls, plus a few videotapes. The order of the lists is alphabetical. Good luck and have fun...

Contacts for Crystal Skull Information

Alan Neuman Productions,
Alan Neuman, 8170 Laurel View Dr., Los Angeles, CA 90069; (213) 656-0754 (Produced a video exploring paranormal and psychic phenomena, including a segment on the Mitchell-Hedges Skull; still available)

AMHREA Foundation, Anna Mitchell-Hedges,
P.O. Box 1541, Station C, Kitchener, Ontario, Canada N2G 4P2; (Research Foundation on Crystal Skulls, Anna is the owner of the Mitchell-Hedges Skull, published book: *The Skull Speaks)*

Andren, Michael, 5670 Walnut Ave., Long Beach, CA 90805; (213) 423-2025 (Crystal teacher, New Age, metaphysics, local contacts, Crystal Skull researcher)

Aquarian Media/The Crystal Visionary, Michael Ney,
P.O. Box 566, Milsons Point, 2061, Sydney, Australia   Tele: (02) 498.5152
(Crystal journal {Crystals in healing/meditation/interviews, dowsing etc.} and
other New Age publications, global crystal contacts, articles/interviews about
Crystal Skulls)

Boddie, Caroline, 65 Brighton St., Rochester, NY 14607; (716) 461-2349
(Crystal teacher, crystal supplier, networker, many national contacts, UFOs,
knows Anna Mitchell-Hedges and helped with the book, *The Skull Speaks*)

Bowen, Sandra, P.O. Box 153, Pinole, CA 94564; (415) 758-8607
(Crystal Skull researcher/lecturer, crystal teacher, UFO contactee/researcher,
co-author, participated in 1985 research with Mitchell-Hedges Crystal Skull)

Cristal Kingdom, Eric Fontzi, 259 Hampton Dr.,Venice, CA 90291;
(213) 396-3919 (Crystal store/supplier, sells carved crystal skulls and
artifacts, art merchant, can have crystal skulls carved to order)

Crystal Awareness, DaEl Walker & Laurie Jelgersma,
110 2nd Ave. So. D-12, Pacheco, CA 94553; (415) 674-9090
(Publisher/Distributor of, *The Crystal Book; The Crystal Healing Book,*
crystal teacher, DaEl participated in research with Mitchell-Hedges Skull,
lecturer, crystal supplier)

Crystal Cosmos Network Directory, Elizabeth Logan,
Box 2386, Winnipeg, Manitoba, Canada R3C 4A6; (204) 661-2551
(Directory of worldwide crystal contacts, crystal researcher)

Deer Tribe Metis Medicine Society, Harley Swiftdeer,
P.O. Box 8204, La Crescenta, CA 91214 (818) 286-2931
(Classes/workshops/lectures on Native American teachings, sells carved
crystal skulls, teaches about Native American legends related to the Crystal
Skulls)

Dorland, Frank, P.O. Box 6233, Los Osos, CA 93402; (805) 528-2886
(Had Mitchell-Hedges Skull for six years of research, crystallographer, crystal
research, author of book, *Holy Ice,* studies world religions and religious
artifacts)

Haberer, Sandra, P. O. Box 249, Lynn, NC 28750
(Trance Medium, channel for two spokepersons of the Sabreena Soul Group. Does public lectures and workshops. Sandra has a personal interest in the Crystal Skulls and the Sabreena Soul Group also shares information.)

J & S Aquarian Networking, P.O. Box 1395, Pacifica, CA 94044; Joshua Shapiro (415) 359-5476; Jeff Cohen (415) 756-0633
(Networking, UFO and Crystal Skull books, crystal contacts, publisher, researchers, lecturers, contact lists)

Jochmans, Joseph, 31 Sumner Park, Rochester, NY 14607;
(New Age lecturer/author, researches ancient Earth ruins, crystals, channel, ley-lines, newsletter, has studied Mitchell-Hedges Crystal Skull)

Lavandar Lines, Beverly Criswell, P.O. Box 1089, Santa Fe, NM 87504; (505) 757-6012 (New Age publisher/book distributor, wrote book on quartz crystals, crystal supplier, UFO contactee, channel, author, networker)

Mehler, Steve, 507 Udovich Lane, Paradise, CA 95969; (916) 877-6642
(New Age and Crystal Skull Researcher/Lecturer, had the Amethyst and Mayan Crystal Skulls in his home, Psychic Archaeologist, Egyptology afficianado, videographer)

Musee De L'Homme, Attn: Phototheque,
Place du Trocadero et du 11-Novembre, 75116 Paris, France
(Occasionally displays the Paris Crystal Skull {Aztec Skull} and sells photographs of it)

Museum of Man, Great Russell St., London WC1B 3DG, England
(Displays the British Crystal Skull)

Mystic Crystal Publications, John Milewski, P.O. Box 8029, Santa Fe, NM 87504 (Published book: *The Crystal Sourcebook,* which includes articles with many crystal teachers)

Plapp, Gary, c/o Seekers Unlimited, 5539 Blossom Acres Dr., San Jose, CA 95124; (408) 264-1492 (Archaeology, research, scientific devices, classes, Crystal Skull studies, has seen the Amethyst Crystal Skull, dowsing, occult, UFO channeling)

Psychic Research Institute, Marcel Vogel,
  1725 Little Orchard St. #C, San Jose, CA 95125; (408) 279-2291
  (Crystal and psychic research, lecturer, audio & video cassettes, newsletter,
  has seen and researched several Crystal Skulls)

Ram Metaphysical Bookstore, Francoise Beaudoin,
  1749 Park Ave., San Jose, CA 95126; (408) 294-2651
  (Metaphysical bookstore, sells crystals, had the Amethyst Skull in her home)

Society of Crystal Skulls, International, a division of the Institute of
  Psychic and Hypnotic Sciences; F. R. 'Nick' Nocerino,
  P.O. Box 302, Pinole, CA 94564; (415) 724-6603 (Founded in 1944, Oldest
  known organization to find, study, research and lecture about ancient Crystal
  Skulls; Courses for the use of quartz crystals and stones since 1944)

Strange Magazine, Mark Chorvinsky, P.O. Box 2246, Rockville, MD 20852
  (301) 468-6133   (Collects bibliography on all books and articles related to
  the Crystal Skulls, his magazine has an article about the British Skull)

Talisman Trading Co., P. Damian Quinn, P.O. Box 1895, La Mesa, CA
  92041;   (619) 236-9525   (Sells crystals and contemporary carved crystal
  skulls from Brazil, gemologist)

List of Crystal Skull Books

Bowen, Sandra; F. R. 'Nick' Nocerino & Joshua Shapiro,
  Mysteries of the Crystal Skulls Revealed,
  J & S Aquarian Networking, Pinole, CA, 1987 (First Edition); Pacifica, CA,
  1988 (Revised Edition)

This book is a combination of interviews and articles by Crystal Skull
researchers and spiritual channels. It tries to work with what is known so
far, then goes beyond by considering the parapsychological perspective as a
valid scientific approach. There are numerous points of view exploring
ancient Crystal Skulls and many photographs of four of them, plus some of
the contemporary carved skulls. Included within the chapters are original
illustrations which portray the various information presented. It is planned
as the beginning of many books which reveal the true purposes of the
Crystal Skulls.

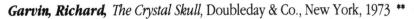

Garvin, Richard, *The Crystal Skull,* Doubleday & Co., New York, 1973 **

Richard Garvin wrote the first book to focus on the investigation of the Crystal Skulls. There are extensive interviews with Frank Dorland, as well as quotes from the first published comparison of the Mitchell-Hedges Skull and the British Skull in the MAN article in 1936. Garvin gives background on F. A. Mitchell-Hedges and his adopted daughter, Anna Mitchell-Hedges, including an interview with her and copies of some of her correspondences about the Crystal Skull. There are photographs of the Lubaantun expedition, the British and Paris Skulls, as well as the Mitchell-Hedges Skull. Garvin discusses the scientific tests that were conducted at Hewlett-Packard in 1970 with the Mitchell-Hedges Skull, including associated psychic phenomena. A most in-depth book on the Mitchell-Hedges Skull and thoroughly researched.

James, Brian Hadley, *The Skull Speaks,* Anna Mitchell-Hedges Research & Exploration Association, Kitchener, Ontario, Canada 1985

This is a channeled book involving nine sessions that trance medium Carole Davis had in the presence of the Mitchell-Hedges Crystal Skull. Since the whole book is written from a parapsychological perspective, there are specific answers given to questions related to the skull's history and use, which few other books address. The main ideas conveyed are that some form of consciousness works and communicates through the skull, and that the skull has an ancient connection to Atlantis and Bimini. There is also a good photo section in the book.

Milewski, John & Virginia Hartford, *The Crystal Sourcebook,* Mystic Crystal Publications, Sedona, Arizona 1987

This book is a compilation of articles by some of the leading authorities on crystals. One of the chapters contains an article by Frank Dorland, summarizing his experiences and research with the Mitchell-Hedges Crystal Skull. There is also a photograph of it included. In Mr. Nocerino's chapter, he discusses his involvement with the Crystal Skulls. Lastly, Lehmann Hisey makes mention of this Crystal Skull in his article in context of the research done by Hewlett-Packard.

Mitchell-Hedges, F. A., *Danger My Ally,* Elek Books LTD., 1954 **

This book is an autobiography of F. A. Mitchell-Hedges. It has thirteen lines of information that specifically refer to the Mitchell-Hedges Crystal Skull and there is a picture of the Crystal Skull in the book.

Morrill, Sibley, *The Mystery of Crystal Gazing* **
(How An Ancient Mayan Skull May Be the Key),
Cadleon Publishing, San Francisco, California 1969

Mr. Morrill is basically concerned with the art of scrying for images in crystal. He refers to the Mitchell-Hedges Skull, which he had an opportunity to see when Frank Dorland had the skull in Marin County, California, as the finest scrying instrument. Also included is some history on the Crystal Skull, as well as photographs.

Morrill, Sibley, *Ambrose Bierce, F. A. Mitchell-Hedges and the Crystal Skull,*
Cadleon Press, San Francisco, California 1972 **

Mr. Morrill's second book focuses on unraveling how the Mitchell-Hedges Skull was found and how Ambrose Bierce and Mitchell-Hedges may have been working together when they found it. He questions the story about how it was purportedly found. Again, background information is given about the Crystal Skull and includes a few photos.

Welfare, Simon & John Fairley, *Arthur C. Clarke's Mysterious World,* **
A & W Publishers Inc., New York, NY 1980, pgs. 50-55

This book is devoted to exploring the mysteries in our world, including the ancient Crystal Skulls. This short article focuses mostly on the Mitchell-Hedges Skull, and in particular on F. A. Mitchell-Hedges. It does mention the British Skull and the Paris Skull, and there are pictures of each of these. Also, on the cover there is a picture of the British Skull.

** --**This book is out of print. Try used-book stores or libraries.**

Crystal Skull Articles

MAN, July 1936, published by Royal Anthropological Institute of Great Britain (Articles by Adrian Digby, G. M. Morant and H. J. Braunholtz comparing the British Skull to the Mitchell-Hedges Skull. The articles are on pages 105-109 and include several pictures of both of these skulls.)

Fate Magazine, March, 1962, and an article by Joe Nickell & John Fischer, "Crystal Skull of Death," Part 1 (July 1984), Part 2 (August, 1984).

Alameda County Weekender, **Morning News and Times Star,** October 3, 1966 (Discusses findings of Anton Szandor LaVey on the Mitchell-Hedges Skull.)

Measure, Hewlett-Packard Company (newsletter), February, 1971
(Shares research results on the Mitchell-Hedges Skull when Frank Dorland and Richard Garvin brought it to their laboratories for analysis in 1970.)

Crystal Visionary, Vol. #3, 1987, Sydney, Australia (Basically looks at the information given in the Garvin book); Vol. #5, 1987-88, (Interview with F.R. 'Nick' Nocerino and excerpts of the book, *Mysteries of the Crystal Skulls Revealed.*)

California UFO, "Crystal Skull Calling," Vol. 2, No. 3, September, 1987
(Interviews with Sandra Bowen, Ron Dickinson, F. R. 'Nick' Nocerino and Joshua Shapiro, plus quotes from the book, *Mysteries of the Crystal Skulls Revealed.*)

Strange Magazine, "The Controversial Crystal Skulls - Part One" (British Museum Crystal Skull), April, 1988, Vol. 1, No. 1, by Mark Chorvinsky

Crystal Pathways, "The Crystal Skulls," Vol. 1, No. 1, April, 1988,
by Joshua Shapiro (Joshua's experiences with the Amethyst Crystal Skull and a short summary about several other ancient skulls.)

The Psychic Journal, "Mysteries of the Crystal Skulls Revealed," June, 1988,
by Joshua Shapiro (assisted by Sandra Bowen)
(Brief definition of quartz crystal and its uses, background information on several ancient Crystal Skulls and theories of their origins.)

Crystal Skull Videos

The Crystal Skull (The Psychic Connection),
Alan Neuman Productions, Alan Neuman,
8170 Laurel View Dr., Los Angeles, CA 90069; (213) 656-0754

(Interviews Anna Mitchell-Hedges and Carole Davis, who was the channel for their book, *The Skull Speaks.* You see Ms. Davis channeling in the presence of the skull. This video was a segment of a large documentary called "The Psychic Connection," done by Mr. Neuman. 30 minutes)

Journey into the Crystal Skulls, by F. R. 'Nick' Nocerino
   The Society of Crystal Skulls, International,
   P.O. Box 302, Pinole, CA 94564; (415) 724-6603

(This is an experiential tape enabling one to view various pictures of the Mitchell-Hedges Skull and the Mayan Skull with music from Steven Halpern's "Crystal Suite." These images are interlaced with many scenes from nature and special computer graphics. 30 minutes)

The Mysteries, Magic & Truths of the Crystal Skulls
   (with F. R. 'Nick' Nocerino)
   Crystal Congress, P. O. Box 5442, Mill Valley, CA 94942; (415) 388-8355

(A seminar given by F. R. 'Nick' Nocerino at the Crystal Congress, July, 1987, sharing his personal experiences with the Crystal Skulls beginning in 1935. This video includes slides of the Mayan and Mitchell-Hedges Skulls.)

It may be possible to obtain a copy of the following cable TV programs which dealt with the Crystal Skulls, by writing to the contacts listed below. These stations arranged for the co-authors to appear on their respective shows:

"Georgi's Psychic Awareness"

(Shown in Dallas, Texas, during the First International Crystal Conference, May of 1986. Georgi's guests were Sandra Bowen, Ron Dickinson, F. R. 'Nick' Nocerino, Joshua Shapiro and DaEl Walker. 60 minutes)
Contact: Georgi's Entertainment, Attn: Georgi Clark,
11525 Goodnight Lane, Dallas, TX 75229

"Space Cities: Mysteries of the Crystal Skulls Revealed"

(Shown in Hayward, California during September of 1987. Space Cities guests were Sandra Bowen, Jeff Cohen, F. R. 'Nick' Nocerino and Joshua Shapiro. 30 minutes)
Contact: Gavegin Video Productions, Attn: Sloopy Barreau,
251 Dohern Ave., San Jose, CA 95116

APPENDIX D

The following is a brief description of each Contributor,
including contact information:

Abbey, Michael - Visionary artist and illustrator. Michael is a gifted artist in a variety of media who also does technical illustrations. He has a connection with crystals and the Crystal Skulls and has created a series of full-feature paintings dealing with the Crystal Skulls. Michael is available for commissioned artwork and projects.

VISUAL COMMUNICATIONS, Michael Abbey,
  P.O. Box 357, Santa Cruz, CA 95061; (408) 458-1984

Birkett, Rodney - Visionary artist whose subjects include crystals, mysticism, shamanism, surrealist and New Age imagery. Several of his paintings have been exhibited in the renowned Illuminarium Gallery in Marin County, California. Rodney's artwork has appeared as cover art on various New Age music tapes and he is available for commissioned projects.

RODNEY BIRKETT, P.O. Box 350, Walnut Grove, CA 95690

Bowen, Sandra - Crystal and Crystal Skull Teacher and Researcher. Sandra was part of the Research Team that went to Canada to work with the Mitchell-Hedges Skull in November of 1985. She is a co-founder of J & S Aquarian Networking, and has lectured with Joshua Shapiro. Sandra has worked very closely with and supported the work of Nick Nocerino. She had a UFO experience in connection with the Crystal Skulls in 1981. Sandra also conducts psychic development classes.

SANDRA BOWEN, P.O. Box 153, Pinole, CA 94564; (415) 758-8607

Cohen, Jeff (J & S Aquarian Networking) - Researcher/teacher/lecturer about UFOs, Sasquatch, crystals and metaphysics. Book editor, planner and transcriber. Executive Director and Partner of J & S Aquarian Networking. Spiritual minister, healer and networker, Jeff currently earns a living as a Field Service Engineer in medical electronics. He helped with the transcription of several of the taped interviews, and provided assistance and guidance with the planning, writing, editing, design and publishing of this book.

JEFF COHEN, c/o J & S Aquarian Networking,
  P.O. Box 1395, Pacifica, CA 94044 (415) 756-0633

Fisher, Barbara - Author of the novel, *Breathing Room,* Barbara is also an editor, journalist, and audio engineer. She works in the Bay Area and New York City, and is particularly interested in the difference in lifestyles on the East and West Coasts and how that affects people psychologically and spiritually.

BARBARA FISHER, P.O. BOX 7488, Berkeley, CA 94707; (415) 848-2337.

Greiner, Li - Book Publisher and book designer. Li is a bibliophile and collector of metaphysical books. He is the Senior Art Director in Publications for Apple Computers, Inc. Li also uses computers to publish his own books and is interested in all fields of mysticism and metaphysics.

NuSIRIUS PUBLISHING, Li Greiner, 471 20th Ave., San Francisco, CA 94121

Kant, Michael - Michael is a Planetary Light Worker who continues to work with the Higher Evolution in key areas of education which make use of Planetary Technologies and the Sacred Sciences. Having been aboard Lightships in times past and learned from a diverse spectrum of beings, Michael continues to work in such key Planetary Technologies such as Atlantean Crystal Sciences, Morphocrystallic Sciences, Lemurian Technologies and Light-based Technologies. Currently, he is in communication and contact with galactic races who originate from the distant star systems of the Pleiades.

MICHAEL KANT, c/o J & S Aquarian Networking,
  P.O. Box 1395, Pacifica, CA 94044

APPENDIX E

Klimo, Jon - Author of a new book entitled, *Channeling*, published by Jeremy Tarcher. This is one of the most in-depth books analyzing the phenomenon of channeling. Jon is interested in speaking to other channels and eagerly explores all fields involved in the New Age.

JON KLIMO, 1209 Ordway, Berkeley, CA 94706; (415) 527-3113

Kokorich, Alexandra - Visionary Artist who offers Spirit and Past Life Drawings. She is available by appointment. Alexandra has a strong past life connection with the Crystal Skulls and would eventually like to research the skulls. She has a major fascination and interest in UFOs.

ALEXANDRA KOKORICH, 231 West Sequoia Dr., Phoenix, AZ 85027

Mehler, Steve - Steve is a Psychic Archaeologist, scientist and researcher. He was a staff member of the Rosicrucian Museum in San Jose, California, and then became involved with the Mayan and Amethyst Crystal Skulls, which he had in his home for short periods of time. Steve had many other crystal researchers come to work with the skulls. Also, since then he has begun to work actively in researching crystals and doing free-lance video work.

STEVE MEHLER, 507 Udovich Lane, Paradise, CA 95969; (916) 877-6642

Nocerino, F. R. 'Nick' - Founder of the Society of Crystal Skulls, International, a division of the Institute of Psychic and Hypnotic Sciences. Nick is known as a teacher of teachers. He can be credited for starting the Crystal Skulls' popularity that is sweeping the metaphysical community today. Nick has been the only known researcher to see and work with many of the skulls discussed in this book, for example, the Rose Quartz Skull and the Templar Skull. He established the first teacher's credential for Parapsychology issued by the California State Board of Education. His qualifications in the field of Parapsychology are attributed to his continuing research and the factual data he has compiled. Nick has worked as a research consultant for documentaries on parapsychology-related films, radio and TV shows, books and magazines. Some of the areas of his expertise are: Crystals and Crystal Skulls researcher/lecturer, psychic development classes, hauntings investigations, exorcisms, private consultations, UFO research and regressions (since 1950). Nick is currently writing his memoirs and completing his second video about Crystal Skulls.

FRANK R. 'NICK' NOCERINO, (Society of Crystal Skulls, International),
   P.O. Box 302, Pinole, CA 94564; (415) 724-6603

Quinn, Damien (Talisman Trading Co.) - Damien has contacts with various carvers throughout the world who are creating small skulls using different types of crystal. He is bringing these skulls into the United States for sale to those who are interested [See Photogallery].

TALISMAN TRADING CO., Attn: Damien Quinn, P.O. Box 1895, La Mesa, CA 92041; (619) 236-9525, (619) 274-4819

Rowe, Neville - Neville is a Channel for a group of dimensional beings named Soli, and for the Dolphins and Whales. He is a past-life regressionist who offers intensive workshops which help many to become open channels to their Higher Selves/Spirit Guides/Teachers.

NEVILLE ROWE, 7985 Santa Monica Blvd. #109/223, West Hollywood, CA 90046; (213) 650-4973

Shapiro, Joshua (J & S Aquarian Networking) - Author/Compiler of *Journeys of an Aquarian Age Networker; UFOs, Space Brothers & the Aquarian Age; Mysteries of the Crystal Skulls Revealed; Directory of New Age Resources (Southern Calif. Edition)* and editor of *The True Story of Bigfoot: Stan Johnson's Close Encounters.* Joshua is an Aquarian Age Networker and Co-founder/President of J & S Aquarian Networking. He has given several lectures with Sandra Bowen and Jeff Cohen about UFOs & Crystal Skulls, is a computer consultant, and designer of directories at Whole Life Expos.

JOSHUA SHAPIRO, J & S Aquarian Networking,
   P.O. Box 1395, Pacifica, CA 94044; (415) 359-5476

Shimwell, John - John is an English-born photographer and writer, empath and fledgling channel. He is interested in energy in all its forms, from UFOs to the human aura, and sees his long involvement with metaphysics as a way to apply these interests to his own spiritual growth. John went to the British Museum and his photographs of the British Skull appear in this book.

JOHN SHIMWELL, 1349 Park Dr. #7 , Mtn. View, CA 94040; (415) 940-1462

Tomas, Matt - Matt is a Macintosh computer enthusiast and computer graphic artist and planner for the City Planning Department of Berkeley, California. His special interest is utilizing computers to create graphic images for various applications and his skills were utilized in several areas of this book.

MATT TOMAS, 3419 Santa Clara Ave., El Cerrito, CA 94530

APPENDIX E

Youngman, R. H. - He is a direct importer and wholesaler of crystals. His company offers custom-cutting of crystals and is commissioning a carver to create contemporary carved crystal skulls [See Photogallery].

R. H. YOUNGMAN, 607 W. Orangethorpe, Fullerton, CA 92632; (714) 526-6780

Thompson, M. B.

APPENDIX F
CHRONOLOGY

This appendix contains the sequence of events which produced this book, the history of how the participating individuals met each other and other pivotal events which shaped the book's contents.

August, 1979: Nick goes to Mexico and meets a Mayan priest who claims to own the Mayan Crystal Skull. He works with the skull for one day.

October, 1979: Nick makes an agreement with the Mayan priest to bring the Mayan Skull into the United States by paying all the expenses. He picks up the skull and brings it to the San Pablo/Pinole area.

October, 1979 - January, 1980: Nick has the Mayan Skull for four months of extensive research, with over thirty other researchers participating. Nick gives his first public lecture about the Crystal Skulls.

February, 1980: Nick participates in the first Crystal Symposium in California in Mountain View and lectures about the Crystal Skulls. Sandra Bowen attends the lecture and sees the slides of the Mayan Skull. Shortly thereafter, she becomes Nick's student.

April, 1980: Joshua leaves Chicago and starts to network with New Age individuals and groups from Chicago to California.

September, 1981: Sandra has her UFO experience during the investigation of a haunted house in Northern California; the group is led by Nick. She meets Akbar and Josephat on a spacecraft, where they reminded her about her life's mission to share information about the Crystal Skulls and research these artifacts.

March, 1982: Sandra has her second direct contact with Akbar and Josephat during the appearance of a mysterious large cloud which hung over many areas of the United States. When she tries to record their messages, three tape recorders jam.

July, 1982: Joshua arrives in California with the first edition of his book, *Journeys of an Aquarian Age Networker,* based on information he collected during his networking travels. He eventually resides in the San Francisco Bay Area.

September, 1982: Joshua's first book is officially published with 1000 copies issued. There is one page about crystals.

November, 1982: Joshua meets Steve Mehler and Francoise Beaudoin at a New Age Renaissance Fair in San Jose. They decide to carry his Networker Book and schedule a lecture at Francoise's bookstore in December.

December, 1982: The Mayan priest contacts Steve Mehler and Francoise Beaudoin about the Amethyst Skull and invites Steve to participate as an expert to authenticate the skull. In the meantime, Nick, Marcel Vogel and others involved with crystals and psychic research come to work with this skull. Steve has the Amethyst Skull in his home for five days.

February, 1983: Nick has a research session with the Amethyst Skull.

April, 1983: Joshua visits Francoise's bookstore in San Jose and drops off more of his networking books. At this time, she shares pictures she had taken when Steve had the Amethyst Skull. Something is catalyzed in Joshua's mind, as he had no interest in crystals or Crystal Skulls prior to this time. Michael Kant writes his first letter to Joshua in response to reading the Networker Book, beginning an on-going correspondence.

May, 1983: A prospective buyer is in San Jose and indicates some interest in seeing the Amethyst Skull. Steve Mehler arranges a session, which Joshua and a few of his friends are invited to attend. This is Joshua's first time to be in the presence of a Crystal Skull.

October, 1983: Sandra meets the Mayan priest at Nick's home. She requests and receives a psychic healing from him in spirit form.

December, 1983: While lecturing at a local New Age Conference sponsored by the Unity & Diversity Council in Los Angeles, Joshua meets DaEl Walker, a well-known crystal teacher and author of, *The Crystal Book.* DaEl is also a student of F. R. 'Nick' Nocerino. Joshua and DaEl trade copies of their respective books. This is the first time Joshua learns of Nick as being a prominent crystal teacher.

March, 1985: Joshua does a lecture about UFOs at (Francoise's) the Ram Metaphysical Bookstore in San Jose, California. He meets artist, Rodney Birkett, a good friend of Francoise.

April, 1985: Joshua meets Sandra at an informal lecture he gives in a private home in Oakland, sharing a video about UFOs dealing with the Billy Meier case.[1] Shortly thereafter, they decide to work together and teach about New Age information, UFOs and the Crystal Skulls. Through Sandra, Joshua finally meets Nick, who begins to help him with some of his projects. Throughout the rest of this year, Nick shares videotapes with Joshua which were recorded during the research of the Mayan Skull, as well as various slides on several of the ancient Crystal Skulls that Nick has seen.

September, 1985: Nick writes to and calls Frank Dorland for material about the Mitchell-Hedges Crystal Skull. Joshua and Sandra later visit Frank and he gives them a copy of a videotape of various TV shows which have shared information about the Mitchell-Hedges Skull. This is the beginning of their friendship.

November, 1985: Sandra and Nick go to Kitchener, Ontario, Canada for three weeks of research on the Mitchell-Hedges Skull. DaEl Walker and Ron Dickinson (Ron was one of the researchers with the Mayan Skull) are the other members of the team. The research team takes photographs, slides and video of the skull, as well as tape-recording all conversations in its presence. While they are in Canada, Joshua begins to create a UFO book from the UFO chapter in his networking book. While the researchers are working with the Mitchell-Hedges Skull, Joshua meditates upon pictures of it (from the Garvin book) and has several interesting inner experiences. When Nick and Sandra return from Canada, for the first time we all see the pictures that were taken of the Mitchell-Hedges Skull, some of which clearly show images of UFOs appearing within it.

---

[1]-One of the most controversial cases of UFO/ET contacts because it involved frequent ongoing contacts between this Swiss farmer and advanced beings from the Pleiades and DAL Universe. It is well-documented with over 2,000 pages of contact notes, photographs and 8mm movie footage.

CHRONOLOGY

December, 1985: Joshua and Sandra give their first public lecture about UFOs and Crystal Skulls at the Wellness Institute in Sacramento, California. The first interview with Michael Kant is arranged, and due to a mix-up of dates, he is not there when Joshua and Sandra come to his apartment in the Sacramento area. They leave Michael a list of questions and he mails the answers back. This information forms the basis of their in-person interview which occurs at the end of the month.

January, 1986: Joshua and Sandra interview Nick about his impressions of the Crystal Skulls from the trip to Canada in 1985.

January, 1986 - October, 1986: The three co-authors do numerous lectures about the Crystal Skulls, mostly located in California. Joshua and Sandra do a lecture tour in Southern California from January through February. They also share information about the Crystal Skulls and their UFO connection at the Rocky Mountain UFO Conference in July, sponsored by Dr. Leo Sprinkle.

April, 1986: The research team to Canada gives a lecture at Shared Visions in Berkeley, California about their findings/conclusions based on their work with the Mitchell-Hedges Crystal Skull. Joshua assists with the lecture. In preparation for this lecture and future engagements, the research team decides to offer a set of photographs for sale, taken during the research with the Mitchell-Hedges Skull.

May, 1986: Nick, Sandra, Joshua, Ron and DaEl all attend the First International Crystal Conference held in Dallas, Texas. The Mitchell-Hedges Skull is on display, so Joshua not only has his first opportunity to be in its presence, but he also meets Anna Mitchell-Hedges. We appear on a cable TV show called "Georgi's Psychic Awareness" and discuss crystals, the Crystal Skulls and UFOs. Nick gives a lecture with Anna Mitchell-Hedges about the Crystal Skulls.

June, 1986: We all attend the Crystal Congress in San Francisco. Nick and DaEl give lectures while Anna Mitchell-Hedges brings the Crystal Skull for display. Sandra, Joshua and Ron work at a booth for the Crystal Skull Society, making the picture packets available. Damien Quinn of Talisman Trading Co. has a booth with many contemporary carved crystal skulls from a Brazilian carver. This is another sign of the interest people are beginning to have in ancient Crystal Skulls. Jeff Cohen contacts us for the first time and purchases some of our books.

APPENDIX F

July, 1986: Sandra and Joshua give their first public class series in Hayward, California, arranged by Nick. In one of the sessions, we focus on the Crystal Skulls.

September, 1986: We rent a Macintosh Computer and begin entering information from all the interviews and articles to create a preliminary version of this Crystal Skull book entitled, *Mysteries of the Crystal Skulls Revealed!!* Nick loans Joshua and Sandra a transcriber to speed up the transcription process of all the taped interviews.

October, 1986: We interview Steve Mehler about his experiences with the Mayan and Amethyst Skulls. Through the help of Larry Byram and Sandra's credit card, we are able to purchase our own Macintosh computer. Joshua and Sandra work with Jeff Cohen to do a joint lecture about UFOs and Crystal Skulls at a local New Age center in San Francisco. At this lecture, Joshua and Sandra meet Janine Smith. Later this month, Jeff decides to join J & S Aquarian Networking.

November, 1986: We have our second interview with Michael Kant to clarify some of his points from the first interview. We ask questions related to some of the most recent information collected from him and also receive his impressions of the various ancient Crystal Skulls by showing slides of them. We meet Rodney Birkett at the New Age Renaissance Faire in San Jose, and discuss the details pertaining to commissioning a painting for the cover of our book. Rodney begins working on the painting in December.

January, 1987: We finish production of the first version of our Crystal Skulls book and have them available at the Whole Life Expo in Los Angeles the next month.

February, 1987: Rodney Birkett finishes the painting to be used for the revised version of the Crystal Skulls book. We sell the first copies of our Crystal Skulls book at the Whole Life Expo in Los Angeles. All co-authors give a lecture and workshop about the Crystal Skulls. Lois Julien buys copy of the book and goes to Joshua and Sandra's lecture, which has an attendance of over 1,000 people. Lois contacts the co-authors before the end of the month to tell them she is planning to go to London and Paris to see the Crystal Skulls in the museums there. She promises to take pictures if she can. Nick does several other Crystal Skull lectures and workshops while in the Southern California area.

April, 1987: A publisher expresses interest in publishing *Mysteries of the Crystal Skulls Revealed,* and talks with Sandra, Joshua and Jeff at the Whole Life Expo in San Francisco. Joshua and Sandra sell the preliminary version of this book at their booth and show slides of the Crystal Skulls during the panel about crystals. Nick was scheduled to lecture at the Expo but was unable to attend due to illness. Also at the Whole Life Expo, a poster print of Rodney's painting is first shown publicly.

May - July, 1987: Nick is scheduled to do some lectures with DaEl Walker in Toronto, which are delayed. He eventually does seminars in Toronto and lectures in Chicago and Detroit about the Crystal Skulls. Nick gives a seminar at the Crystal Congress in Santa Monica, California about the Crystal Skulls. At the Congress, Lois Julien gives us photographs she took of the British Skull, and pictures (she bought) of the Paris Skull while in the Trocadero Museum. The prospective publisher decides not to publish our revised book, so the principals look at self-publishing. Sandra and Joshua do a lecture about the Crystal Skulls in San Jose, CA, at a local Dr. Who / Star Trek conference and they meet John Shimwell.

August, 1987: Sandra and Joshua meet Li Greiner, the Senior Art Director of Publishing for Apple Computers, Inc., at a local bookstore in San Francisco while they are filling an order for the Crystal Skull book. Li indicates an interest in helping to design the book and also has a strong interest in the Crystal Skulls.

September, 1987: Li volunteers to help with the book. Sandra, Nick, Joshua and Jeff appear on a local cable TV show in Hayward, California and talk about crystals and Crystal Skulls. An article appears about the Crystal Skulls in the magazine, "California UFO," out of Santa Monica, California.

October, 1987: All three co-authors lecture at the Whole Life Expo in Los Angeles about the Crystal Skulls. Nick introduces a meditative videotape showing pictures of the Mitchell-Hedges and Mayan Skulls. Sandra, Janine, Joshua and Jeff interview Neville Rowe, channeler of the dolphins, at the hotel where the Whole Life Expo is held. John Shimwell donates photographs and slides (for our book) which he took of the British Skull while he was in England. Sandra, Joshua and Jeff conduct a third interview with Michael Kant.

APPENDIX F

November - December 1987: Jon Klimo, a friend of Joshua and author of the book, *Channeling*, published by Jeremy Tarcher, agrees to write a short definition of channeling for this book. All written material for this book is compiled and the first-draft version is edited. Li Greiner begins the design and layout of the book. Michael Abbey starts creating the artwork and illustrations. Joshua and Sandra lecture about the Crystal Skulls at the "Focus on You" Conference in Phoenix, Arizona. They meet Alexandra Kokorich, a visionary artist who draws spirit guides she sees around people. They also place the Crystal Skulls book into the first book/crystal stores in Arizona.

1988: In February, the second draft of the book is completed. A professional editor is sought. Catherine Valentine recommends Barbara Fisher, of Berkeley, California. In March the group meets Barbara and decides to work with her. In April, Michael Abbey completes seven paintings which will be used as illustrations for the book. Alexandra Kokorich agrees to do several drawings for the book. In May, Barbara Fisher completes the editing for the book. In June, the final design is begun and all work is completed in November for printing to proceed.

GLOSSARY

366 Keys of Enoch: Enoch is mentioned in the old testament as a Hebrew Prophet who ascended into the Heavens and did not experience a physical death. The 366 Keys of Enoch refer to secret teachings which allow an individual to discover the hidden dimensions of Spirit. It is believed by many that without these key teachings, a spiritual seeker cannot enter the Inner Heavens.

Apports (From the Higher Dimensions) / Projected Directly: An object or being which physically appears, apparently from nowhere.

Ascended Master: A soul who has achieved a master vibration of consciousness and may reside in a physical or spiritual body, teaching universal truths on all levels.

Atlantean Fire Crystals: Special Atlantean quartz crystals used by the so-called Higher Evolution for the holographic projection of thoughtforms and information storage.

Atlantean Time Vaults: Ancient Atlantean record chambers created to store knowledge and scientific/technological devices to be used by future generations.

Atoma: The Central Sun which is located at the core of our planet, implying that our Earth is hollow. The citizens of the Inner Earth have continuous sunlight unless it is blocked by clouds which surround this sun.

Aurameter: A sensitive metal instrument similar in use to a dowsing rod. As this instrument meets the edge of an energy field or aura, its rod will be pushed away by this field, thus indicating the distance the aura extends.

Axis of the Crystal: Within quartz crystals, the individual molecules of silicon dioxide have a specific symmetry of alignment. This alignment is referenced against an imaginary median line called the Axis of the Crystal.

Ayurvedic Medicine: An ancient East Indian healing system which utilizes essences of plants and minerals to effect homeopathic remedies.

Bach Flower Remedies: Tinctures composed of various flower essences to be used for healing.

Biocrystalline Body of Light: *(See definition under "Light.")*

Biocrystalline Computer: A computer composed of Living Thought Crystals which are activated by Planetary and Galactic Intelligences. This computer is not automated, nor a machine, as are our modern computers. We believe that the Crystal Skulls fit into this category.

Biocrystalline Structure: The complete crystalline skeleton of a once-living being which is associated with its respective Crystal Skull.

Chana Energies: The name of energy which is emitted through our hands. Each finger sends out a different type of vibration. The Chana energies, also known as Mudras, were very important in rituals for the Tibetan Buddhist and Hindu cultures.

Chronomonitors: Biocrystalline computers created by the Higher Evolution to monitor Planetary Evolution. They also record key historical events of planetary civilizations and prevent war.

Color Wheel: A motorized multi-colored wheel which emits various frequencies of color and sound.

Color Codes: The sequence of color harmonics present in various key crystal artifacts which are used by the Higher Evolution to communicate with planetary species.

Communicator: A term used to describe a person who is able to project their awareness and psychically see events occurring far away from where their physical body resides.

Cosmic Pyramids of Light: *(See definition under "Light.")*

Crystal Ark of the Covenant: A crystalline structure programmed by extraterrestrials which contains the Divine Plan for the spiritual evolution of the Earth. This crystal ark should not be confused with the Biblical Ark.

Crystal Dais: A crystal disk frequently used on Light Ships and various worlds for teleportation. It also serves as a key lens for the amplification of the energy of crystalline artifacts.

Egyptian-Tibetan Tribunal: The Planetary Tribunal which is responsible for the implementation of Cosmic Law and is maintained by members of the Higher Evolution still present on Earth.

Elders/Elohim/Els: Members of the Higher Evolution who arrived on our Life Station through Zionic Beaming from the Orion constellation.

En-hydro: A mineral that contains natural pockets of water within its structure.

Fire Letters: The Universal Language of Light (See definition of *"Light."*) through which the Scriptures of Light are holographically projected to planetary or galactic evolution. Since the Fall of Man, aspects of the Fire Letters have been involved in the written languages of many cultures, such as Egyptian, Hebrew, Sanskrit, Tibetan and modern Chinese.

Fourth & Fifth Dimensions/Dimensional Frequencies: Accelerated vibrational dimensions of our world which co-exist with our third dimensional reality. As the Earth becomes more spiritually oriented, we will enter into these levels.

Frequency Stations: A physical or etheric structure capable of broadcasting multi-dimensional energies of Light which is assisting our planet in its spiritual evolution. One such frequency station (mentioned in this book as Tribal Light) is located beneath the Potala in Lhasa, Tibet. This is where the thirteen Master Crystal Skulls were once located.

Genetic Light Programming/Coding: *(See definition under "Light.")*

Halls of Records: There are many locations upon and within our world, where records of knowledge have been stored by past civilizations. These halls would be similar to our modern libraries, except that the manner of recording their information is in a totally different form. A Hall of Records would be similar to the Atlantean Time Capsules.

Harmonic Grid System/Ley Lines/Planetary Grid: A grid pattern of electromagnetic energy which covers the Earth, and whose points of intersection are considered power spots.

Higher Evolution: A term which describes etheric Light Beings who exist multidimensionally and exemplify the spiritual wisdom of the Divine Creator.

Higher Self: A form of spiritual guidance reflecting a link to one's own soul-knowledge, which can be reached through meditation or hypnotic regression.

Inner Earth: A theory which states that our planet is hollow with the crust of the Earth being approximately 800 miles thick. Also, there are openings at the poles which have a diameter of 1200 miles. At the core of our planet is an inner sun (the Atoma). Thus, gravity emanates from the center of the Earth's crust and holds all objects to the outer and inner surface.

Jerusalem Command: The name given to Interdimensional and Galactic Beings from Orion, who are assisting our planet in its vibrational shift into a higher level of awareness and harmonious existence.

GLOSSARY

Light: Throughout many of the world's religions, the word *Light* is used to refer to goodness, enlightenment and Truth. In a spiritual context, this word is used to describe the basic building block which composes all matter and energy. Light represents how we humans might perceive a being of a higher vibration from another dimension. We would see them as a light, because their energy would hurt our eyes. Those individuals who have a near-death experience, see a blinding white Light when their consciousness is out-of-body. Thus, some people say that if we could understand what God is, we would perceive God to be pure loving Light.

In concert with this meaning, we have defined the following terms which use the base word of Light.

Biocrystalline Light Body: The Living Light surrounding all our planetary species.

Cosmic Pyramids of Light: A pyramidal structure which exists in the etheric energy levels of the Earth and resonates with key earth energy areas. These pyramids help to broadcast higher vibrational frequencies of Light which aid in raising the consciousness of our planet.

Genetic Light Programming/Coding: Light Programs used by the Inner Earth and Galactic Civilization which preserve their genetic codes and matrix.

Light Beings/Bodies/Races: Beings or Races who are so advanced spiritually and of such a high vibrational rate, that our physical sight can only register them as being a color of light with no defined form.

Light Codes/Functions/Frequencies/ Programs: Universal Knowledge or information existing interdimensionally within various ancient crystalline artifacts. These Light codes or programs can be activated through the proper sequence of events in tandem with an individual's spiritual energy. All ancient crystalline tools have light programs inside, which protect them from unauthorized intrusions.

Light Ships: Interdimensional spacecraft used by higher intelligences or extraterrestrials. Attributes of the Light energies allow these craft to instantaneously transverse through many dimensions because time and space, as we understand them, do not exist in the Light dimensions.

Light Spectrums/Universes: Term used to describe dimensional levels where the most spiritually evolved masters or Higher Evolution reside. These universes may co-exist side by side with our physical world, but their higher frequencies of vibration make them seem invisible to us unless one is using psychic or spiritual awareness.

Lightworkers: Those individuals who are dedicated to teaching spiritual truths and using this knowledge to create a world of peace and love. These people receive guidance as to the nature of their missions on the Earth, through their inner gifts from spirit guides or their higher selves.

Pillar of Light: Powerful etheric energy vortexes which take on the form of a spiralling pillar of Living Light. These pillars of Light can be generated by Light Ships and the Crystal Skulls, as well as within the Twelve Crystalline Fields of Light that surround our planet.

Pyramidal Light Codes: Scriptures of Living Light which are used extensively in programming our planetary evolution. If one could inwardly see these energy particles they would have a pyramidal shape. An example of Pyramidal Light Codes would be the Ten Commandments of Light.

Scriptures of Light: Higher Universal Teachings existing in the inner dimensions being broadcast by Pyramids of Light, Pillars of Light and the Ten Commandments. These scriptures contain the spiritual and scientific technologies which help a planetary evolution to raise in consciousness and move into the Light Dimensions.

Ten Commandments of Light: The ten key frequencies or light codes which an individual must understand and incorporate into their essence, to pass into the next octave or dimension of spiritual growth.

Twelve Crystalline Fields of Light: The Living Light which surrounds our world. These Twelve Fields of Light form a grid pattern and are a sheath which can receive and step down the broadcast of higher vibrational frequencies from other galaxies. The Ten Commandments of Light and the Crystal Skulls help to keep these fields of Light in steady alignment.

Magic Mirrors: Mirrors used to create psychic visions of other places and dimensions.

Maldek: In Legend, Maldek was the thirteenth planet in our solar system, situated between Mars and Jupiter. It was destroyed through a nuclear fusion explosion and its remains are supposedly the asteroid belt found between Mars and Jupiter.

Melchizedek Brotherhoods/Schools: An ancient order in charge of the Earth's education which helps to link physical creation with the externalization of the Divine Hierarchy.

Metal Books: Encoded information on various types of metal which are unknown to our current technology and are used as a form of book by extraterrestrials and ancient civilizations.

Mind Bodies/Link: It is said that all people possess several bodies through which their consciousness moves. One of these is the mind (or mental) body. We as human beings are a simultaneous integration of all these bodies and parts of our consciousness move in and out of each one. By working with these various levels, we can merge with other sentient beings.

New Jerusalem: A term used to refer to the new capital of the Earth, after we have completed our transformation into the Age of Aquarius.

Peruvian Whistles: Whistles fashioned in the form of people and animals, made by the people of Peru, which emit unusual high-pitched sounds when a person blows on them.

Pillar of Light: *(See definition under "Light.")*

Population II System: A solar system which has two Suns, consisting of a higher frequency of Light vibration and inhabitants which are more spiritually advanced.

Pyramidal Light Codes: *(See definition under "Light.")*

Sacred Sciences: A term used to describe the ancient technologies created through a combination of metaphysics and science.

Sananda: The name which represents the soul who was the Biblical Jesus. This is his name on the higher vibrational dimensions.

Scanners: A person who is able to project his/her consciousness and watch events and people at a different physical location.

Scripture of Light: *(See definition under "Light.")*

Solar Cross: A symbol consisting of an equal-armed cross within a circle. The cross represents the seeking of Truth and the circle represents no beginning or end (The Great Spirit).

Space Needle: A station which acts as a transmitter and receiver of higher dimensional energies allowing communication with Galactic Beings and the Higher Evolution.

Ten Commandments of Light/Ten Key Frequencies: *(See definition under "Light.")*

Thought Crystals/Thought Forms: Thought Crystals are the same as recording crystals. They are crystals in which people's knowledge can be directly stored and then received telepathically by others.

Twelve Crystalline Fields of Light: *(See definition under "Light.")*

Wicca: An ancient worldwide religion that deals with the Goddess or the feminine aspect of reality. The Wicca are aware of life's mystical side and the intricate balance within all kingdoms of the planet, and they have reverence for the Mother Earth.

Windows: In this book, windows refer to dimensional openings which appear in various types of scrying/gazing stones.

Zionic Energy Beams/Light Projection: An energy beam which allows extraterrestrials to project themselves or their artifacts between locations or dimensions.

GLOSSARY

INDEX

(Italicized page numbers indicate Photographs or Illustrations)

294

INDEX

INDEX

INDEX